SMALL BASIC
FOR KIDS

Edward H. Carlson
Philip Conrod
Lou Tylee

Illustrations by Kevin Brockschmidt

Adapted from "Kids and the IBM-PC/PCjr"
By Edward H. Carlson

Kidware Software LLC
PO Box 701
Maple Valley, Washington 98038
1.425.413.1185
www.kidwaresoftware.com
www.computerscienceforkids.com

Printed in the United States of America

2Nd Edition Color Illustrations by Kevin Brockschmidt

ISBN-13: 978-1-937161-82-8 (Paperback)
ISBN-13: 978-1-937161-89-7 (Electronic)

Adapted from "Kids and the IBM-PC/PCjr", By Edward H. Carlson

This guide was developed for the course, "Small Basic for Kids" produced by Kidware Software, Maple Valley, Washington. It is not intended to be a complete reference to the Small Basic language. Please consult the Microsoft website for detailed reference information.

This guide refers to several software and hardware products by their trade names. These references are for informational purposes only and all trademarks are the property of their respective companies and owners. Microsoft, Visual Studio, Small Basic, Visual Basic, Visual J#, and Visual C#, IntelliSense, Word, Excel, MSDN, and Windows are all trademark products of the Microsoft Corporation. Java is a trademark product of the Oracle Corporation.

The example companies, organizations, products, domain names, e-mail addresses, logos, people, places, and events depicted are fictitious. No association with any real company, organization, product, domain name, e-mail address, logo, person, place, or event is intended or should be inferred.

About The Authors

Edward H. Carlson is a Professor Emeritus at Michigan State University. His interest in computers started in 1960 and he was involved in many University Projects until his retirement. Edward authored eight computer programming books including "Kids and the Apple," "Kids and the Commodore 64," and "Kids and the IBM PC/PCjr". Over 700,000 copies of these computer programming books were sold. Edward also established several Computer Camps for Children.

Philip Conrod has authored, co-authored and edited numerous computer programming books for kids, teens and adults. Philip holds a BS in Computer Information Systems and a Master's certificate in the Essentials of Business Development from Regis University. Philip has held various Information Technology leadership roles in companies like Sundstrand Aerospace, Safeco Insurance Companies, FamilyLife, Kenworth Truck Company, PACCAR and Darigold. Philip serves as the President & Publisher of Kidware Software, LLC. He is also the proud father of three "techie" daughters. Philip and his lovely family live in Maple Valley, Washington.

Lou Tylee holds BS and MS degrees in Mechanical Engineering and a PhD in Electrical Engineering. Lou has been programming computers since 1969 when he took his first Fortran course in college. He has written software to control suspensions for high speed ground vehicles, monitor nuclear power plants, lower noise levels in commercial jetliners, compute takeoff speeds for jetliners, locate and identify air and ground traffic and to let kids count bunnies, learn how to spell and do math problems. He has written several on-line texts teaching Visual Basic, Visual C# and Java to thousands of people. He taught a beginning Visual Basic course for over 15 years at a major university. Currently, Lou works as an engineer at a major Seattle aerospace firm. He is the proud father of five children and proud husband of his special wife. Lou and his family live in Seattle, Washington.

1

TABLE OF CONTENTS

GRAPHICS

ADVANCED PROGRAMMING AND GAMES

APPENDICES

PREFACE

In the late 1970's and early 1980's, it seems there were computers everywhere with names like Apple II, Commodore 64, Texas Instruments 99/4A, Atari 400, Coleco Adam, Timex Sinclair and the IBM PC-Jr. Stores like Sears, JC Penneys and even K Mart sold computers. One thing these machines had in common was that they could be programmed with some version of Microsoft's Basic language. Each computer had its own fans and own magazines. Users would wait each month for the next issue of a magazine with Basic programs you could type into your computer and try at home. Just about anyone could write and run a simple Basic program in minutes.

At this same time, a series of landmark books teaching kids how to program in the Basic language was also introduced and published by Ed Carlson at Michigan State University. There were eight books in all. Titles like "Kids and the Apple," "Kids and the Commodore 64," and "Kids and the IBM PC/PCjr" could be found on bookstores shelves. Over 700,000 copies of these books were sold. These books allowed kids to quickly learn to write programs they could have fun with. The books encouraged learning about programming.

This was a fun and exciting time for the beginning programmer, but the fun times ended shortly after the introduction of the IBM-PC in the early 1980's. Bigger and faster computers brought forth bigger languages and bigger development environments. These new languages were expensive to acquire and difficult for the beginning programmer to grasp.

Let's fast forward to today. In an attempt to rekindle the days when just about anyone could sit down at a computer and write a simple program using the Basic language, Microsoft has introduced a new language – Small Basic. It is an updated version of the 1980's product with modern syntax and a very nice development environment. But, it still has simplicity. And, it's a great environment to use for teaching kids about programming.

When I first saw Small Basic, I recalled the series of books by Ed Carlson. I contacted Ed (he's retired now) and we are producing this new book which is an adaptation of his "Kids and the IBM PC/PCjr" book published by Datamost in 1983:

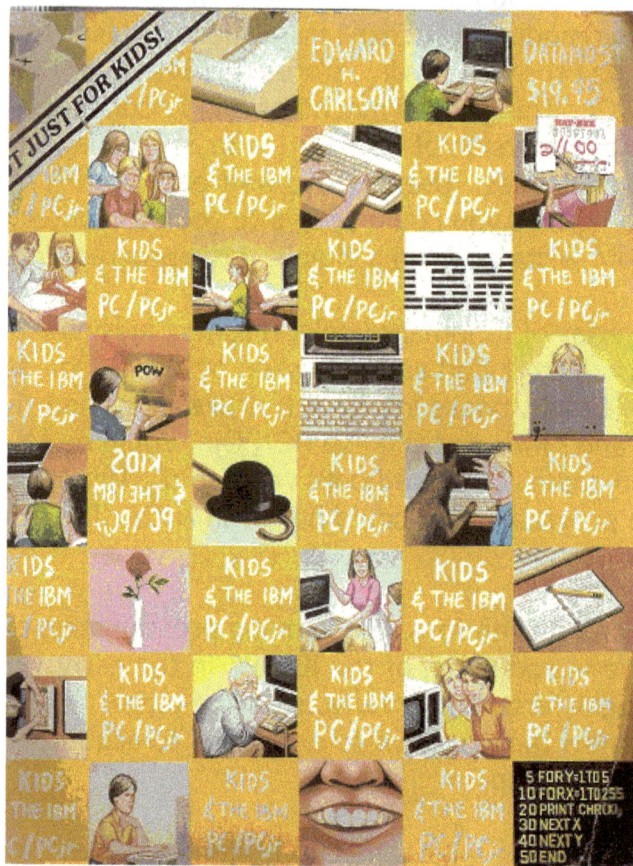

Many of the instructor notes and descriptions in this adapted work are taken verbatim from the original book. Most of the lessons follow Ed's older book. What he taught kids about programming in 1983 still applies today. We hope that a new generation of programmers is spawned by this new Small Basic language and this reworking of the original "Kids and the ..." books for learning it.

Lou Tylee
Seattle, Washington

TO THE KIDS

This book teaches you how to write computer programs using Small Basic.

You will learn how to make your own word and action games. You may entertain your friends with challenging games and provide some silly moments at your parties with short games you invent.

Perhaps your DVD collection or your home's recipes needs the organization your special programs can provide. If you are working on the school yearbook, maybe a program to handle the finances or records would be useful.

You may help your younger sisters and brothers by writing drill programs for arithmetic facts or spelling. Even your own schoolwork in history or foreign language may be made easier by programs you write.

How to Use This Book: Do all the examples. Try all the assignments. If you get stuck, go back and reread the lesson carefully, from the top. You may have overlooked some detail. After trying hard to get unstuck by yourself, you may go ask a parent or teacher for help.

There are review questions for each lesson. Be sure you can answer them before announcing that you have finished the lesson!

MAY YOU FIND ALL THE BUGS IN YOUR PROGRAMS!

TO THE PARENTS

This book is designed to teach Small Basic programming to youngsters from 8 to 15 years old. It gives guidance, explanations, exercises, reviews, and "quizzes." Some exercises have room for the student to write in answers that you can check later. Answers are provided in the back of the book for program assignments.

Your child will probably need some help in getting started and a great deal of encouragement at the sticky places. Learning to program is not easy because it requires handling some sophisticated concepts, as well as accuracy and attention to detail, which are not typical childhood traits. For these very reasons, it is a valuable experience for children. They will be well rewarded if they can stick with the book long enough to reach the fun projects that are possible once a repertoire of statements is built up.

How to Use This Book: The book is divided into lessons for the kids to do. Each lesson is preceded by a **Notes** section which you should read. It outlines the things to be studied, gives some helpful hints and provides questions which you can use verbally (usually at the computer) to see if the skills and concepts have been mastered.

These notes are intended for the parents and teachers, but the older students may also profit by reading them. The younger students will probably not read them, and can get all the material they need from the lessons themselves. For the youngest children, it may be advisable to read the lesson out loud with them and discuss it, before they start working.

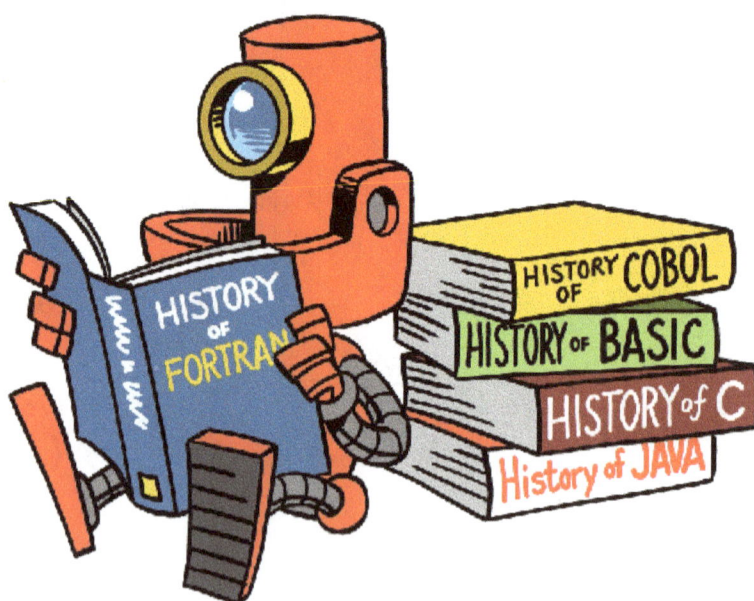

TO THE TEACHER

This book is designed for students, starting about the fifth grade. It teaches Small Basic programming for Windows computers.

The lessons contain explanations, examples, exercises and review questions. Notes for the instructor which accompany each lesson summarize the material, provide helpful hints and provide good review questions.

The book is intended for self study, but may also be used in a classroom setting.

We view this book as teaching programming in the broadest sense, using the Small Basic language, rather than teaching Small Basic. Central is the idea that procedures are entities in themselves. They can be named, broken down into elementary parts and debugged. Some other concepts include: "chunking" ideas into "mind-sized bites," organizing such modules in a hierarchical system, looping to repeat modules, and condition testing (the **If** statement). These powerful ideas about procedures extend naturally into many situations in life.

Verbal and visual metaphor is used to make the new material familiar to the student. Each concept is tied to the student's everyday experiences through the choice examples, the language chosen to express the idea and through cartoons.

ABOUT PROGRAMMING

There is a common misconception about programming a computer. Many people think that ability in mathematics is required – not so. Computing is analogous to the childhood activities of playing with building blocks and writing an English composition.

Like a block set that has many copies of a few types of blocks, Small Basic uses a relatively small number of standard statements. Yet the blocks can be formed into unique and imaginative castles and Small Basic can be used to write an almost limitless variety of programs. Like an essay on the theme "How I Spent My Summer," writing a program involves skill and planning on all scales. To write a theme, the child organizes her thoughts on several scales, from the overall topic, to lead and summary paragraphs and sentences, and on down to the grammar and punctuation in sentences and spelling of words.

Creativity in each of these activities: blocks, writing, and Small Basic, has little scope at the lowest level: individual blocks, words, or statements. At best, a small "bag of tricks" is developed. For example, a child may discover that the triangle block, first used to make roofs, makes splendid fir trees. What is needed at small scale is accuracy in syntax. Here computing is an almost ideal self-paced learning situation, because syntax errors are largely discovered and pointed out by the Small Basic environment as the child builds and tests the program.

At larger scales, creativity comes into full scope and many other latent abilities of the child are developed. School skills such as arithmetic and language arts are utilized as needed, and thus strengthened. But the strongest features of programming are balanced between analysis (why doesn't it work as I want?) and synthesis (planning on several size scales, from the program as a whole down through loops and subroutines to individual statements). The analytical and synthesis skills learned in programming can be transferred to more general situations and can help the child to a more mature style of thinking and working.

INTRODUCTION

INSTRUCTOR NOTES 1 GETTING STARTED

Before starting, one obvious need is for each student to have the Small Basic environment installed on the computer they are using. Either you or an aide can do this or you can lead the student through the steps. Make sure you are using Version 0.9 or higher.

DOWNLOADING AND INSTALLING SMALL BASIC

Start up your web browser (Internet Explorer, Netscape or other). Small Basic is hosted on Microsoft's Small Basic website:

http://www.smallbasic.com

On the Small Basic web page, you should see a button on the top right corner of the webpage that allows you to download Small Basic:

Download

Click this download button and then one more download button. This window should eventually appear:

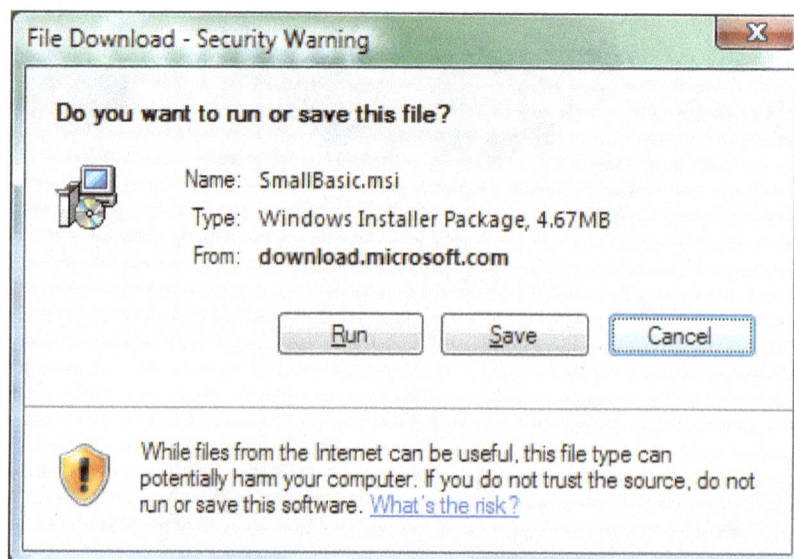

Click **Run** and the download of the installer begins. When complete, you should see:

Again, click **Run** to see the Setup Wizard:

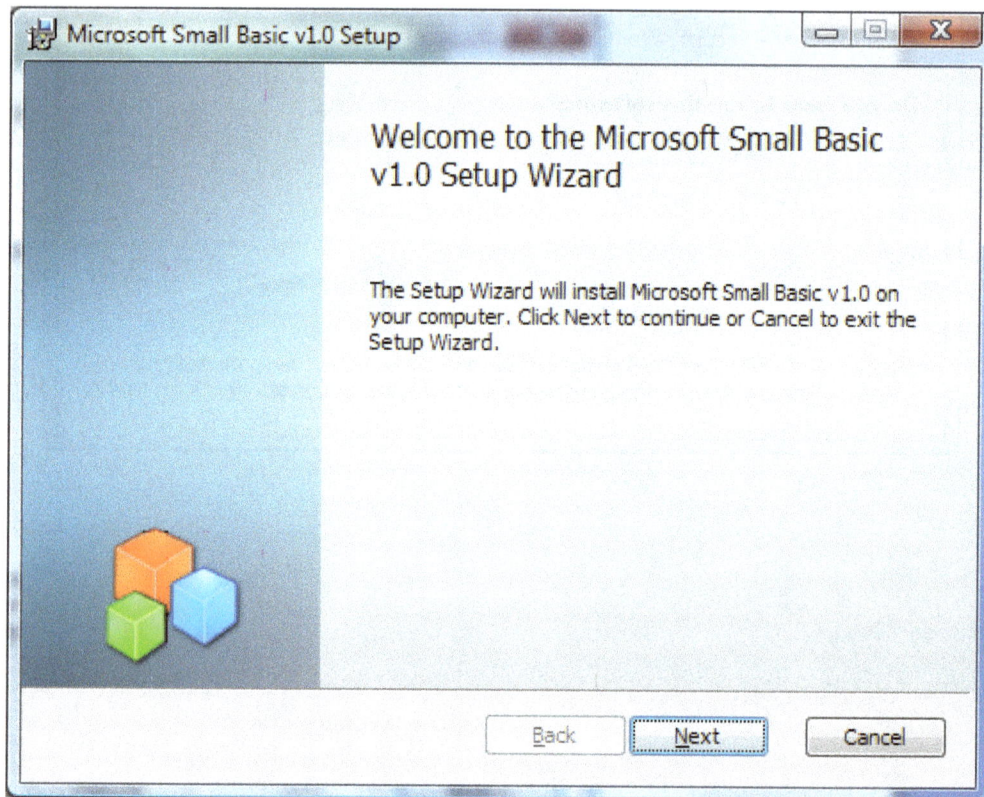

Click **Next** to start the installation process. Accept the licensing agreement. Then, for each screen afterwards, accept the default choice by clicking **Next**.

When done you should see a screen announcing a successful installation.

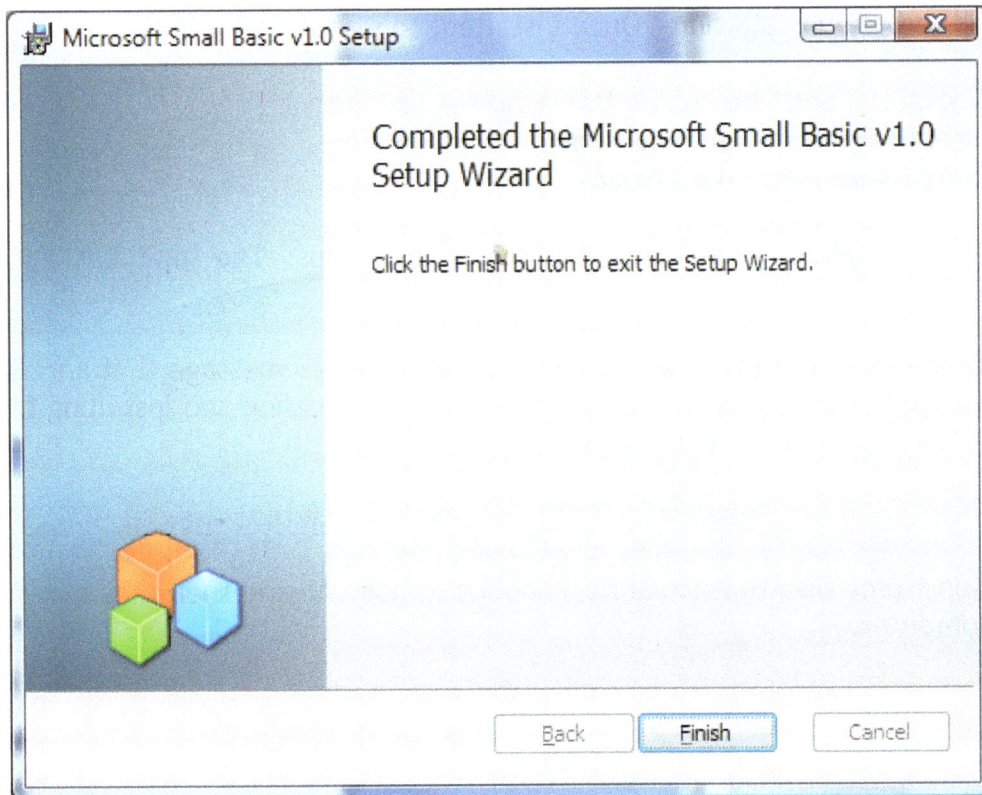

STARTING SMALL BASIC

You should test the installation. Once installed, to start Small Basic:

- Click on the **Start** button on the Windows task bar
- Select **Programs**, then **Small Basic**
- Click on **Microsoft Small Basic**

You should also make sure your students know these steps. The Small Basic program should start.

After installation and trying to start, you may see an error message that announces Small Basic cannot be started. If this occurs, try downloading and installing the 4.5 version of the Microsoft .NET framework at:

https://www.microsoft.com/en-us/download/details.aspx?id=30653

This contains some files that Small Basic needs to operate and such files may not be on your computer.

GETTING STARTED

Once installed, there are many questions your student may have in the beginning, so pull up a chair and help in the familiarization.

Make sure the students know they cannot damage the computer by typing incorrect code. Help your students find familiar keys on the keyboard (punctuation, **Enter**, **Shift** keys).

The contents of the lesson:

1. Start Small Basic.
2. Finding the toolbar and the editor window.
3. Understanding what a program is.
4. Using the **New** toolbar button.
5. **Comment** and **WriteLine** statements.
6. Entering a program.
7. Using the **Run** toolbar button.
8. Understanding that the computer processes statements one at a time in the order they are written.

We introduce the **comment** statement early on. This can sometimes be a little confusing to new students. It needs to be distinguished from program statements.

1. Write a program that will print your name.

2. Run the program.

3. Write a program that will say hello to your teacher.

4. Run that program.

LESSON 1   GETTING STARTED

HOW TO GET STARTED

Sit down at your computer and click **Start** on the Windows taskbar. Select **Programs**, then the **Small Basic** folder. You will see:

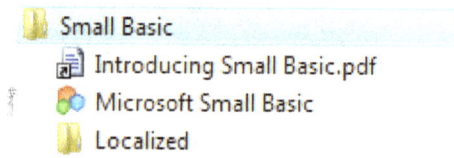

Click **Microsoft Small Basic**. You will see this:

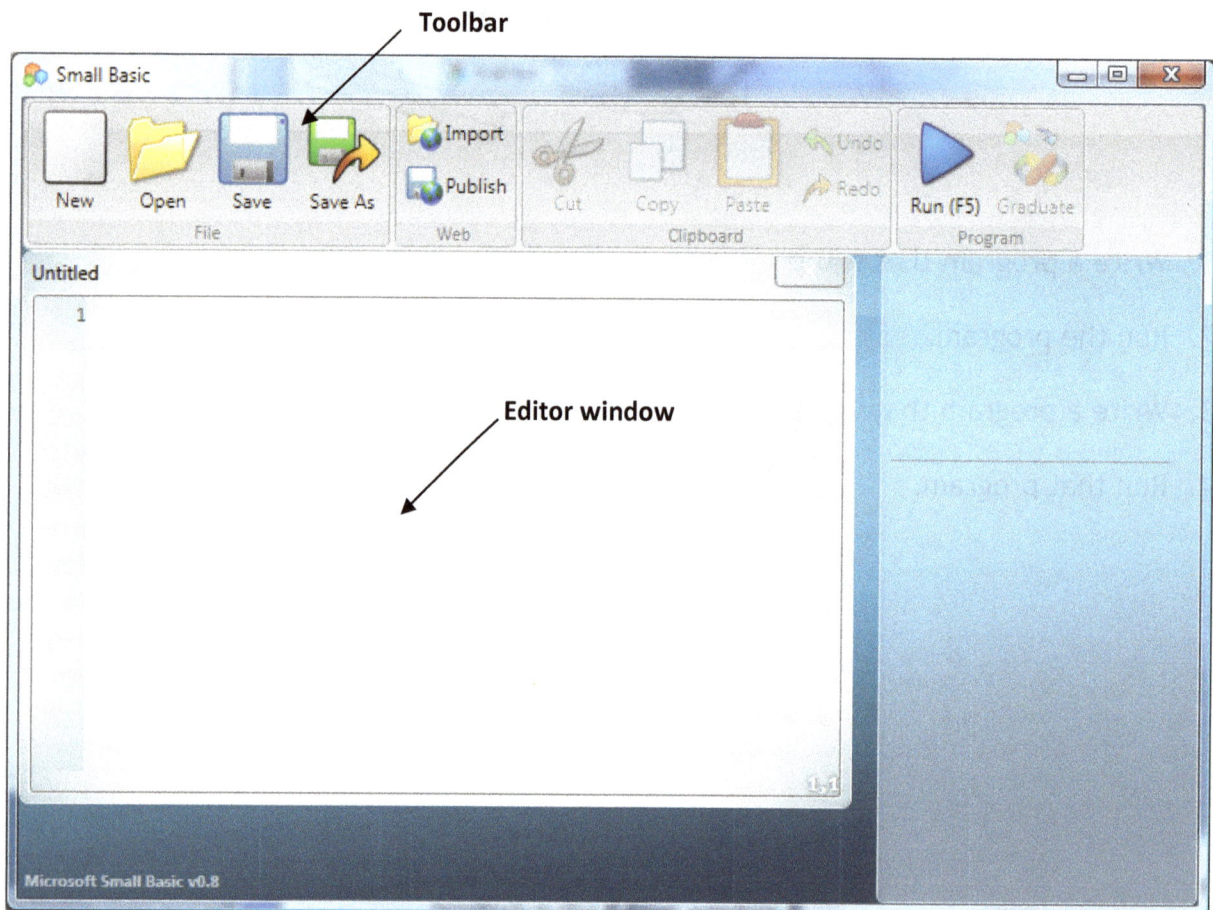

The **Toolbar** is used to control your computer program. First you will write your computer program in the **Editor window**, then you will tell the computer to run your program.

WHAT IS A PROGRAM?

A program is a list of statements telling the computer what to do when you run the program. Each statement is on a line in the editor. The editor puts a number next to the line in the gray area on the left side of the editor window.

HOW TO ENTER A LINE

Click in the editor window. Next to Line 1 is a vertical flashing line. This line is called the **cursor**. When you see it flashing, it means the computer is waiting for you to type something in. Cursor means runner. The cursor runs along as you type, showing where the next letter will appear.

When we say "enter a line" we always mean to do these two things:

1. Type a line
2. Press the **Enter** key

The **Enter** key has a bent arrow on it like this:

The **Enter** key is at the right end of the middle row of the keyboard.

Type this line in the Small Basic editor:

```
TextWindow.WriteLine("Hello")
```

The dot, parentheses and quotation marks are punctuations that must be put in the correct places for the computer to understand the statement.

Press **Enter** after typing the line. The editor window will look like this:

```
Untitled *
   1  TextWindow.WriteLine("Hello")
   2
```

CAPITAL LETTERS

You can use either capital or small letters in a statement. Small Basic acts like **WriteLine** and **writeline** is the same command.

THE NUMBER ZERO AND THE LETTER "O"

Small Basic always writes a zero like this:

Zero   0

And the letter O like this:

Letter O   O or o

You have to be careful to do the same.

Right - TextWindow.WriteLine("Hello")

Wrong - TextWind0w.WriteLine("Hell0")

HOW TO RUN A PROGRAM

After you type a program, you want to see what it will do. So click the **Run** button in the Small Basic Toolbar:

Run (F5)

Clicking this button tells the computer to obey the statements listed in the editor. Go ahead – click **Run**.

If you typed the statement correctly, you should see (I have resized this window to fit it on the page – your window will be larger):

The editor window disappears and a new window, the text window, appears. In it the computer shows what the program did.

The program you wrote told the computer to "write the line that says Hello into the text window." After the computer ran your program, it left a message for you:

"Press any key to continue ..."

So press a key. The text window disappears and the editor window reappears, with your program in it. If you want, you can add some statements to your program, or repair anything you did not like about what it did.

THE NEW TOOLBAR BUTTON

New

Each time you click the **New** button in the toolbar, a new empty editor window opens, letting you start another program. A new editor window also appears when you start Small Basic.

Click **New** to try it. To close an editor window, click the **X** in the upper right corner.

Click Here to Close Editor

Untitled

```
1 |
```

You may be asked if you want to save your program. We will learn how to do this later. For now, just answer **No** when asked to save.

COMMENTS

Click the **New** button to open a new editor window. Enter this program:

```
' Hello program
TextWindow.WriteLine("Hello")
TextWindow.WriteLine("My Friend")
```

This program has three lines. The first line starts with a single apostrophe and is called a **comment**. It is used to write little notes to yourself. The computer itself ignores your comments. The editor will look like this:

```
t Untitled *

  1  'Hello program
  2  TextWindow.WriteLine("Hello")
  3  TextWindow.WriteLine("My Friend")
  4  |
```

Click the **Run** button and you will see:

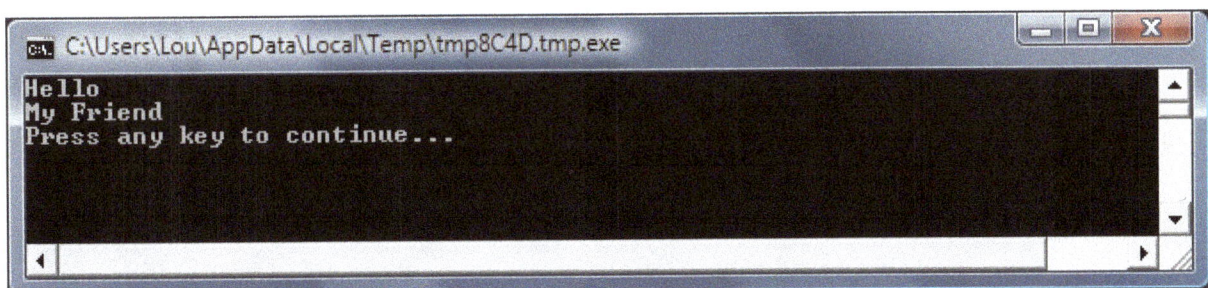

```
C:\Users\Lou\AppData\Local\Temp\tmp8C4D.tmp.exe

Hello
My Friend
Press any key to continue...
```

The computer processes the program statements in the editor. It starts with the first statement (ignoring the comment) and goes down the list in order.

Did you notice, as you typed your program in, a little window like this kept popping up:

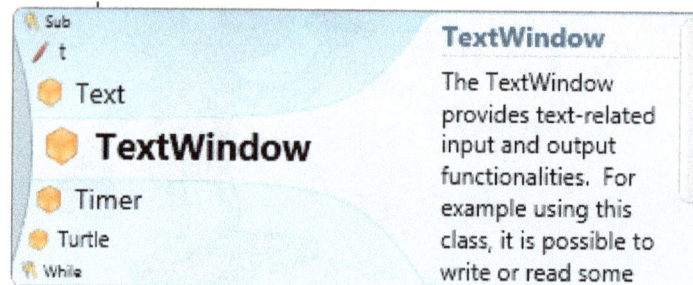

Small Basic tries to figure out what you want to type. Instead of actually typing a statement, you can choose from this list. Just use the up and down arrows to go through the list. When your choice appears, press **Enter**.

Assignment 1:

1. Explain what the **New** toolbar button does.

2. Write a program that uses one comment and two **WriteLine** statements. **Run** your new program.

The **Sound** object has available sounds to play. We use the **PlayBellRingAndWait** sound. You should let the students use lots of "bells and whistles" to increase program richness.

The **Clear** statement clears the text window.

The **BackgroundColor** property changes the text window color (it must be followed by a **Clear**). The **ForegroundColor** property changes the color of text printed from that point on. It doesn't change any characters already in the window.

The idea of a **string constant**, used in Lesson 1, is explained. The numbers appearing in a string, for example "19", cannot be used directly in arithmetic.

QUESTIONS:

1. How do you do each of these things:

    Make the computer ring a bell?
    Clear the text window?
    Print your name?

2. What is a **string**?

3. What keyboard key do you use to enter a program line?

4. Write a program that prints FIRE! FIRE! on a red background. Make a bell ring.

LESSON 2   SOUNDS AND STRINGS

Start Small Basic. Make sure you have an empty editor window. If you don't, click the **New** button in the toolbar.

THAT RINGS A BELL!

Enter this program in the editor:

```
' Bell
TextWindow.Clear()
Sound.PlayBellRingAndWait()
TextWindow.WriteLine("Dinner time!")
```

Run the program. You will see this after hearing a bell ringing:

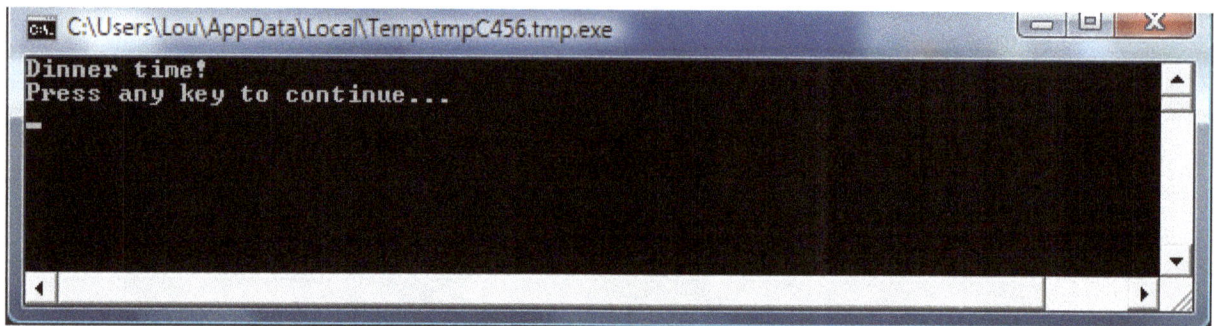

This is the line that made the bell sound play:

```
Sound.PlayBellRingAndWait()
```

This statement makes a bell ring and waits until it is finished before continuing the program.

Here are other sounds it can play:

```
Sound.PlayChimeAndWait()
Sound.PlayChimesAndWait()
Sound.PlayClickAndWait()

Sound.PlayBellRing()
Sound.PlayChime()
Sound.PlayChimes()
Sound.PlayClick()
```

There are two types of sounds. The sounds with "AndWait" at the end of the statement play until completion then continue with the program. The sounds without "AndWait" start playing and continue immediately with the program. So, the "AndWait" sounds take longer, putting some delay in a program.

CLEARING THE TEXT WINDOW IN A PROGRAM

When the program is running, if it gets to a **Clear** statement, it erases the text window.

Start a **New** program. Type in these statements:

```
' Wipe that smile off
TextWindow.WriteLine("Smile!")
Sound.PlayBellRingAndWait()
TextWindow.Clear()
TextWindow.WriteLine("That's better!")
```

Run the program. You will first see **Smile!**, then hear a bell. The window will clear and you will see:

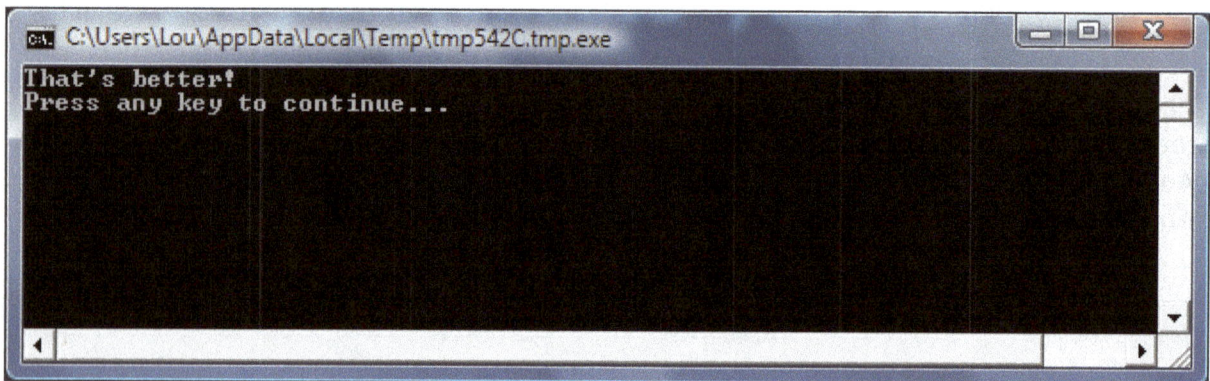

Do you see how this works?

WRITING AN EMPTY LINE

Start a **New** program. Type in these statements:

```
' skipping lines
TextWindow.Clear()
TextWindow.WriteLine("Here is the first line")
TextWindow.WriteLine("")
TextWindow.WriteLine("Here is the second line")
```

Run the program. You'll see:

To write a blank line, use:

```
TextWindow.WriteLine("")
```

COLOR THE WINDOW RED

Start a **New** program. Type these statements:

```
'Red screen
TextWindow.BackgroundColor = "Red"
TextWindow.Clear()
```

Run the program. You should have a red text window:

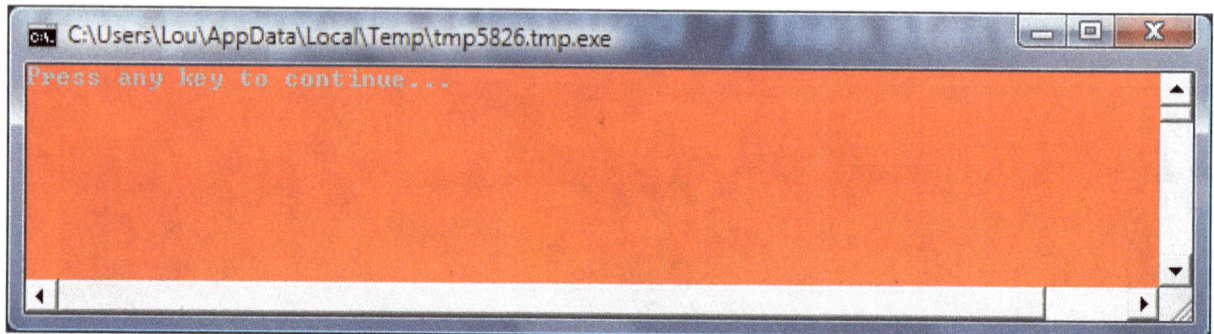

Remember, your comment *'Red screen* is ignored by the computer when the program runs. The red color really comes from the statement:

```
TextWindow.BackgroundColor = "Red"
```

The window color is the **BackgroundColor.** Small Basic has many colors you can use. Some others are: Pink, Yellow, Orange, Purple, Green, Aqua, Blue, White, Brown, Gray, Black.

COLOR THE TEXT

Gray letters on Red background? It's hard to read! Add two more lines to your program:

```
'Red screen
TextWindow.BackgroundColor = "Red"
TextWindow.Clear()
TextWindow.ForegroundColor = "Yellow"
TextWindow.WriteLine("This is yellow")
```

Run the program. You should now have yellow text in a red window:

The text color is the **ForegroundColor.**

PICTURE DRAWING

You can use the **WriteLine** statement to draw pictures. This code will draw a car. Start a **New** program and enter this code:

```
'Car
TextWindow.WriteLine("")
TextWindow.WriteLine(" XXXXXX")
TextWindow.WriteLine("XXXXXXXXXXX")
TextWindow.WriteLine(" O          O")
TextWindow.WriteLine("")
```

Don't forget to put the spaces in the **WriteLine** statements! They are part of the drawing.

Run the program. Here's the car:

STRING CONSTANTS

Look at these **WriteLine** statements:

```
TextWindow.WriteLine("Joe")
TextWindow.WriteLine("  XXXXXX")
TextWindow.WriteLine("#s47%*$")
TextWindow.WriteLine("19")
TextWindow.WriteLine("3.141592653")
TextWindow.WriteLine("I'm 14")
```

The letters, numbers, and punctuation marks are called **characters**. Even a blank space is a character, as in the statement to write a blank line:

```
TextWindow.WriteLine("")
```

Characters in a row make a **string**. The characters are stretched out like beads on a string.

A string between quotation marks is called a **string constant**. It is a **string** because it is made of letters, numbers, and punctuation marks all in a row. It is a **constant** because it stays the same. It doesn't change as the program runs.

1. Write a program that prints your first, middle and last names. Make the letters black on a yellow screen.

2. Now, add a "bell ring" before it prints each name.

3. Write a program that draws three flying birds in the text window.

INSTRUCTOR NOTES 3   EDITING LINES

This lesson concerns typing lines in the code editor. We discuss use of the mouse and arrow keys to move the cursor. Characters in the editor are not affected by the cursor moving over them. Wherever the cursor stops, you can type in new characters.

Holding down any key for a short time starts the auto repeat feature of the keyboard. This is very useful for making repeated characters, such as a line of characters or spaces in a line, or for moving the cursor fast with the arrow keys.

QUESTIONS:

1. What is the cursor? What is it good for?

2. Have your student demonstrate the following:

    Edit existing line
    Add line
    Delete line
    Copy a line

3. Show the repeating feature of the keyboard.

LESSON 3   EDITING LINES

THE CURSOR IS A FLASHING LINE

In the editor, the little vertical flashing line is called the **input cursor**. It shows you where the next letter you type will appear.

MOVING THE CURSOR

There are several ways to move the cursor. First, you can use the mouse. Simply click the mouse at the position where you want the cursor. You can also use the arrow keys on the keyboard. They are usually at the lower right of your keyboard near the right **Shift** key.

Once the cursor is somewhere in a statement line, pressing the **Home** key moves the cursor to the beginning of the line. Pressing **End** moves the cursor to the end of the line.

Start a **New** program. Enter this code:

```
'editing
TextWindow.WriteLine("This is line 1")
TextWindow.WriteLine("This is line 2")
```

The code window looks like this:

```
Untitled *

1  'editing
2  TextWindow.WriteLine("This is line 1")
3  TextWindow.WriteLine("This is line 2")
4
```

Click with the mouse to put the cursor after the dot (.) in Line 2. Use the arrow keys to move the cursor around. Press the **Home** and **End** keys to try out how they work.

38

Run the program to see:

```
C:\Users\Lou\AppData\Local\Temp\tmp202B.tmp.exe
This is line 1
This is line 2
Press any key to continue...
```

REPEATING KEYS

Position the cursor in the code window. Hold down the right arrow key. Notice the cursor just goes whizzing along! We call this a **repeating key**. This works for most keys on the keyboard. Hold down the H key and see what happens.

ADDING A LINE TO A PROGRAM

You can add a line anywhere in the program. You just need to make space for it. To put a line before an existing line, place the cursor at the beginning of that line (use the mouse, arrow keys, or else press **Home** while the cursor is in that line), then press **Enter**. A blank line will open up before the existing line.

Return to the editor window. Place the cursor at the beginning of this line:

```
TextWindow.WriteLine("This is line 2")
```

Press **Enter**. A blank line will appear above it:

```
Untitled *
1  'editing
2  TextWindow.WriteLine("This is line 1")
3
4  TextWindow.WriteLine("This is line 2")
5
```

Move the cursor up and type into the empty line:

```
TextWindow.WriteLine("This is middle line")
```

The code window will now be:

```
Untitled *
1  'editing
2  TextWindow.WriteLine("This is line 1")
3  TextWindow.WriteLine("This is middle line")
4  TextWindow.WriteLine("This is line 2")
5
```

Run the program to see:

```
C:\Users\Lou\AppData\Local\Temp\tmpDC98.tmp.exe
This is line 1
This is middle line
This is line 2
Press any key to continue...
```

In a similar manner, putting the cursor at the end of a line, and then pressing **Enter**, puts a blank line below it.

DELETING A LINE

What if you want to delete an entire line? You can use the mouse and **Delete** key to do this. Put the cursor at the beginning of the line, press the **Left** mouse button and drag the cursor to beginning of the following line. This highlights the line. Now click **Delete** and it will disappear.

Return to the editor window. Highlight the line you added:

```
Untitled *
1  'editing
2  TextWindow.WriteLine("This is line 1")
3  TextWindow.WriteLine("This is middle line")
4  TextWindow.WriteLine("This is line 2")
5
```

Press **Delete** and its gone!

```
Untitled *
1  'editing
2  TextWindow.WriteLine("This is line 1")
3  TextWindow.WriteLine("This is line 2")
4
```

I WANT THAT LINE BACK!

What if you delete a line then decide you want it back? There is a cool button on the toolbar called the **Undo** button:

Clicking this button will make the editor forget (or undo) the last thing you did. If you click it first thing after making some change to your program, that change will be undone.

If you change your mind again and want to delete the line, click the **Redo** button:

Clicking this button will repeat (redo) the last thing you did in the editor.

ANOTHER WAY TO DELETE A LINE

Highlight a line in the code editor. Then, click the **Cut** button in the toolbar:

This button works like the **Delete** button, except it deletes (cuts) whatever text is highlighted using the mouse.

COPYING A LINE

As you continue writing programs, you will see many of the lines look very much alike. To save typing effort, you might like to copy lines. To do this, first highlight the line you want to copy. Then click the **Copy** button in the toolbar:

Next, put the cursor where you want the copied line to go. Click the **Paste** button:

You will get a copy of the line - at this point you might need to make some changes to the copied line. We see how to do this in the next lesson.

Assignment 3:

1. Start a **New** program. Type a line in the program. Move the cursor around in the line. Use the **Home** and **End** keys. Press **Enter** when done.

2. Try adding, deleting and copying lines in a program.

INSTRUCTOR NOTES 4   FIXING LINES AND SYNTAX ERRORS

This lesson concerns basic editing. We reexamine use of the mouse and arrow keys to move the cursor.

There are two erasure keys: **Backspace** and **Delete**. Make sure the student understands how each works.

We talk briefly about syntax errors. Help the students understand the error messages. Emphasize to students the need to type exactly to avoid syntax errors.

TASKS:

1. Demonstrate use of the **Backspace** and **Delete** keys. Explain how they differ.

2. Purposely have students introduce errors so they see how the syntax checking works.

3. Write a program that draws a smiley face.

LESSON 4   FIXING LINES AND SYNTAX ERRORS

FIXING MESSED UP LINES

To add characters to any spot on a line, put the cursor at that spot, and just type.

To erase part of a line, there are two keys to use, **Backspace** and **Delete**.

The **Backspace** key is on the top row of your keyboard (there is an arrow on it):

It erases "backward" that is, it erases characters to the left of the cursor.

Start a **New** program. Type this single line:

```
TextWinEow.WriteLine("Test program")
```

Notice I had you type **TextWindow** with an 'E' instead of a 'd'. Move the cursor to the right of the 'E'. Press the **Backspace** key. The letter disappears! Now type 'd' and the line is correct.

Delete key means take away:

This key is bigger on some keyboards. It erases letters to the right of the cursor. Go ahead and try it.

Start a **New** program. Type this single line:

```
TextWindow.WWriteLine("Test program")
```

This time we have an extra 'W'. Move the cursor to the left of the extra 'W' – press **Delete** and it's gone!

Both the **Backspace** and **Delete** keys are repeating keys. If you hold them down too long, you may erase more letters than you want.

So, remember: **Backspace** erases what is next to cursor on the left and then goes on whizzing along to the left, erasing as it goes. **Delete** erases what is to the right of the cursor and then sits there eating up letters as long as you hold the key.

SYNTAX ERRORS

So how do you know if you need to fix a line in your program? One way is that you notice the error before running the program. Examples are the extra letters we just saw.

Sometimes you don't see an error. In these cases, the computer will point out your error to you – these are called **syntax error** messages.

Start a **New** program. Once again, type the line with the extra 'w':

```
TextWindow.WWriteLine("Test program")
```

Run the program. You will see:

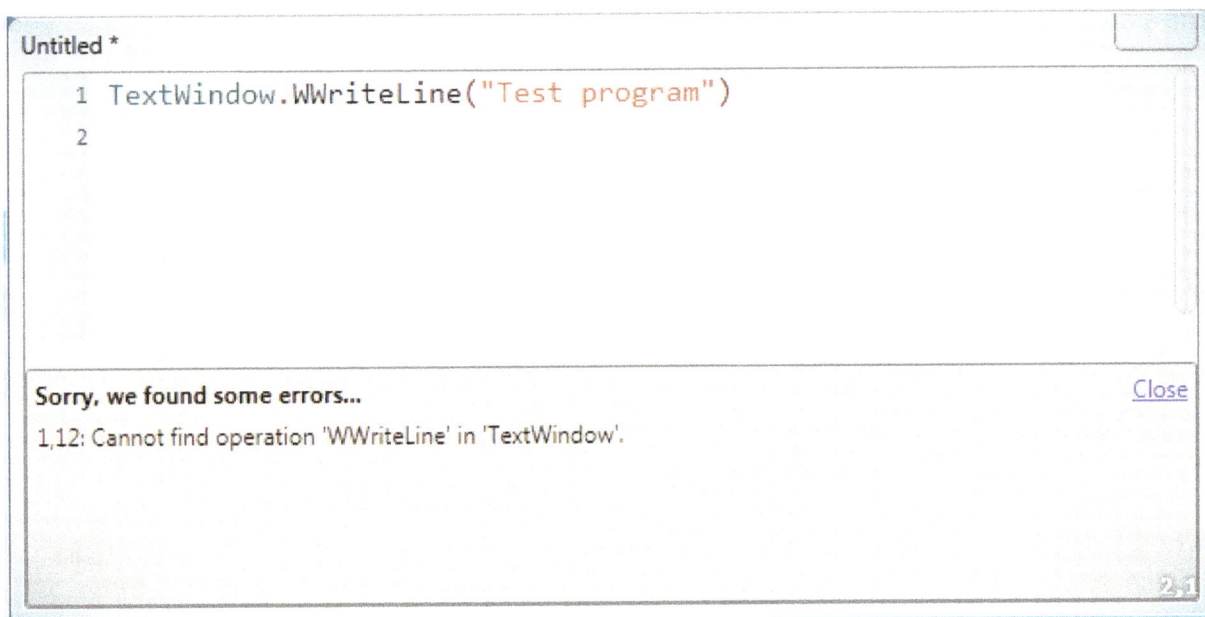

```
Untitled *
 1  TextWindow.WWriteLine("Test program")
 2
```

Sorry, we found some errors...   Close

1,12: Cannot find operation 'WWriteLine' in 'TextWindow'.

Below the code you wrote is a syntax error message that says:

1,12: Cannot find operation 'WWriteLine' in 'TextWindow'

Let's see what this is telling us. The first number (1) tells us which line the error has occurred in. The second number (12) tells us which column in the line the error starts at. It says it doesn't recognize the word **WWriteLine**. Of course it doesn't!

Return to the code window and fix the error. **Run** the program again. It should run correctly, showing:

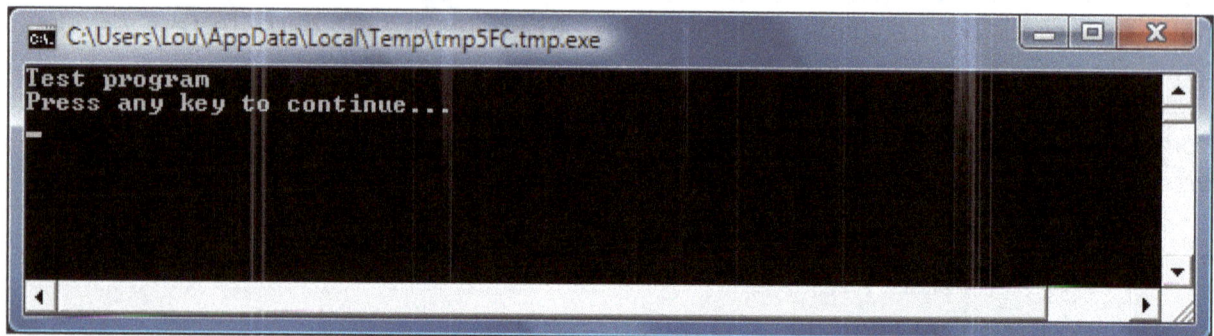

Let's try one other example. Change the line by adding an additional parenthesis at the end of the **WriteLine** statement:

```
TextWindow.WWriteLine("Test program"))
```

Try running and you will see:

Sorry, we found some errors...
1,37: Unexpected token) found.

The problem is clear - you have one too many right parentheses in Column 37 of Line 1.

When you try to run with syntax errors, Small Basic will kindly point out your errors to you so you can fix them. Syntax errors usually result because of incorrect typing, misspellings. Errors may also result from misunderstanding how to use certain statements.

1. Start a **New** program. Type a line in the program. Move the cursor around in the line. Use the **Backspace** and **Delete** keys to change letters. Press **Enter** when done.

2. Fix this line so the comment is CAT and not CAAT

   'CAAT

3. Try to draw a heart using characters. Use red text on a white background.

INSTRUCTOR NOTES 5   READ STATEMENT

This lesson is about the **Read** statement and string variables. We just introduce the statement. Similarly, we will give only the essential feature of each statement as they are introduced. We want the student to "see the forest" before going into details.

String variables are introduced using "box" concept. For the time being, variable names are single letters to avoid naming rules.

The "two hats" of the student, programmer and user of the programs, is introduced. WRITELINE is the programmer speaking, while the user can only speak when invited by a READ statement put there by the programmer.

1. What does the computer put into a box?

2. How does the program ask the user to type in something?

3. How do you know the computer is waiting for an answer?

4. Write a short program using **WriteLine** and **Read**.

Use the **Read** statement to make the computer ask the user to type something.

Start a **New** program. Type in these lines:

```
'Talky-talk
TextWindow.Clear()
TextWindow.WriteLine("Say something")
A = TextWindow.Read()
TextWindow.WriteLine("")
TextWindow.WriteLine("You said")
TextWindow.WriteLine(A)
```

Run the program and you will see:

```
C:\Users\Lou\AppData\Local\Temp\tmp1354.tmp.exe
Say something
_
```

The underscore (_) is flashing, meaning the computer is waiting for you to type something. Type **Hello there** and press **Enter**. You will see:

```
C:\Users\Lou\AppData\Local\Temp\tmp1354.tmp.exe
Say something
Hello there

You said
Hello there
Press any key to continue...
```

Let's see what happened here. After the message **Say something** was printed, the next program line is:

```
A = TextWindow.Read()
```

This is the line waiting for your input (as the user). It is the program **Read** statement. It reads whatever a user types and stores the input in a "box" named **A**. After getting the input, it writes out whatever is in this box A using:

```
TextWindow.WriteLine(A)
```

Run the program again and this time say something funny.

STRING VARIABLES

A is the name of a **string variable**. The computer stores string variables in memory boxes. The name is written on the front of the box and the string is put inside the box.

The box **A** is called a variable because you can put different strings into the box at different times in the program. The box can only hold one string at a time.

Putting a new string into a box automatically erases the old string that was in the box.

YOU WEAR TWO HATS, USER AND PROGRAMMER

You are a PROGRAMMER when you write a program. The person who runs the program is a USER.

Of course, if you run your own program, then YOU are the USER.

When the programmer writes a **WriteLine** statement, she is speaking to the user by writing on the computer monitor.

When the programmer writes a **Read** statement, she is asking the user to say something to the computer.

It is like a game of "May I?" The only time the user gets to say something is when the programmer allows it by writing a **Read** statement in the program.

1. Write a program that asks for a person's name and then says something silly to the person, by name.

2. Write a program that asks you to **Read** your favorite color and put it into a box called C. Now the program asks your favorite animal and puts this into box C too. Have the program write C. What will be written? **Run** the program and see if you are right.

In this lesson:

> **Write** statement
> The "invisible" write cursor
> **ReadNumber** statement

When a program begins to run, we imagine an invisible cursor in place at the upper left of the screen. This is called the "output cursor." It is not really imaginary, though it is invisible. There has to be a variable hidden within the computer which keeps track of where the next character is to appear on the screen. It is useful to pretend that there is an actual cursor, invisible, that represents this hidden variable. The output cursor moves along as things are written on the screen, and remain in place at the end of each written text.

Sometimes what the running program prints on the screen is its own text, for example **Read**. We are most concerned with what we want to write on the screen using the **Write** or **WriteLine** command. The output cursor is an idea important with these statements.

When a given **Write** statement has finished writing, the output cursor remains in place at the end of what has been written. Here is why this idea is useful. The program may now want to use another **Write** (or more generally, some other statement) to write further things on the screen.

The **WriteLine** statement is a **Write** statement with an additional step. After the end of the **Write**, the **WriteLine** statement causes a "carriage return." (Remember the old mechanical typewriters with the carriage return lever on the left side? You never saw such a machine? Ouch!)

The **WriteLine** statement will advance the output cursor to the beginning of the next line, as its last official act.

Any spaces desired in output, as in the "jam and toast" example, must be put into the strings explicitly.

The **ReadNumber** statement is used to input numerical information. It does "key trapping" not allowing any non-numeric input.

1. Which cursor is a flashing line? What statements put it in the text window?

2. Which cursor is invisible? What statements use it?

3. How do you make two statements write on the same line?

4. Will these two words have a space between them when run?

```
TextWindow.Write("Hello")
TextWindow.WriteLine("there!")
```

   If not, how do you put a space between them?

5. When would you want to use **ReadNumber** instead of the **Read** statement?

LESSON 6   WRITE AND READNUMBER

There is another way to write to the text window and another way to read inputs from the user.

ONE LINE OR MANY?

Start a **New** program in Small Basic. Enter this program:

```
' food
TextWindow.WriteLine("toast")
TextWindow.WriteLine("and")
TextWindow.WriteLine("jam")
TextWindow.WriteLine("")
```

Run the program. You will see:

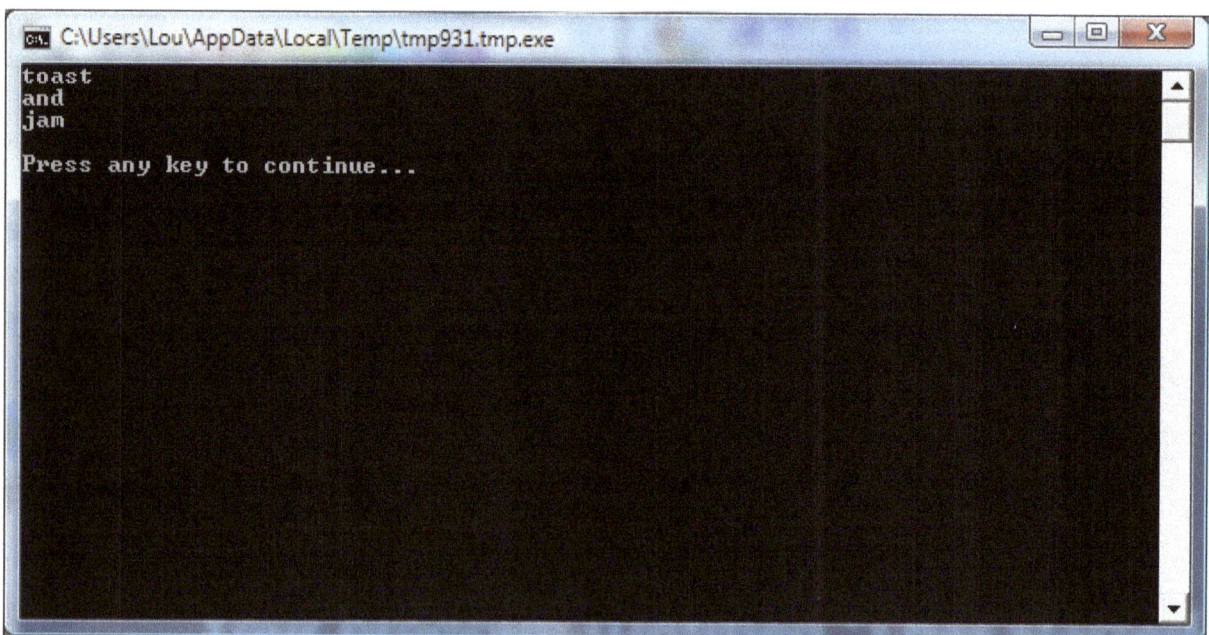

Each **WriteLine** statement prints a separate line.

Change the lines writing toast and jam so they now read:

```
TextWindow.Write("toast ")
TextWindow.Write("and ")
```

We have changed **WriteLine** to **Write** and added a space at the end of "toast" and at the end of "and". Don't change the other lines.

Run the program. Now you see:

What was different from the first time?

_____

_____

THE HIDDEN CURSOR

Remember the flashing line when using the **Read** statement? It is an input cursor and shows where the next input character will appear on the screen when you type.

The commands to write text to the text window (**WriteLine** and **Write**) also have a cursor, but it is invisible. It marks where the next character will appear.

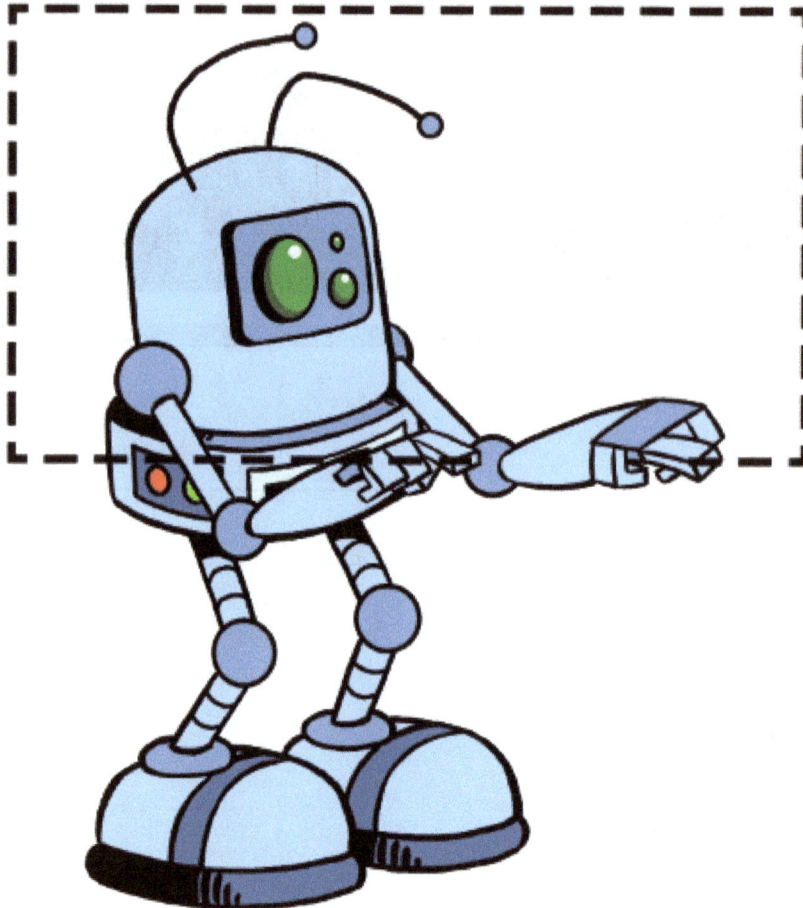

Rule: After a **WriteLine** statement, the invisible cursor moves down to the next line. After a **Write** statement, the invisible cursor waits in place at the end of the line. The next **WriteLine** or **Write** statement adds on to what has already been written on the same line.

FAMOUS PAIRS

Start a **New** program. Enter this code:

```
'famous pairs
TextWindow.Write("Enter a name ")
A = TextWindow.Read()
TextWindow.Write("Enter another ")
B = TextWindow.Read()
TextWindow.WriteLine("")
TextWindow.Write("Presenting that famous twosome ")
TextWindow.Write(A)
TextWindow.Write(" and ")
TextWindow.WriteLine(B)
```

Make sure there is a space before and after the "and".

Run the program. When asked, enter names. Here's what you should see:

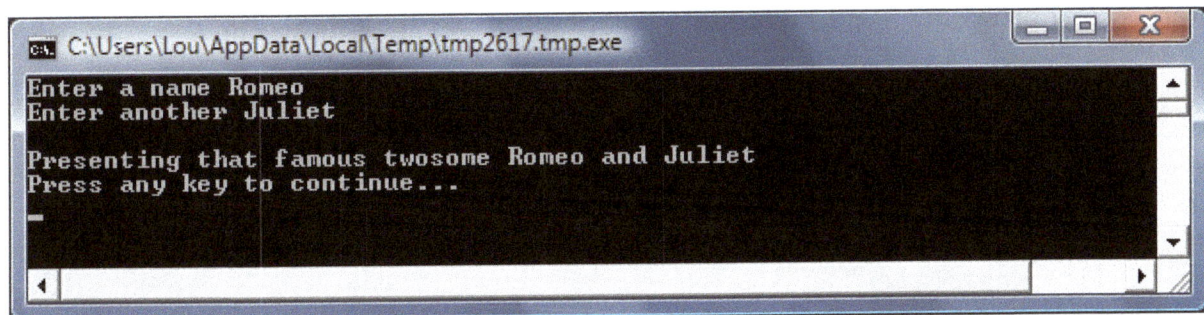

Notice how using **Write** before a **Read** puts the input information on the same line asking for input.

The **Read** statement lets you input a string of characters. The **ReadNumber** statement lets you input a number. It only lets you type a digit (0 – 9), a minus sign (-) or a decimal point (.).

Start a **New** program. Type this code:

```
'input numbers
TextWindow.Write("What's your name? ")
A = TextWindow.Read()
TextWindow.Write("How old are you? ")
B = TextWindow.ReadNumber()
TextWindow.WriteLine("")
TextWindow.Write("So, ")
TextWindow.Write(A)
TextWindow.Write(" you said you are ")
TextWindow.Write(B)
TextWindow.WriteLine(" years old")
```

Run the program. Answer the questions. When asked for your age, try typing characters other than numbers - the computer won't let you! When the program runs, you will see something like this:

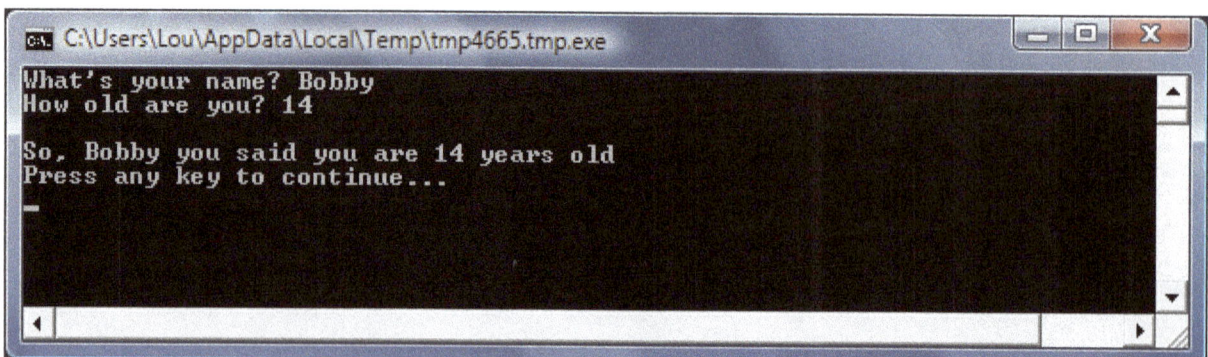

1. Write a program that asks for the name of a musical group and one of their tunes. Then, write the group name and the tune name, with the word "plays" in between.

2. Write a program that asks for a famous person's name and the year they were born? Write out the input information.

The assignment statement is introduced using the concept of memory boxes. Concatenation using the plus sign (+) is called "gluing the strings."

The model is used to emphasize the assignment statement is a replacement command, not an "equal" relationship in the arithmetic sense.

The box idea nicely separates the concepts of "name of the variable" and "value of the variable." The name is on the label of the box, the value is inside. The contents of the box may be removed for use, and new contents inserted.

More exactly, a copy of the contents is made and used; when a variable is used, the original contents remain intact. This point is explained.

QUESTIONS:

1. The assignment statement puts things in boxes. So do Read and ReadNumber statements. How are they different?

2. In this program line:

   Q = "MOM"

   What is "MOM" called? What is the name of the string variable in this line? What is the value of the string variable after the program runs?

3. If you **Run** this little program:

   H = "fat"
   K = " sausage"
   P = H + K

   What is in each box after it runs?

LESSON 7   ASSIGNMENT STATEMENT

The **assignment statement** puts things into boxes. Start a **New** program and enter these lines:

```
Q = "truck"
TextWindow.WriteLine(Q)
```

Run the program. You will see:

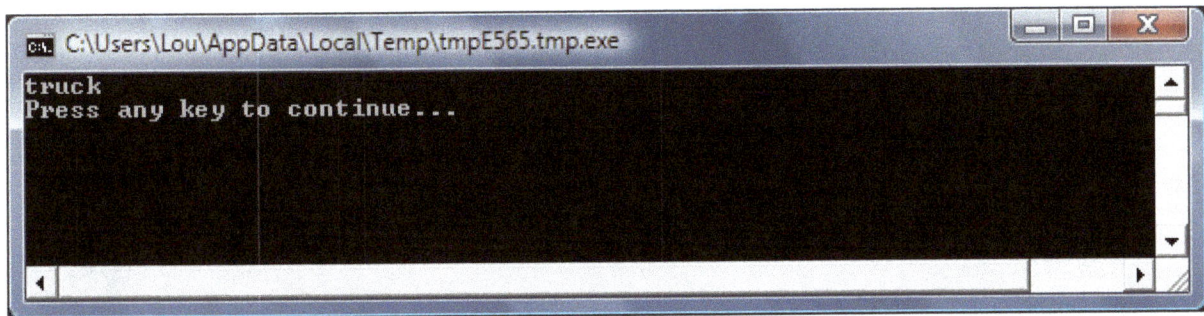

```
C:\Users\Lou\AppData\Local\Temp\tmpE565.tmp.exe
truck
Press any key to continue...
```

Here is what the computer does:

First Line: It sees that a box named **Q** is needed. It looks in memory for it. It doesn't find one because **Q** has not been used in this program before. So it takes an empty box, writes **Q** on the front, and then puts the string "truck" into it.

Second Line: The computer sees that it must write whatever is in box **Q**. It goes to the box and makes a copy of the string "truck" that it finds there. It puts the copy in the text window. The string "truck" is still in box **Q**.

66

NAMES AND VALUES

This line makes a string variable:

```
W = "MOPSEY"
```

The name of the variable is **W**.
The value of the variable is put into the box.
In this line, the value of **W** is "MOPSEY"

ANOTHER EXAMPLE

Start a **New** program. Use this code (I show it in the code window so I can refer to the line numbers):

```
Untitled *

1 D = "pickles"
2 A = " and "
3 TextWindow.Write("What goes with pickles? ")
4 Z = TextWindow.Read()
5 TextWindow.WriteLine("")
6 TextWindow.Write(D)
7 TextWindow.Write(A)
8 TextWindow.WriteLine(Z)
9
```

Explain what the computer does in each line:

1 _____

2 _____

3 _____

4 _____

5 _____

6 _____

7 _____

8 _____

Run the program and see if it does what you thought. Here's what I got:

```
C:\Users\Lou\AppData\Local\Temp\tmp4EC5.tmp.exe

What goes with pickles? hamburgers

pickles and hamburgers
Press any key to continue...
```

GLUING STRINGS

Here is how to stick two strings together to make a longer string. Start a **New** program. Type in this code:

```
Untitled *

1 W = "HAR DE "
2 X = "HAR "
3 A = W + X
4 TextWindow.WriteLine(A)
5 TextWindow.WriteLine("")
6 A = A + X
7 TextWindow.WriteLine(A)
8
```

Before you **Run** the program, try to guess what will be written at Line 4 and Line 7:

4 _____

7 _____

Now, **Run** the program to see if you were right. You should see this:

```
C:\Users\Lou\AppData\Local\Temp\tmp92CA.tmp.exe

HAR DE HAR

HAR DE HAR HAR
Press any key to continue...
```

Rule: The plus sign (+) sticks to strings together.

1. Write your own program which uses an assignment statement and explain how it stores things in "boxes."

2. Write a program that reads two strings, glues them together and writes them in the text window.

The **Goto** statement allows a "dumb" loop that goes on forever. It also helps in the flow of command in later programs, after the **If** is introduced. It provides a slow and easy entrance for the student into the idea that the flow of command ned not just go down the list of lines. Make sure students also understand the concept of a **line label**.

For now, its main use is to let programs run on for a reasonable length of time. In each loop through, something can be modified.

The problem is how to stop it. The X in the upper corner of the text window does this nicely. You can also use the **End Program** button on the overlay that opens when a program runs.

Goto is tolerant of "spaghetti" programming. Examples of "spaghetti" are shown to the students, and although some fun is had with them, the idea is to make the student aware of the mess that undisciplined use of **Goto** can make.

We now have most of the major elements that lead to "real" programming. Lacking is the **If** structure, which will change the computer from some sort of a record player into a machine that can evaluate situations and make decisions accordingly.

1. In this little program:

```
TextWindow.WriteLine("Hi ")
Goto PrintDaddy
PrintBig:
TextWindow.WriteLine("Big ")
PrintDaddy:
TextWindow.WriteLine("Daddy ")
```

What will appear in the text window when it is run?

2. And this one:

```
Print1:
TextWindow.Write("Incredible ")
Print2:
TextWindow.Write("Big Machine ")
Goto Print2
```

3. How do you stop the program in Question 2?

4. Write a short program that plays a bell sound, asks your favorite movie star's name and then does it over and over again.

JUMPING AROUND IN YOUR PROGRAM

Start a **New** program. Try this code:

```
TextWindow.Write("What is your name? ")
N = TextWindow.Read()
WriteName:
TextWindow.WriteLine(N)
Goto WriteName
```

There are two new things in the program. One is the label – **WriteName:**. The other is the command **Goto**. They work as a team.

Run the program. Enter your name. It never stops by itself! Here's what I got:

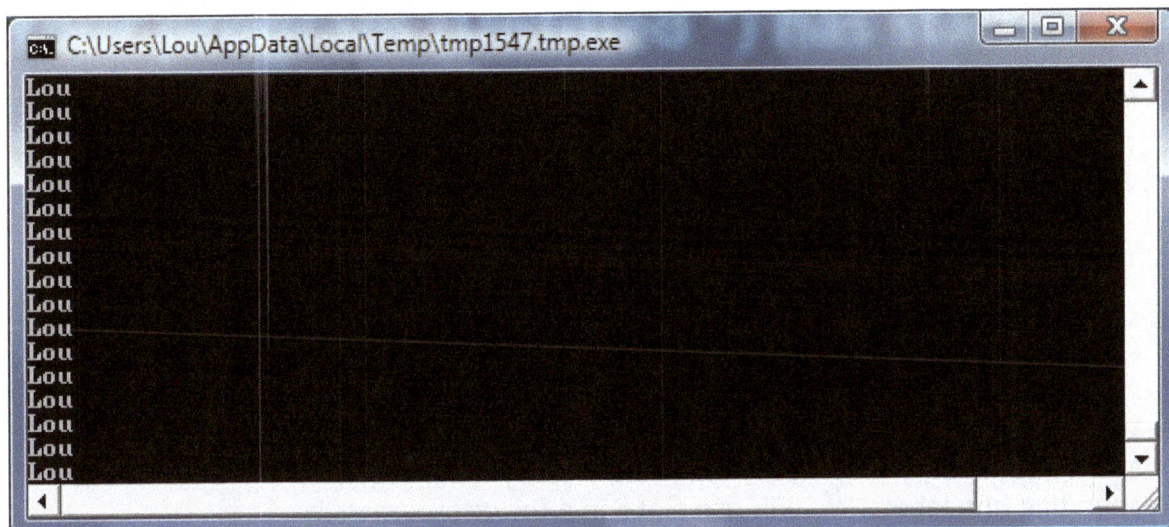

To stop your name from whizzing past your eyes: click the **X** in the upper right corner of the text window:

Click here to stop

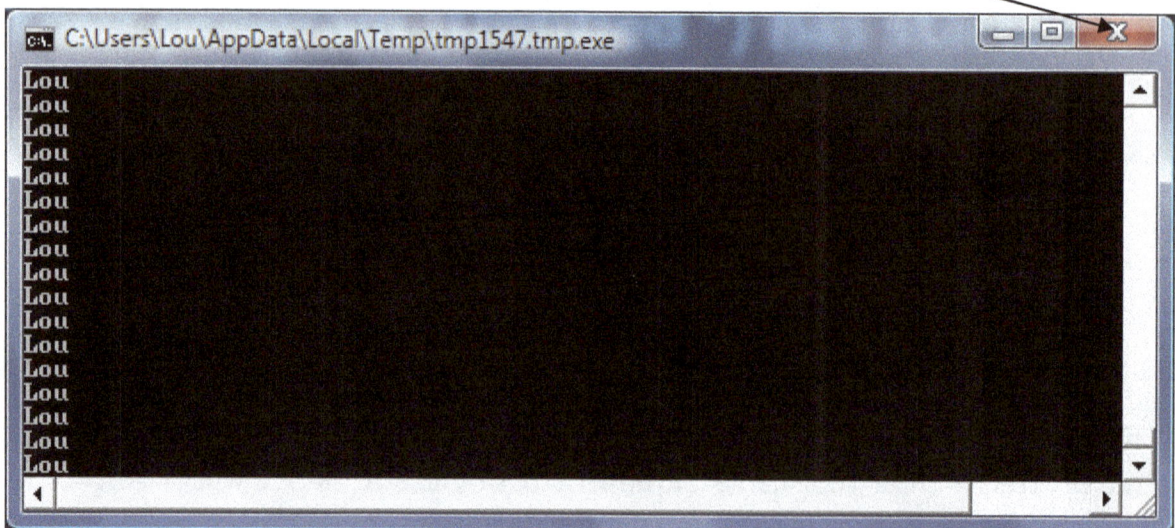

Notice this line of code:

```
Goto WriteName
```

This is the **Goto** command. It is like "Go To Jail" in the game of Monopoly. Every time the computer reaches this line, it goes back to the line labeled **WriteName** and writes your name again.   Look at the **line label:**

```
WriteName:
```

To make a line label, you write a name followed by a colon (:). Every **Goto** needs a corresponding line label. We will use **Goto** in a lot of programs.

MORE JUMPING

Start a **New** program. Type in this code:

```
' Shut up!
GetInput:
  TextWindow.Write("Say something - ")
  S = TextWindow.Read()
  TextWindow.WriteLine("")
  TextWindow.WriteLine("Did you say " + S + "?")
  TextWindow.WriteLine("")
  Goto GetInput
```

Run the program. Keep typing answers whenever you are asked. Click the **X** in the upper corner of the text window to stop the program. Here's what I got:

```
C:\Users\Lou\AppData\Local\Temp\tmp8BB2.tmp.exe
Say something - how are you

Did you say how are you?

Say something - i am having fun

Did you say i am having fun?

Say something - _
```

The arrow in the code listing shows just what the **Goto** statement does. Also look at how we glued the strings together in this line:

```
TextWindow.WriteLine("Did you say " + S + "?")
```

KINDS OF JUMPS

There are only two ways to jump: ahead or back.

Jumping back gives a **loop**:

```
WriteHi:
  TextWindow.WriteLine("Hi!")
  Goto WriteHi
```

The computer goes around and around in this loop, writing Hi! each time. Click the **X** in the upper corner of the text window to stop the program.

Jumping ahead lets you skip part of a program. It is not useful yet, but we will use it later when we explain a very important statement – the **If** statement.

ANOTHER WAY TO STOP

We see when programs are in loops, the **X** in the upper right corner of the text window is a life saver. Whenever you need to stop the program, you can click this X.

There is one other way to stop a program. When a program is running in Small Basic, this window appears:

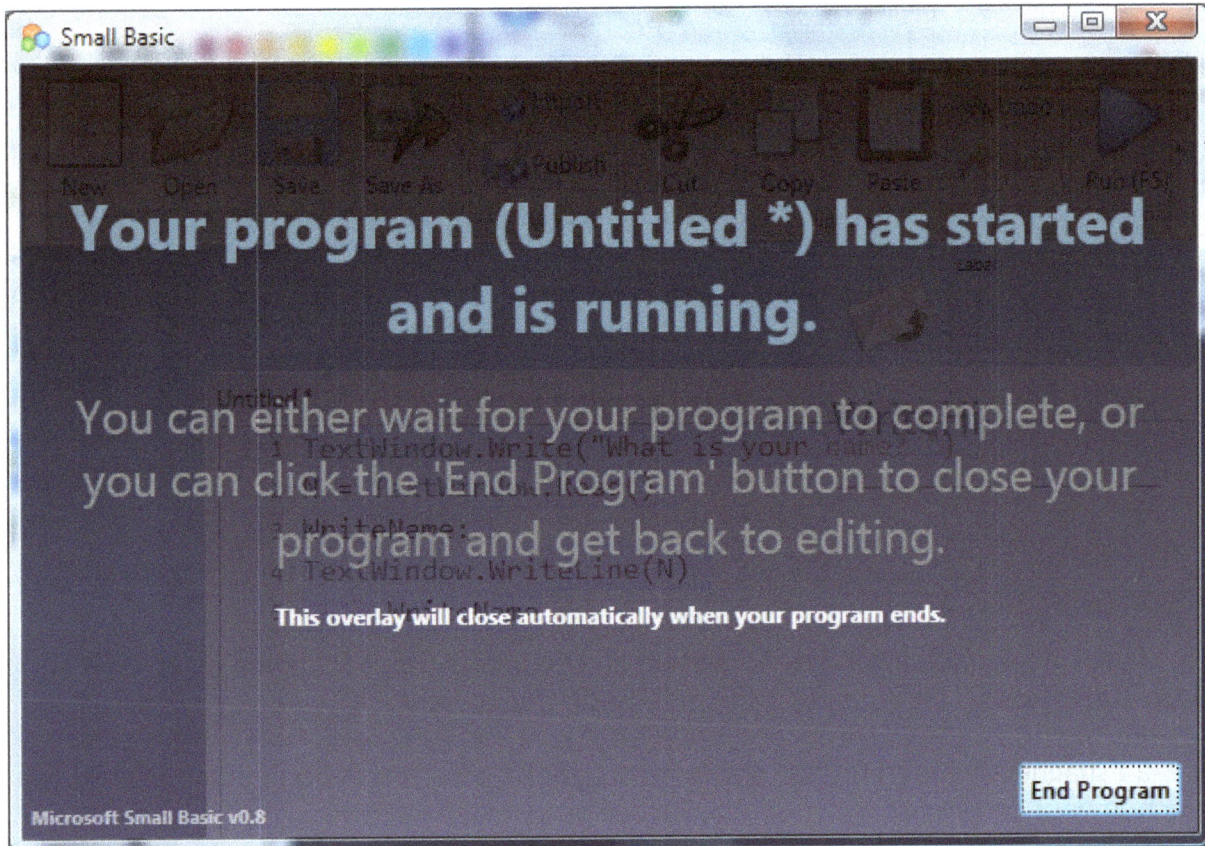

Clicking the **End Program** button will stop your program.

A CAN OF SPAGHETTI

Look at this code:

```
' Spaghetti
Goto PrintSpaghetti
Printa:
TextWindow.WriteLine("a")
Goto Printu
PrintS:
TextWindow.WriteLine("S")
Goto Printa
Printc:
TextWindow.WriteLine("c")
Goto Printe
Printu:
TextWindow.WriteLine("u")
Goto Printc
PrintSpaghetti:
TextWindow.WriteLine("Spaghetti")
Goto PrintS
Printe:
TextWindow.WriteLine("e")
' end
```

This is not a good, clear program! Notice all the labels (lines followed by colons) and **Goto** statements. Try running it in Small Basic if you want.

It is a "spaghetti" program. Do not write spaghetti programs! Don't jump around too much in your programs.

Assignment 8:

1. Just for practice in understanding the **Goto** statement and line labels, draw the road map for this spaghetti program:

```
' Forked Tongue
Goto PrintS
PrintN:
TextWindow.WriteLine("N")
Goto PrintA
PrintS:
TextWindow.WriteLine("S")
Goto PrintN
PrintE:
TextWindow.WriteLine("E")
Goto PrintBite
PrintA:
TextWindow.WriteLine("A")
Goto PrintK
PrintK:
TextWindow.WriteLine("K")
Goto PrintE
PrintBite:
TextWindow.WriteLine("Bite")
' end
```

2. Rewrite the snake program above, leaving out the **Goto** statements, making the program "clean and lean."

3. Write a program that writes "Teen Power" over and over.

4. How do you stop a program in a loop?

5. Write another program that prints your name on one line, then a friend's name on the next, over and over. Sound a ringing bell as each name is written. Stop the program.

6. Write a program that uses **WriteLine**, **Read**, assignment statements and **Goto**. It also should glue strings together.

INSTRUCTOR NOTES 9   IF STATEMENT

If is a powerful but intricate command that is at the very heart of the computer as a logic machine.

Both verbal (the "cake" cartoon) and visual (the "fork in the road" cartoon) metaphors help in understanding the **If** statement.

The **Goto** statement has already introduced the idea that the flow of control down the program list may be altered. To that idea is now added the conditional test: if an assertion is true, one thing happens, if it is false, another.

Condition is used for the assertion of truth. **Statement** is used for the statement to be executed if the assertion is true. Small Basic allows multiple statements between the **If** and the **EndIf**. For simplicity, our examples show a single statement. We also do not study the **ElseIf** or **Else** statements.

Two levels of abstract ideas occur in the assertions. On the literal level we have "equal" and "not equal":

$$A = B$$
$$C <> D$$

On the next level up, we have the truth or falsity of the assertion. Some care may be needed to separate and clarify these notions.

When you see "A = B", it may not really be true that A equals B because the assertion may actually be false.

The larger set of relations:

$$< \quad > \quad = \quad =< \quad => \quad <>$$

will be treated in later lessons.

1. How do you make this program write **That's Fine**?

```
GetAnswer:
TextWindow.Write("Does your toe hurt? ")
T = TextWindow.Read()
If (T = "nah") Then
   TextWindow.WriteLine("That's fine")
EndIf
If (T = "some") Then
   Goto GetAnswer
EndIf
```

2. Write a short program which asks if you like chocolate or vanilla ice cream. Answers could be "C" or "V". For the "C" write "Yummy!" For the "V" answer, print "Mmmmmmmmm!"

3. In the **If** statement example, what is meant by Condition? What is meant by Statement? Where is the "fork in the road" in an **If** statement?

LESSON 9   IF STATEMENT

Start a **New** program. Enter this code:

```
Ask:
TextWindow.WriteLine("")
TextWindow.Write("Are you happy?  (yes or no) ")
A = TextWindow.Read()
If (A = "yes") Then
  TextWindow.WriteLine("I'm glad")
EndIf
If (A = "no") Then
  TextWindow.WriteLine("Too bad")
EndIf
Goto Ask
```

Run the program. Try answering yes, no, or maybe. What happens each time? Here is what I found when I ran it:

Stop the program by clicking the **X** in the upper right corner of the text window.

83

THE IF STATEMENT

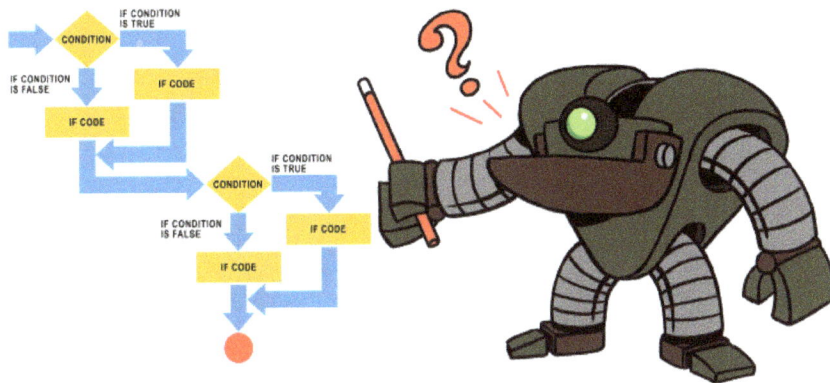

The **If** statement has three important parts: **If**, **Then** and **EndIf**.

```
If (Condition) Then
   Statement
EndIf
```

First, the computer looks at **Condition**.

If it is "true", the computer processes the **Statement**.

If Condition is not true, or "false", the computer goes on to the line following the **EndIf** and does not process the Statement.

In English, we would say:

> If Condition is "true", then process Statement and go on to the next line after the **EndIf** line.

> If Condition is "false", then go on to the next line after the **EndIf** line.

THE "IF" IN ENGLISH AND SMALL BASIC

In English:

> **If** your homework is done, **Then** you may have some cake.

In Small Basic:

```
If (A = "done") Then
   TextWindow.WriteLine("Eat Cake!")
EndIf
```

1. Start a **New** program. Write code that asks if you are a "BOY" or a "GIRL". If the answer is "BOY", the program prints "SNIPS AND SNAILS". If the answer is "GIRL", write "SUGAR AND SPICE".

A FORK IN THE ROAD

When it sees **If**, the computer must choose which road to take.

If Condition is "true", it goes past **Then** and executes the Statement it finds there. Then it goes to the next line after the **EndIf**.

If Condition is "false", it goes to the next line after the **EndIf**.

Look at this example:

```
If (A = "HUNGRY") Then
    TextWindow.WriteLine("Eat!")
EndIf
```

THE "NOT EQUAL" SIGN

Two signs: = means "equal"
        <> means "not equal"

To make the "<>" sign:

> Hold down the **Shift** key
> Then, press the "<" key, then the ">" key

USING THE <> SIGN

Remember how the **If** statement is written:

```
If (Condition) Then
  Statement
EndIf
```

Choose B <> "FIRE" for the Condition. Put it in this **If** statement:

```
If (B <> "FIRE") Then
  TextWindow.WriteLine("Feed him hot chili!")
EndIf
```

How does this work?

If the **B** box holds "COLD", then **B** is not equal to "FIRE".
In this case, the condition B <> "FIRE" is "true".
Since the condition is "true", the computer writes "Feed him hot chili!"

If the **B** box holds "FIRE", then **B** is equal to "FIRE".
In this case, the condition B <> "FIRE" is "false".
Since the condition is "false", the computer will not write anything.

Let's try it in a program. Start a **New** program. Use this code:

```
TextWindow.WriteLine("With dogs, it's a cold nose.")
TextWindow.WriteLine("With dragons, it's ...")
TextWindow.Write("How is your dragon's breath (FIRE or COLD)? ")
B = TextWindow.Read()
If (B <> "FIRE") Then
  TextWindow.WriteLine("Feed him hot chili!")
EndIf
If (B = "FIRE") Then
  TextWindow.WriteLine("Watch out!")
EndIf
TextWindow.WriteLine("Nice dragon")
```

Run the program. Answer FIRE or COLD to see what's printed. Here's what you should see with COLD:

```
C:\Users\Lou\AppData\Local\Temp\tmpA330.tmp.exe
With dogs, it's a cold nose.
With dragons, it's ...
How is your dragon's breath (HOT or COLD)? COLD
Feed him hot chili!
Nice dragon
Press any key to continue...
```

1. Write a "pizza" program. Ask what topping is wanted. You can choose mushrooms, pepperoni, anchovies, green peppers, etc. You can also ask what size.

2. Write a color guessing game. One player inputs a color in string C and the other keeps inputting guesses into string G. Use two **If** statements to tell the user if their guess is right or wrong.

INSTRUCTOR NOTES 10   INTRODUCING NUMBERS

Numeric variables and operations are introduced. Assignment statements, **ReadNumber**, **Write** and **WriteLine** are revisited.

The idea of memory as a shelf of boxes is extended to numbers. Again, variable names are limited to single letters for the time being.

We illustrate arithmetic operations. The asterisk (*) for multiplication will probably be unfamiliar to the student. Division will usually give decimal numbers, so it is nice if your student is familiar with them. But most arithmetic will be addition and subtraction, with a little multiplication. A student unfamiliar with decimal numbers will not experience any disadvantage.

Here is an issue that we will NOT expose the student to. Because a string is different from a number, you normally create an error if you try to do math with a string. However, sometimes in a mixed expression, Small Basic converts a string to a number and uses it in arithmetic. For example: ("6.7" + 2) is changed to (6.7 + 2) and evaluates to the number 8.7. The practice is very dangerous, as it can easily be misused and then causes errors that are very hard to find.

Similarly in **Write** and **WriteLine** statements with mixed string and numeric quantities, a number can sometimes be converted to a string and the whole thing evaluated as a string.

Students should be strongly discouraged against mixing strings and numbers in the same expression.   You may wish to experiment with this conversion issue, to become aware of its occasional usefulness, as well as its frequent generation of errors.

The non-standard use of the equal sign (=) in Small Basic, that it means "replace" and not "equal," shows up strongly in the statement:

$$N = N + 1$$

The cartoon uses the box idea to illustrate this meaning of "=".

1. What are the different kinds of "boxes" in memory? (That is, differing by the kinds of things stored in the boxes).

2. Explain why N = N + 1 for a computer is not like "7 = 7 + 1" in arithmetic.

3. Give a bad example of arithmetic in an assignment statement.

4. Explain what is meant by the "name of a variable" and the "value of a variable" for both numeric and string variables.

So far we have only used strings, except when we briefly looked at the **ReadNumber** statement. Numbers can be used too. Start a **New** program. Enter this program:

```
' Bigger
TextWindow.Write("Give me a number ")
N = TextWindow.ReadNumber()
A = N + 1
TextWindow.WriteLine("")
TextWindow.Write("Here is a bigger one ")
TextWindow.WriteLine(A)
```

Run the program. Enter a number. Here's what I see:

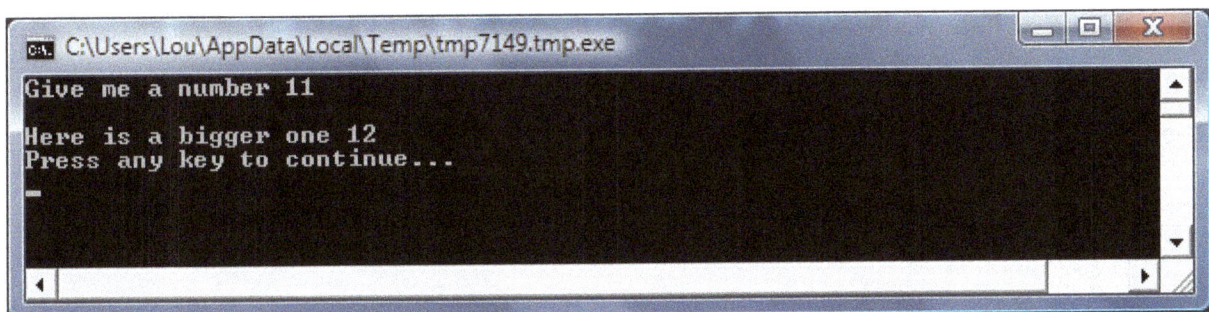

ARITHMETIC

+	addition	*	multiplication
-	subtraction	/	division

The + and – signs are on the far right side of the top row of the keyboard.

Computers use "*" instead of "x" for a multiplication sign. Try this. Change this line in the code above:

A = N + 1

to

A = N * 5

(Find the "*" above the 8 on the keyboard). Now, A is equal to 5 times N.

Run the program to check the result. Here, I multiplied 7 times 5:

Computers use "/" for a division sign. Many times, division answers are decimal numbers. Try this. Change this line in the code above:

```
A = N + 1
```

So that N is divided by 5:

```
A = N / 5
```

Run the program to check the result. Here, I divided 93 by 5:

```
C:\Users\Lou\AppData\Local\Temp\tmp190F.tmp.exe

Give me a number 93

Here is a bigger one 18.6
Press any key to continue...
```

VARIABLES

Just as you have to name a box that holds a string variable, you need a name for a box that holds a number. The thing that you put into the box is the "value" of the variable. An example is a price of a bicycle:

```
Bicycle = 54.00
```

ARITHMETIC IN THE ASSIGNMENT STATEMENT

Start a **New** program. Type in this code:

```
A = 2001
B = 1983
C = A - B
TextWindow.WriteLine("How much longer Hal?")
TextWindow.Write(C)
TextWindow.WriteLine(" years")
```

Run the program to see:

```
C:\Users\Lou\AppData\Local\Temp\tmp9E66.tmp.exe
How much longer Hal?
18 years
Press any key to continue...
```

Numbers and strings are different. Example: 1984 is a number, but "1984" is not a number. It is a string constant because it is in quotes.

Rule: Even if a string is made up of numeric characters, it is still not a number.

Some numeric constants: 5, 22, 3.14, -50

Some string constants: "Hi", "7", "TWO", "3.14"

Rule: You should not do arithmetic with the numbers in strings.

Correct: A = 3 + 7
Incorrect: A = "3" + "7"

So, there are two types of variables: string and numeric. You cannot put a string in a number box or a number in a string box.

STRINGS AND NUMBERS IN SMALL BASIC

Remember – it is not proper to do arithmetic with strings – only numbers. However, there are times that Small Basic will let you get away with this improper arithmetic.

Start a **New** program. Use this code:

```
A = 5
B = "10"
C = A + B
TextWindow.WriteLine(C)
```

Notice you are trying to add a number (5) with a string ("10"). **Run** the program. You would think you might get an error, but try it. Do you see this?:

You will get 15.

Rule: If a string contains proper numeric data, and you are doing arithmetic, Small Basic will first copy the string from its box. Then it will convert the copy to a number to do the arithmetic. That's what happened here – the string "10" was converted to the numeric 10.

Use this conversion ability of Small Basic with great care, because variations on it sometimes cause incorrect results.

Change the first line in the code so it's no longer a numeric string:

```
A = "A5"
B = "10"
C = A + B
TextWindow.WriteLine(C)
```

Now you are "adding" two strings. **Run** the program and you see:

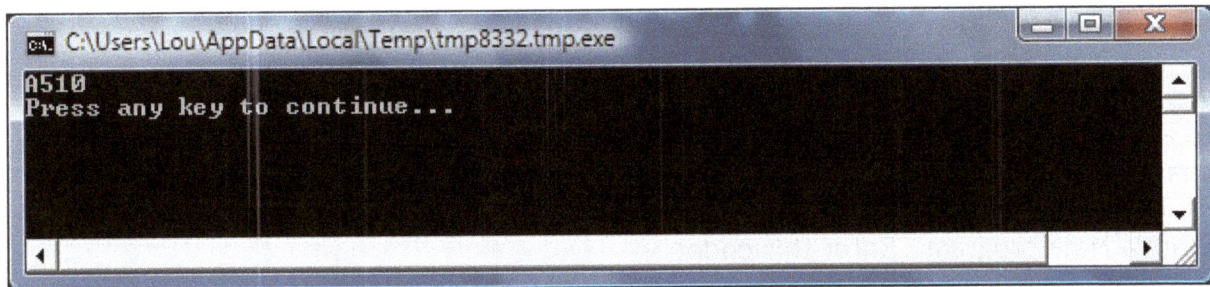

```
C:\Users\Lou\AppData\Local\Temp\tmp8332.tmp.exe
A510
Press any key to continue...
```

Remember the plus sign (+) is also used to glue strings – that's what happened here.

Now, change the code to:

```
A = "A5"
B = "10"
C = A * B
TextWindow.WriteLine(C)
```

Here we are trying to "multiply" two strings. **Run** the program to see:

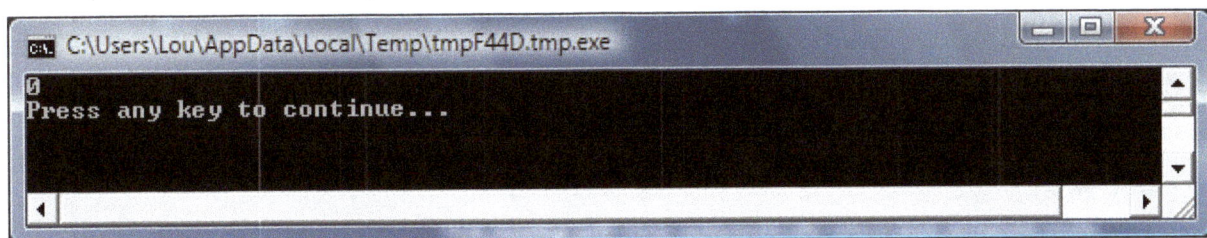

```
C:\Users\Lou\AppData\Local\Temp\tmpF44D.tmp.exe
0
Press any key to continue...
```

We get a zero! Small Basic was not able to convert the strings to proper numbers and, rather than stop with an error, it just computed a zero. This is not a good result – you may not know what's going on.

Rule: Avoid doing arithmetic with strings, especially when using the plus (+) sign.

One of these statements will <u>not</u> write the number 8 – which one?

```
TextWindow.WriteLine(8)
TextWindow.WriteLine("8")
TextWindow.WriteLine("5 + 3")
TextWindow.WriteLine("5" + "3")
TextWindow.WriteLine(5 + 3)
```

MIXTURES IN PRINT

We just saw that when doing arithmetic, Small Basic will (if possible) change a string to a number. You will also find that when writing out numbers, Small Basic will change numbers to strings if needed.

Start a **New** program. Enter this code:

```
A = 5
TextWindow.WriteLine("My hand has " + A + " fingers.")
```

We are "gluing" a number inside a string. **Run** the program to see:

The program properly put the number in the string before writing the result.

A FUNNY THING ABOUT THE EQUAL SIGN

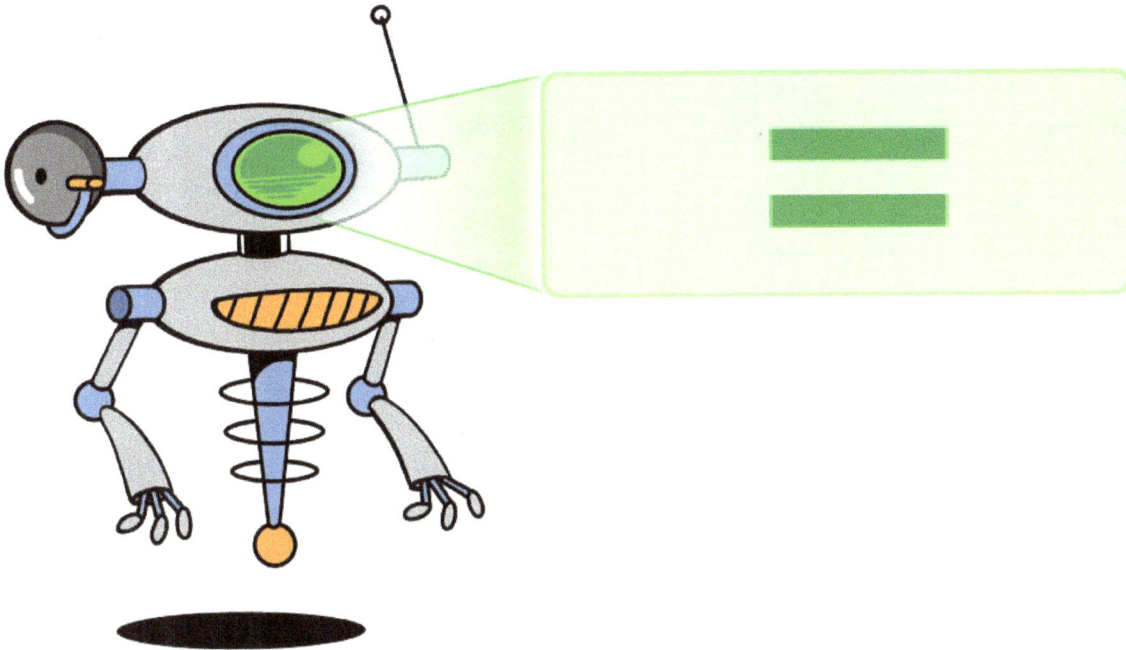

The equal sign (=) in computing does not exactly mean "equals." Look at this program line:

```
N = N + 1
```

This does not make sense in arithmetic. Suppose N is 7. This would say that:

```
7 = 7 + 1
```

which is not correct.

But it is okay in computing to say N = N + 1 because the "=" really means "replace" (or assign). Look at this line again:

```
N = N + 1
```

Here is what happens if N is 7:

The computer goes to the box with **N** written on the front.
It takes the number 7 from the box.
It adds 1 to the 7 to get 8.
Then it throws away the 7 that was in the box, and puts 8 in the box.

Another way to say the same thing is: (New N) equals (Old N) plus one

DON'T BE BACKWARD!

In arithmetic, you can put two numbers on whichever side of the equal sign you want. But in assignment statements, you cannot.

Arithmetic:	N = 3 3 = N	means the same as
Small Basic:	N = 3 3 = N	correct incorrect
Small Basic:	N = B B = N	is not the same as Why not?

N = B means _____

B = N means _____

Assignment 10:

1. Write a program that asks for your age and the current year. Then subtract and write out the year of your birth. Be sure to use **Write** or **WriteLine** statements to tell what is wanted and what the final number means.

2. Write a program that asks for two numbers and then writes out their product (multiplies them). Be sure to use lots of **WriteLine** statements to tell the user what is happening.

INSTRUCTOR NOTES 11   DELAYS AND RANDOM NUMBERS

Two important methods are introduced: **Delay** and **GetRandomNumber**. These are used in games and graphics.

This lesson introduces the **Delay** method used to slow the program down so that its operation can be more easily observed. The concept of a millisecond may need extra explanation.

The **GetRandomNumber** method generates random numbers from 1 to a limit specified by the method argument. Illustrate that to get any a range starting with another integer than 1 just requires a simple addition or subtraction.

QUESTIONS:

1. How would you delay for two seconds in a program?

2. What is the argument in this statement?

    ```
    Program.Delay(3500)
    ```

3. What does this line do:

    ```
    Math.GetRandomNumber(8)
    ```

4. How can you generate random numbers from 0 to 9?

LESSON 11   DELAYS AND RANDOM NUMBERS

Here is a way to slow down a program. It uses the **Delay** statement. Start a **New** program. Type this code in the editor:

```
' Game
TextWindow.WriteLine("Hide")
Program.Delay(2000)
TextWindow.WriteLine("Ready or not, here I come!")
```

Run the program. When it first starts you see:

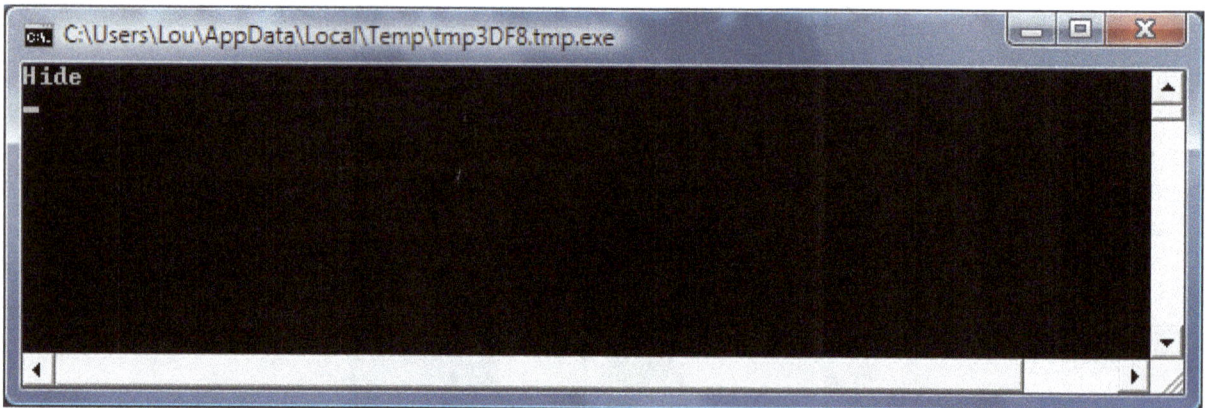

```
C:\Users\Lou\AppData\Local\Temp\tmp3DF8.tmp.exe

Hide
```

Then after a brief wait (like counting when you are "it" in a game of hide and seek), the program ends with this message:

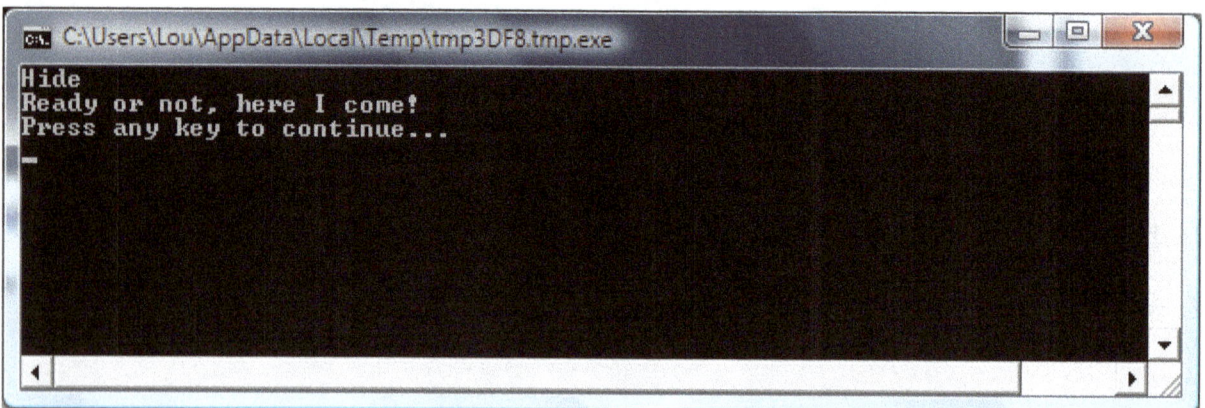

```
C:\Users\Lou\AppData\Local\Temp\tmp3DF8.tmp.exe

Hide
Ready or not, here I come!
Press any key to continue...
```

The wait was caused by this statement:

```
Program.Delay(2000)
```

This is the Small Basic **Delay** statement. The number in parentheses tells the computer how long to delay, or wait, before going on to the next program line.

The delay value is measured in something called **milliseconds**. **Milli** means one-thousandth so there are 1000 milliseconds in one second of time. The 2000 used in this example told the computer to delay 2000 milliseconds, or 2 seconds. Try other values.

Let's build a timer. Start a **New** program. Use this code:

```
' Tick tock
TextWindow.Write("Wait how long? ")
S = TextWindow.ReadNumber()
T = S * 1000
Program.Delay(T)
TextWindow.WriteLine("")
Sound.PlayBellRing()
TextWindow.WriteLine(S + " seconds are up")
```

Run the program. When asked, enter how long you want to wait (in seconds). The program waits that amount of time (using **Delay**), then rings a bell and prints a message. Here's what I got for 10 seconds:

METHODS DON'T FIGHT BUT THEY HAVE ARGUMENTS

The **Delay** statement is also called a **method.** Small Basic has many such methods that help us with our programs. The **WriteLine** and **Read** statements we have used are also methods.

The number inside the parentheses is called the **"argument** of the method." **Delay** tells the computer to wait and the argument tells it how long to wait.

RANDOM NUMBERS

When you throw dice, you can't predict what numbers will come up.

When dealing cards, you can't predict what cards each person will get.

The computer needs some way to let you "roll dice" and "deal cards" and do many other unpredictable things. The **GetRandomNumber** method lets you do this.

Start a **New** program. Use this code:

```
'Random numbers
GetNumber:
N = Math.GetRandomNumber(100)
TextWindow.WriteLine(N)
If (N < 95) Then
  Goto GetNumber
EndIf
```

Run the program. You will see lots of numbers in the text window:

```
C:\Users\Lou\AppData\Local\Temp\tmpF375.tmp.exe
69
81
58
30
92
9
21
14
34
77
19
16
20
73
78
55
15
48
98
Press any key to continue...
```

This line created those numbers:

```
N = Math.GetRandomNumber(100)
```

The **GetRandomNumber** method gives random numbers from 1 to the argument value (100 here).

Change the program above to:

```
'Random numbers
GetNumber:
N = Math.GetRandomNumber(52)
TextWindow.WriteLine(N)
If (N < 46) Then
  Goto GetNumber
EndIf
```

Run this program and you will get numbers from 1 to 52. These could be used for choosing 52 cards in a standard deck.

ROLLING THE DICE

Usually dice games use two dice. A single one of them is called a "die." Here is a program that acts like a single die. Start a **New** program and enter the code:

```
'One die
RollDie:
D = Math.GetRandomNumber(6)
TextWindow.WriteLine("Die shows " + D)
TextWindow.WriteLine("")
TextWindow.Write("Roll again <y/n>? ")
A = TextWindow.Read()
If (A = "y") Then
  Goto RollDie
EndIf
```

Run the program and roll the die a few times to see how the **GetRandomNumber** method works. Here's an example:

```
C:\Users\Lou\AppData\Local\Temp\tmp3B8D.tmp.exe
Die shows 4

Roll again <y/n>? y
Die shows 6

Roll again <y/n>? y
Die shows 4

Roll again <y/n>? y
Die shows 3

Roll again <y/n>? y
Die shows 1

Roll again <y/n>? y
Die shows 6

Roll again <y/n>?
```

Click the **X** in the upper corner of the text window to stop the program.

109

RANDOM NUMBERS IN THE MIDDLE

Suppose your game has a funny die that only show 6, 7 or 8 when you roll it.

Start a **New** program. Use this code (it just changes the line computing D in the previous program):

```
'Funny die
RollDie:
D = Math.GetRandomNumber(3) + 5
TextWindow.WriteLine("Die shows " + D)
TextWindow.WriteLine("")
TextWindow.Write("Roll again <y/n>? ")
A = TextWindow.Read()
If (A = "y") Then
  Goto RollDie
EndIf
```

Run the program and you see:

Notice you only get 6, 7 or 8.

How it works:

Math.GetRandomNumber(3)	Possible Values: 1, 2, 3
Math.GetRandomNumber(3) + 5	Possible Values: 6, 7, 8

1. Write a "slow poke" program that prints out a three word message with a couple of seconds between each word. Have the computer ring a bell before each word.

2. Write a program that rolls two dice. Show the number on each die and the sum. Maybe add a delay between displaying the two values.

3. Write a "coin flipping" game, you against the computer. If you get heads and computer gets tails, you win. If computer gets heads and you get tails, the computer wins. If you both get the same, it's a tie. Use the computer to flip a coin, choose 1 or 2 using **GetRandomNumber**: 1 is heads, 2 is tails. Let the computer figure out who wins and keep score.

The **If** statement is extended to numeric expressions. The logical relations used in this lesson are:

=   >   <   <>

It is a good idea to get the student to pronounce these expressions out loud. "A < B" makes a lot more sense when pronounced "A is less than B," than when just allowed to flow in the eyeballs. Of course, the "point" of the < and the > symbols (that is, the little end) is at the side of the smaller of the two numbers.

The use of nested **If** statements is demonstrated. This is a very powerful construction, but may be confusing. It is worthwhile to go through the example with your student to make sure that the construction is understood.

A loop is demonstrated in the Guessing Game, but is not discussed. You might like to work through this with your student.

QUESTIONS:

1. What part of the **If** statement is "true" or "false"?

2. What follows the **Then** in an **If** statement?

3. After this little program runs, what will be in Box D?

    ```
    D = 4
    If (3 < 7) Then
       D = 9
    EndIf
    ```

4. Same question, but for 3 > 7?

LESSON 12   THE IF STATEMENT WITH NUMBERS

Start a **New** program. Try this code:

```
' Teenager
TextWindow.Write("Your age? ")
A = TextWindow.ReadNumber()
If (A < 13) Then
  TextWindow.WriteLine("Not yet a teenager!")
EndIf
If (A > 19) Then
  TextWindow.WriteLine("Grown up already!")
EndIf
```

Run the program and enter your age. If you are 11, you see:

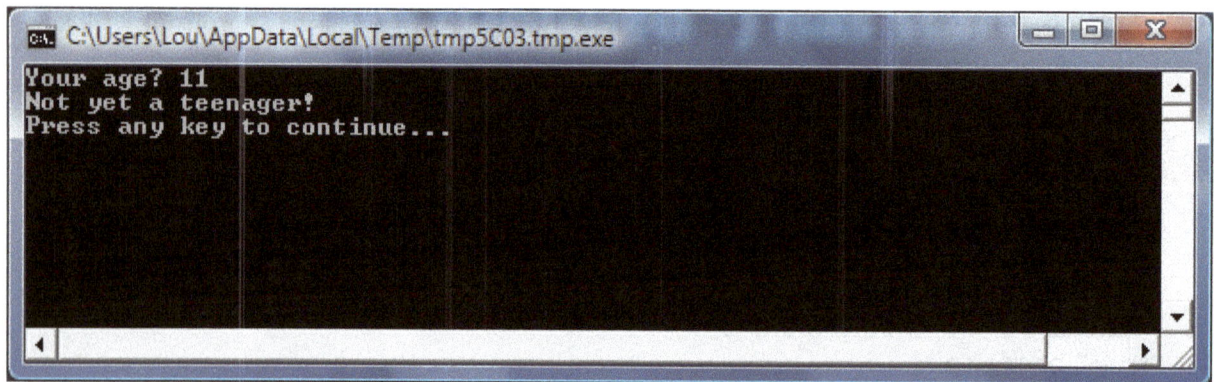

This **If** command is like the one that you used before with strings. Again, we have:

```
If (Condition) Then
  Statement
EndIf
```

Recall this means if **Condition** is "true" then process the **Statement**. With numbers, the Condition can have these arithmetic symbols:

=	equal to
>	greater than
<	less than
<>	not equal to

Each Condition is written in "math language," but you should say it out loud in English. For example:

A <> B	is pronounced	"A is not equal to B"
5 < 7	is pronounced	"five is less than seven"

PRACTICE

For these examples, let A = 7, B = 5, C = 5

Say each Condition out loud and tell if it is "true" or "false":

A = B	true false	B = C	true false
A > B	true false	B < C	true false
A < B	true false	B <> C	true false
A = C	true false	A <> C	true false

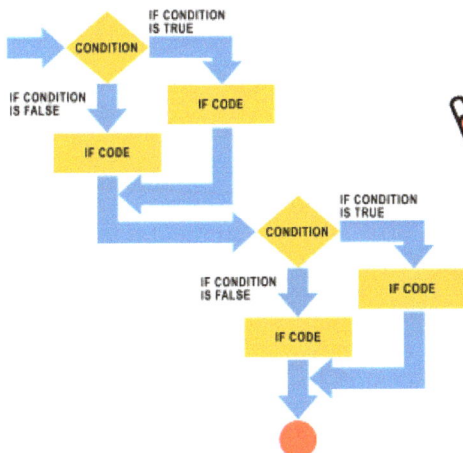

AN IF INSIDE AN IF

The teenager program above is missing something – there is no message if you are a teenager! Let's fix that. Add this code at the end:

```
If (A > 12) Then
  If (A < 20) Then
    TextWindow.WriteLine("Teenager!")
  EndIf
EndIf
```

The first line asks "is the age greater than 12?"

If the answer is "yes" the line gets to ask the second question – "is the age less than 20?"

If the answer again is "yes" the computer writes "Teenager!"

If the answer to either question is "no," the **WriteLine** statement is not reached so nothing is printed.

Run the new program. Answer 15 to make sure the new code works:

```
C:\Users\Lou\AppData\Local\Temp\tmp1D9E.tmp.exe

Your age? 15
Teenager!
Press any key to continue...
```

GUESSING GAME

Start a **New** program. Use this code:

```
' Guessing Game
N = Math.GetRandomNumber(100)
TextWindow.WriteLine("I have a number between 1 and 100")
GetGuess:
TextWindow.Write("Make a guess ")
G = TextWindow.ReadNumber()
If (G < N) Then
  TextWindow.WriteLine("Too small")
EndIf
If (G > N) Then
  TextWindow.WriteLine("Too big")
EndIf
If (G = N) Then
  Goto GotIt
EndIf
Goto GetGuess
GotIt:
'game is over
TextWindow.WriteLine("")
TextWindow.WriteLine("That's it!")
```

In this game, the computer picks a random number from 1 to 100. You try to guess it with clues from the computer. Study the code and understand what happens once a guess is entered. If you want to save this program, look ahead to the next lesson.

Run the program and play it. Here's a game I played:

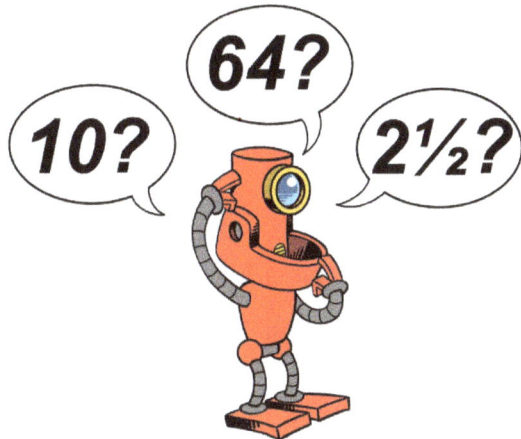

```
C:\Users\Lou\AppData\Local\Temp\tmp455.tmp.exe
I have a number between 1 and 100
Make a guess 50
Too small
Make a guess 75
Too small
Make a guess 87
Too big
Make a guess 81
Too small
Make a guess 84
Too small
Make a guess 85

That's it!
Press any key to continue...
```

116

1. Here is another program. What will it write to the text window and how many times?

```
N = 1
GoAgain:
If (N = 13) Then
   TextWindow.WriteLine("Unlucky!")
EndIf
N = N + 2
If (N > 30) Then
   Goto Done
EndIf
Goto GoAgain
Done:
TextWindow.WriteLine("Done")
```

Run it to check your answer. What happens if you change the first line to:

```
N = 2
```

2. Write a program that says something about each number from one to ten. The player enters a number and the computer prints something about each number: "three strikes, you're out" or "seven is lucky" etc.

3. Add to the **Guessing Game** program so that it prints "You're Hot" whenever the guesser is close to the right number.

4. Write a game for guessing a card that the computer has selected. Have the computer select the suit (club, diamond, heart, or spade) and the value (1 through 13). First, you guess the suit, then the program goes on to ask the value.

INSTRUCTOR NOTES 13   FOR LOOPS

A **For** loop is made up of a **For** statement (which may contain a **Step** statement) and a **EndFor** statement. These statements may be separated by several lines, and yet be strongly interdependent. The student learns the utility of repeating a set of commands in the middle of a loop. Nested loops are introduced.

Small Basic detects whether an exit condition of a **For** loop is satisfied before the loop is run even once. This makes for cleaner logic in our programs.

The **For** statement is evaluated just once at the time the loop is entered. It puts the starting value of the loop variable into variable storage where it is treated like any other numeric variable. The **Step** value, the ending value and the address of the first statement after the **For** are put on a memory stack.

From then on, all the looping action takes place at the **EndFor** statement. Upon reaching **EndFor**, the loop variable is incremented by the value of **Step** (one if no **Step** is specified) and compared with the end value. If the loop variable is larger than the end value (or smaller in the case of a negative **Step**), **EndFor** passes control to the statement after itself. Otherwise, it sends control to the next statement after the **For** statement.

Because the loop variable is treated like any other variable, it can be used or changed in the body of the loop. Jumping into the middle of a loop is usually a disaster. Jumping out of a loop before reaching **EndFor** is commonly done, but in some cases (especially where subroutines are involved) may give hard-to-find bugs.

QUESTIONS:

1. What is the "loop variable" in this line?

```
For Q = 1 To 10
   TextWindow.WriteLine(Q)
EndFor
```

2. Write a loop that writes the numbers from 0 to 20 by twos.

3. Write a "Ten Little Indians" program loop that print from 10 down to zero Indians.

4. Write a pair of nested loops to write MINI in the outside loop and HA in the inside loop. Write three MINIs and for each MINI, print two HAs.

LESSON 13   FOR LOOPS

Remember the **Goto** loop?

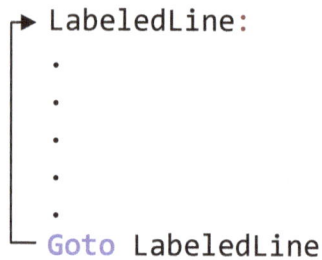

```
LabeledLine:
  .
  .
  .
  .
  .
Goto LabeledLine
```

In this loop the code between the **LabeledLine** and **Goto** statement repeats forever. What if you know how many times you want a loop to repeat? The **For** loop can do this counting.

Start a **New** program. Type this code:

```
' Counting
For I = 1 To 10
  TextWindow.WriteLine(I)
EndFor
TextWindow.WriteLine("Done counting")
```

Run the program. You will see:

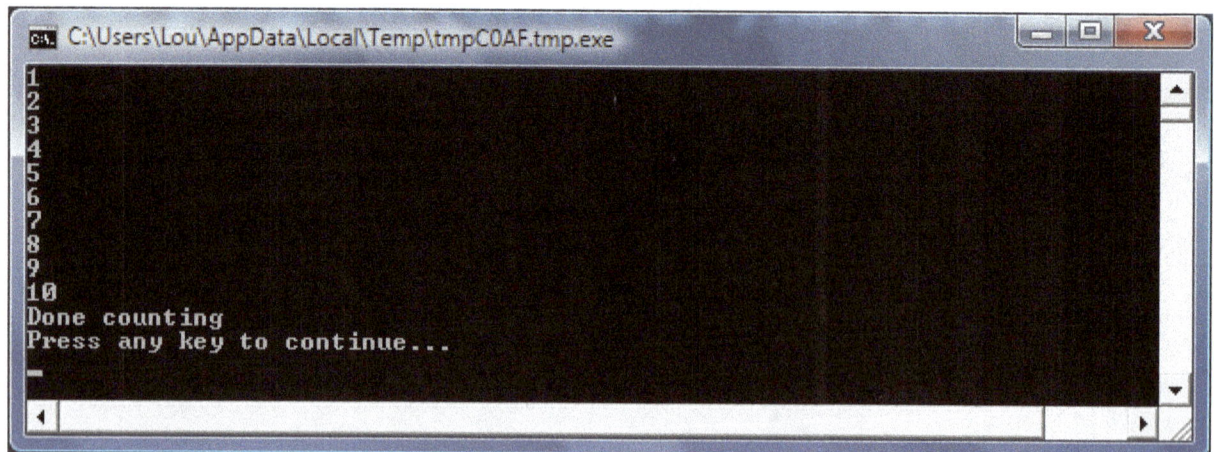

```
C:\Users\Lou\AppData\Local\Temp\tmpC0AF.tmp.exe
1
2
3
4
5
6
7
8
9
10
Done counting
Press any key to continue...
```

The computer counts from 1 to 10 before going on to the next line after the **EndFor** statement.

The numbers in the **For** statement tell the loop what value to start with (1 in this example) and what to end with (10 in this example). The loop can start on any number and end on any higher number. Try changing the **For** statement to:

```
For I = 5 To 20
For I = 100 To 101
For I = 7 To 13
For I = 1.3 To 5.7
```

Run the program for each example to see how the loop works.

THE STEP STATEMENT

The computer was counting by ones in the above examples. To make it count by twos, change the program to this:

```
' Counting by twos
For I = 1 To 10 Step 2
  TextWindow.WriteLine(I)
EndFor
TextWindow.WriteLine("Done counting")
```

Run the program to see:

```
1
3
5
7
9
Done counting
Press any key to continue...
```

The **Step** statement sets the value it counts by. If you don't set **Step**, it uses one.

Assignment 13A:

1. Have the computer count by fives from 0 to 100.

COUNTDOWN LOOPS

You can make the computer count down by using a negative **Step**.

Start a **New** program. Enter this code:

```
' Apollo 11
TextWindow.WriteLine("T minus 12 seconds and counting")
For I = 12 To 0 Step -1
  TextWindow.WriteLine(I)
  Sound.PlayClick()
  Program.Delay(1000)
EndFor
TextWindow.WriteLine("All engines running. Lift off.")
Program.Delay(1000)
TextWindow.WriteLine("We have lift off.")
Program.Delay(1000)
TextWindow.WriteLine("32 minutes past the hour.")
Program.Delay(1000)
TextWindow.WriteLine("Lift off on Apollo 11.")
TextWindow.WriteLine("")
```

Run the program. You will hear a little "clock tick" with each new display. Here is the text window when complete:

NESTED LOOPS

You can have one loop inside another. These are "nested loops." It is like the baby's set of toy boxes that fit inside each other.

Start a **New** program. Enter this code:

```
'nested loops
'Times tables
For M = 0 To 9
  For N = 0 To 9
    TextWindow.WriteLine(M + " X " + N + " = " + M * N)
  EndFor
EndFor
```

This program prints out all the multiplication facts for the digits zero to nine. We have an outside loop (using M as the mulitplicand) and an inside loop (using N as the multiplier). Each **For** loop has a matching **EndFor** statement. The Small Basic editor "indents" the loop code making it easier to read.

Run the program. You will see something like this:

Scroll up to see all the math facts. Can you do your facts that fast?

NONSENSE LOOPS

Small Basic will skip loops that are not supposed to run.

Start a New program. Enter this code:

```
' Nonsense
TextWindow.WriteLine(I)
For I = 5 To 3
  TextWindow.WriteLine(I)
EndFor
TextWindow.WriteLine(I)
```

This is a nonsense loop. The **For** statement says to start at 5 and get bigger, until it is larger than 3. But it is larger than 3 in the first place! What will Small Basic ever do here? It will just skip the whole loop!

Run the program. You will see:

It first writes the initial value of I. Since the variable is never defined, Small Basic assumes it is a blank space. The For statement sets I to 5, then notices the loop should not run, so it skips down to the line after the EndFor statement. There it prints the value of I, which is 5.

1. Write a program that writes your name 15 times.

2. Now, make it write your name on one line, your friend's name on the next and keep switching until each name is written five times.

3. Write a program that writes out addition facts using the digits from zero to nine.

This lesson shows how to save programs and how to open them again. This lesson can be used anytime after Lesson 1.

Your students may need extra help in finding and creating folders on the computer hard drive.

We put this late in the book because most programs up to this point are relatively short and uninteresting, not worth saving. The process of programming was being emphasized, not the end result of useful programs.

However, your own judgment should prevail, and you can insert this lesson at an earlier point in the flow of lessons so that your student can save some programs he or she is particularly proud of.

QUESTIONS:

1. What is a file?

2. What are the rules for a file name?

3. Can you have more than one program at a time open in Small Basic? If so, how do you switch from one program to another?

ENTERING A PROGRAM

If you already have a program in the Small Basic editor, skip this step. If you don't have a program, start a **New** one and type these two lines:

```
' Hi
TextWindow.WriteLine("Hi!")
```

SAVING A PROGRAM

You save a program by clicking the **Save** button in the Small Basic toolbar:

When you click this, a dialog box like this will appear.

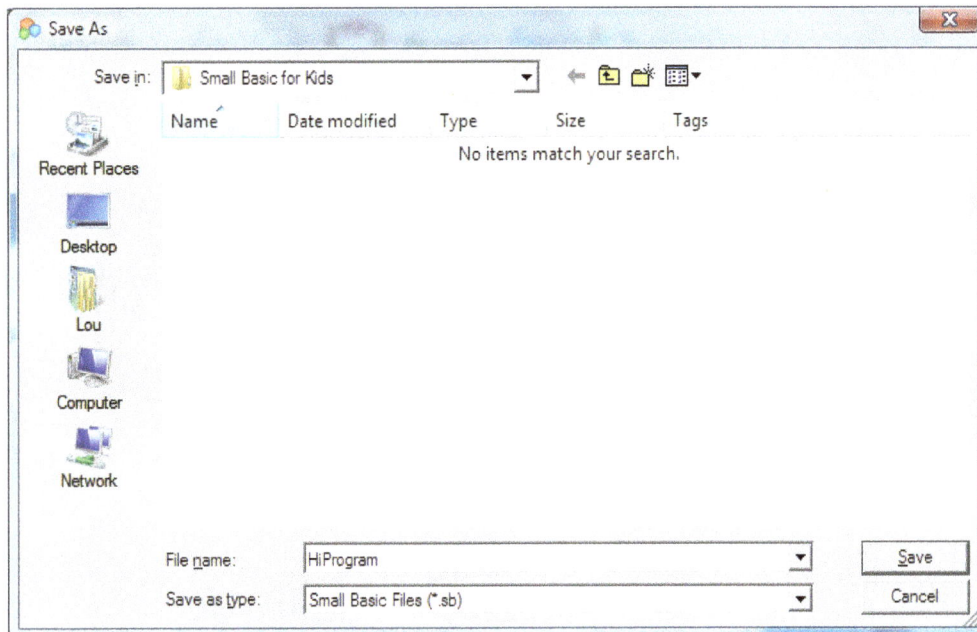

You pick a folder on your computer's hard drive (I chose **Small Basic for Kids**) and type a **File name**. Use **HiProgram** for this example. Then, just click the **Save** button in the lower right corner of the dialog box.

128

FILE NAMES

You can name your program file anything you want. The name must begin with a letter. The name can contain letters, numbers, and the underscore character (_). You find the underscore by pressing **Shift** and the key to the right of the zero.

Make sure you give your program a name you can remember.

OPENING A PROGRAM

Now that you have saved your program, you can close it by clicking the **X** in the upper right corner of the editor window.

To open a Small Basic program, click the **Open** button in the toolbar:

Open

A dialog box will appear:

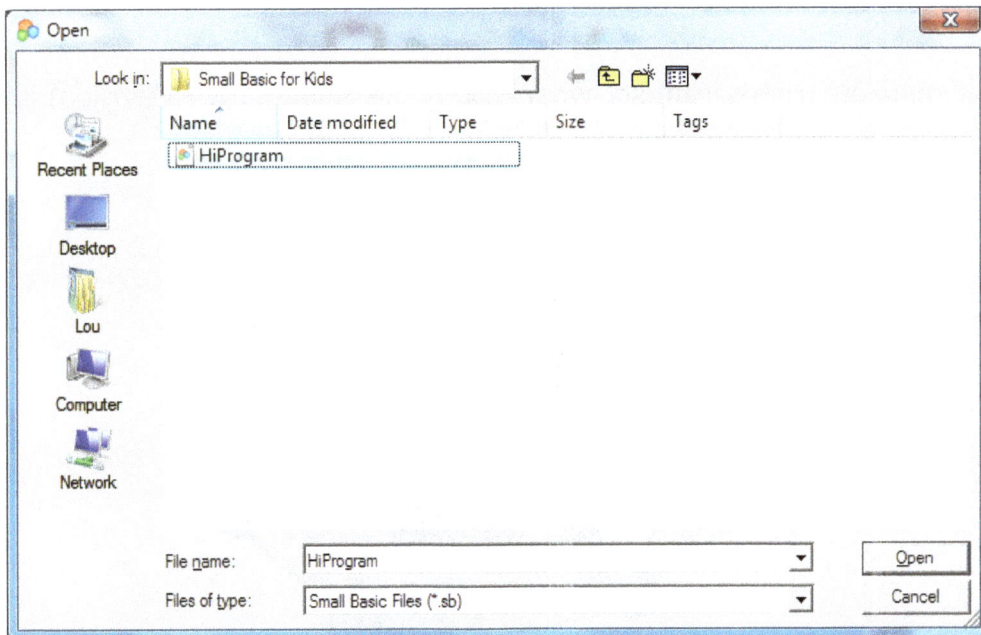

Move the cursor to the folder holding your program, select the program, then click **Open**. The code will be loaded into the editor.

If you used the simple example program, you will see:

```
HiProgram.sb - C:\Small Basic for Kids\HiProgram.sb
1  'Hi
2  TextWindow.WriteLine("Hi!")
```

Notice the filename (**HIProgram.sb**, where **.sb** is the Small Basic extension) is shown in the title bar for the code window.

Assignment 14:

1. Write and short program and save it.

2. Start a **New** program and write another program. Save it.

3. Close Small Basic. Now, restart Small Basic and try opening one or both of the programs you just saved.

GRAPHICS

INSTRUCTOR NOTES 15   TEXT GRAPHICS

The **CursorLeft** and **CursorTop** properties are used to move the output cursor to any point on the text window. These properties allow flexible manipulation of text in the window and also allow a simple form of graphics.

To make effective use of **CursorLeft** and **CursorTop**, you need to think of the text window as an 80 characters across by 25 lines down array. **CursorLeft** sets the across value (the column), while **CursorTop** sets the down value (the row). The one tricky thing is that **CursorLeft** numbers the columns from 0 to 79, while **CursorTop** numbers the rows from 0 to 24. You need to mentally subtract one from physical column and row values to use these two positioning properties properly.

Although lessons on more detailed graphics are presented after this lesson, we show graphics here to get used to several ideas, one being the "across, down" concept of positioning, and another being how to make moving pictures. And, one more idea is that the "origin" of a graphic system is at column 0 and row 0.

Moving characters can be displayed and moved using **CursorLeft** and **CursorTop** in a loop. It is necessary to erase the old object with a space character of the text window background color before the new character is drawn.

It is best to delay the erasing until just before the new character is drawn, to reduce flicker in the picture.

QUESTIONS:

1. If you want to write the next word on row 12 at the left, what statements would you use?

2. If you want to print the next character on row 6, column 20, what statements would you use?

3. How can you print "never again!", wait a second then erase just the word "again"?

4. Show how to write the two words "FAT" and "CAT" on the same line with "CAT" written first, starting at column 25, then after a delay "FAT" printed starting at column 5.

LESSON 15   TEXT GRAPHICS

When you use the "unresized" text window in Small Basic, there is room for 80 characters in each line. The characters (or columns) are numbered from 0 at the left to 79 at the right. This is a little tricky – notice the third "actual" column will be column number 2 (you always need to mentally subtract one).

There is room for 25 lines (or rows) in the text window. They are numbered from 0 at the top to 24 at the bottom. Like the column numbers, you always need to remember to subtract one to identify the row you want.

Start a **New** program. Type this little program:

```
' CursorLeft Demo
TextWindow.CursorLeft = 0
TextWindow.Write("Column 0")
Program.Delay(1000)
TextWindow.CursorLeft = 20
TextWindow.Write("Column 20")
Program.Delay(1000)
TextWindow.CursorLeft = 50
TextWindow.WriteLine("Column 50")
```

Run the program. You should see:

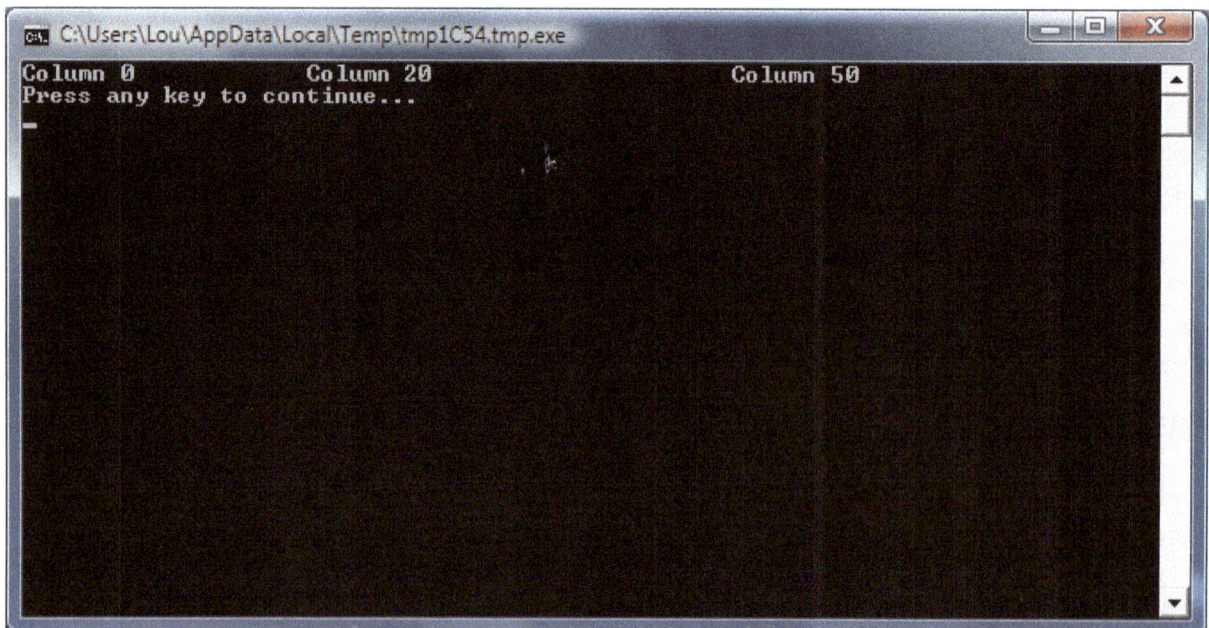

135

The **CursorLeft** value identifies the column the writing cursor will go to. Note to write in the first column, you use:

```
TextWindow.CursorLeft = 0
```

Since **CursorLeft** numbers the columns from 0 to 79 (not 1 to 80), you need to subtract one from the true column you want to write at. A **Write** statement will set **CursorLeft** to the end of the text written; a **WriteLine** statement will return **CursorLeft** to 0 after execution.

Start a New program. Try this code:

```
' CursorTop Demo
TextWindow.CursorTop = 9
TextWindow.WriteLine("Line at Row 9 first")
Program.Delay(1000)
TextWindow.CursorTop = 0
TextWindow.WriteLine("Line at Row 0 next")
Program.Delay(1000)
TextWindow.CursorTop = 16
TextWindow.WriteLine("Line at Row 16 last")
```

Run the program. You will see:

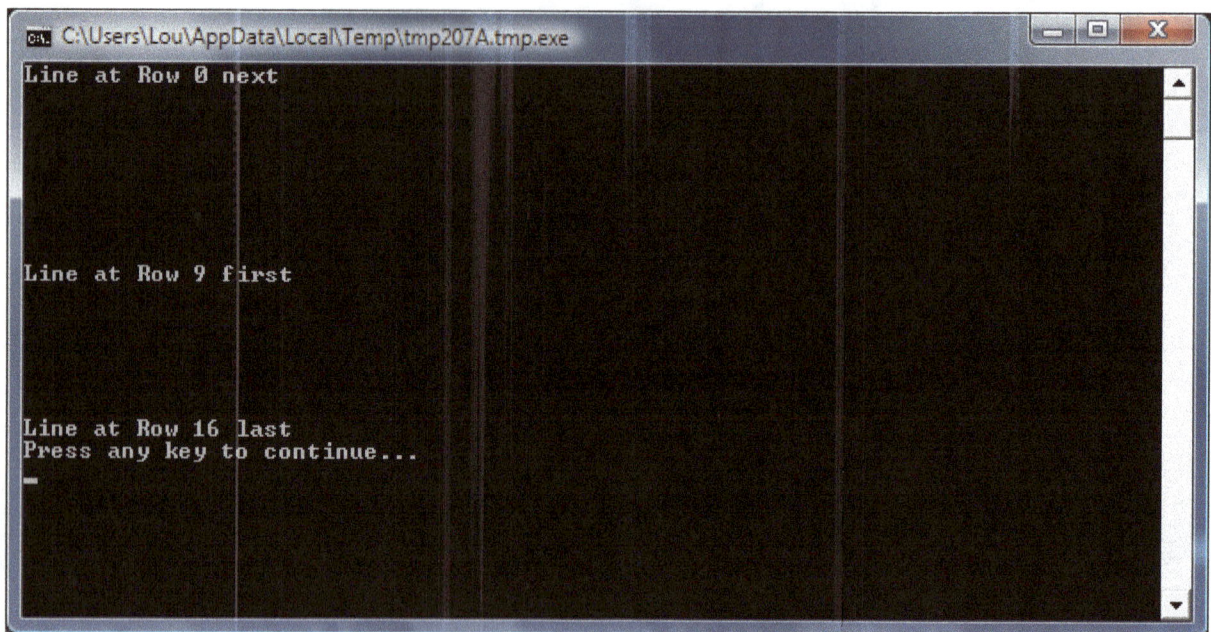

The **CursorTop** value identifies the row the writing cursor will go to. Note to write in the 10th row, you use:

```
TextWindow.CursorTop = 9
```

Again, because the rows are numbered starting at zero, you need to subtract one from the row you want to write at. A **Write** statement will not change **CursorTop**; a **WriteLine** statement will set **CursorTop** to the next line in the text window.

Start a **New** program. Type this code:

```
' column and row
GetValues:
TextWindow.Write("Which column? ")
C = TextWindow.ReadNumber()
TextWindow.Write("Which row? ")
R = TextWindow.ReadNumber()
TextWindow.CursorLeft = C
TextWindow.CursorTop = R
TextWindow.Write("*")
Program.Delay(2000)
TextWindow.Clear()
Goto GetValues
```

Run the program. Enter a column value and a row value. An asterisk will be printed at the location – then, after a delay, you can enter another set of values. Here's what I got for column 62, row 15:

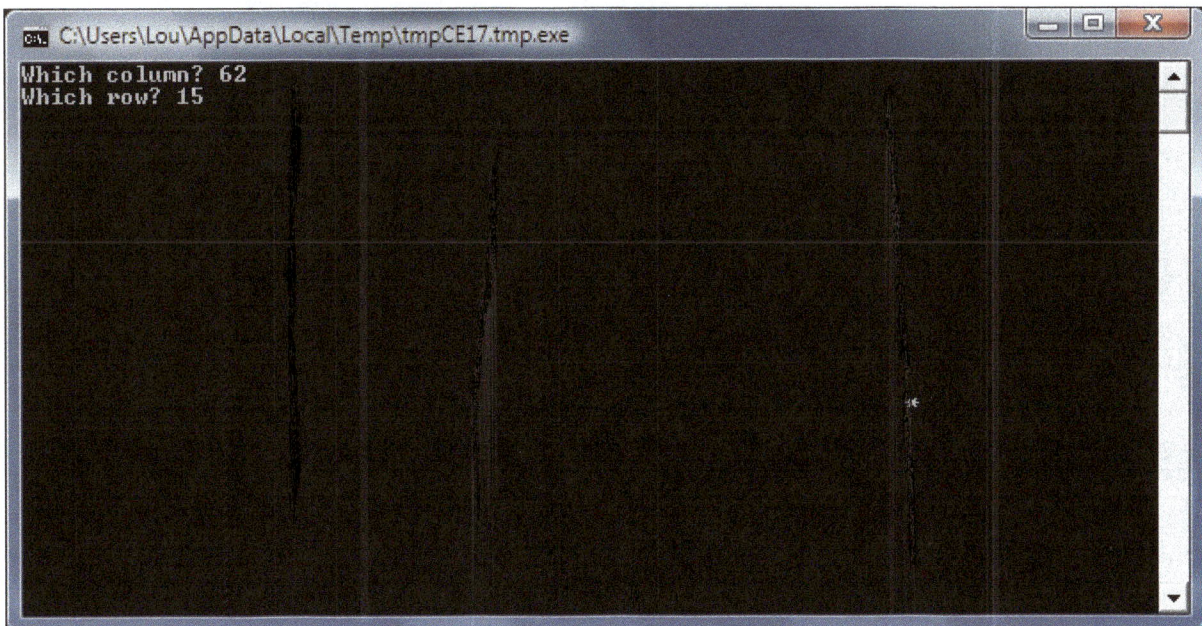

ERASING WHAT YOU WRITE

Start a **New** program. Type in this code:

```
' jumping here
GetAnother:
C = Math.GetRandomNumber(75) - 1
R = Math.GetRandomNumber(23) - 1
TextWindow.CursorLeft = C
TextWindow.CursorTop = R
TextWindow.Write("HERE")
Program.Delay(2000)
TextWindow.CursorLeft = C - 1
TextWindow.CursorTop = R - 1
TextWindow.Write("     ")
Goto GetAnother
```

Run the program. The word HERE will appear at different places in the text window, then disappear.

How do you stop this program?

YELLOW BALLOON

Start a **New** program. Type this code:

```
' Yellow balloon
C = 0
R = 24
TextWindow.ForegroundColor = "Yellow"
DrawBalloon:
TextWindow.CursorLeft = C
TextWindow.CursorTop = R
TextWindow.Write("O")
Program.Delay(500)
'erase
TextWindow.CursorLeft = C
TextWindow.CursorTop = R
TextWindow.Write(" ")
C = C + 3
R = R - 1
If (R > 0) Then
   Goto DrawBalloon
EndIf
```

Run the program. You will see:

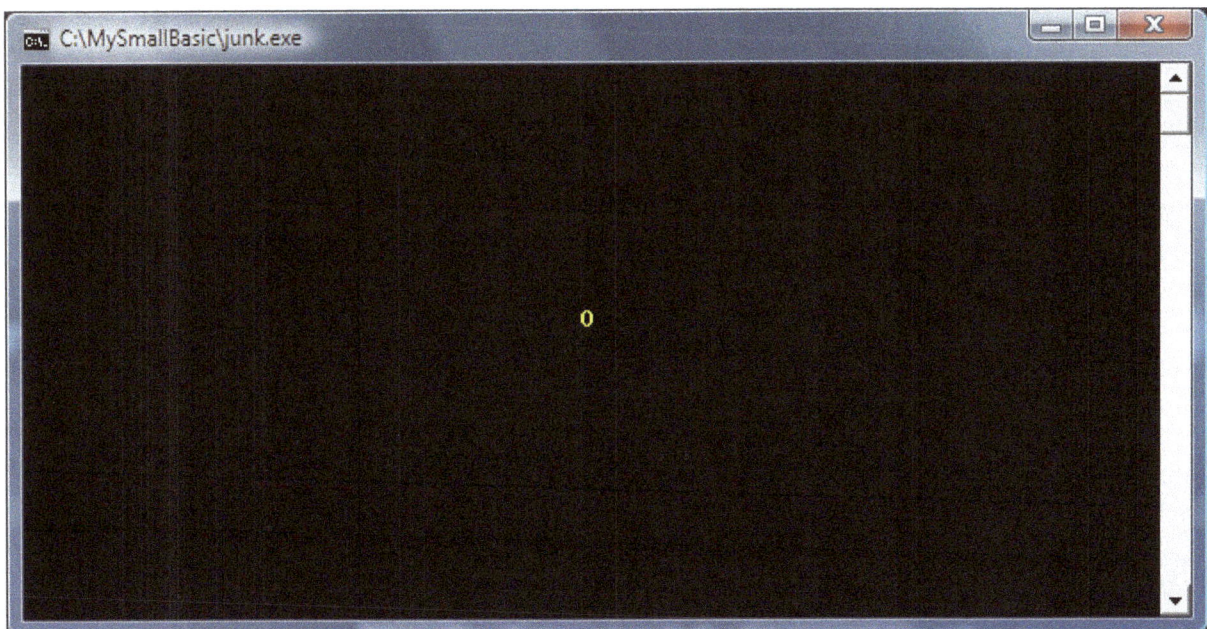

The yellow balloon flies up the screen. Each time, before we draw the balloon, it is erased at its last position to give the impression of motion.

RANDOM COLORED BLOCKS PROGRAM

This program draws random "walking" blocks of color. Start a **New** program. Enter this code (yes, it's long):

```
' Random sketcher
' start near center
C = 40
R = 12
GetDirection:
'get random direction (-1, 0, +1)
D = 2- Math.GetRandomNumber(3)
C = C + D
If (C < 0) Then
  C = 0
EndIf
If (C > 79) Then
  C = 79
EndIf
D = 2- Math.GetRandomNumber(3)
R = R + D
If (R < 0) Then
  R = 0
EndIf
If (R > 24) Then
  R = 24
EndIf
' pick one of five random colors
N = Math.GetRandomNumber(5)
If (N = 1) Then
  TextWindow.BackgroundColor = "Yellow"
EndIf
If (N = 2) Then
  TextWindow.BackgroundColor = "Blue"
EndIf
If (N = 3) Then
  TextWindow.BackgroundColor = "Red"
EndIf
If (N = 4) Then
  TextWindow.BackgroundColor = "Green"
EndIf
If (N = 5) Then
  TextWindow.BackgroundColor = "Magenta"
EndIf
TextWindow.CursorLeft = C
TextWindow.CursorTop = R
```

```
TextWindow.Write(" ")
Program.Delay(50)
Goto GetDirection
```

Save the program. **Run** the program and just watch the little box walk around the screen leaving one of five colors behind. Here's my text window after a few minutes:

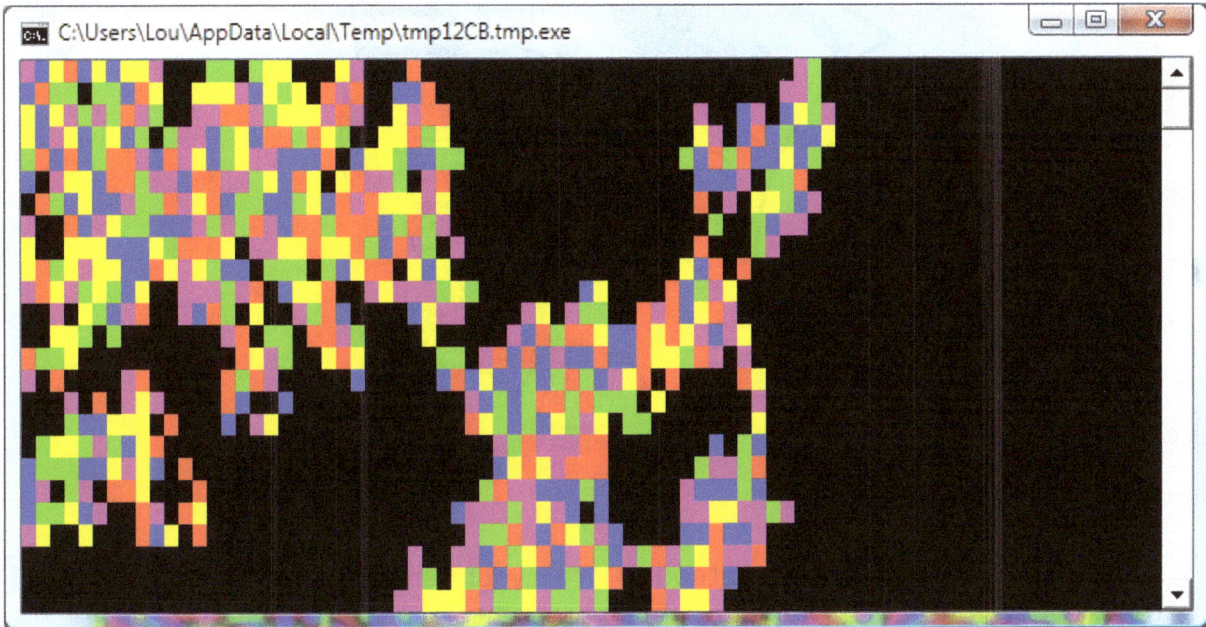

The code is pretty easy to follow. We'll explain a little.

A random direction is assigned to the row:

```
D = 2- Math.GetRandomNumber(3)
```

This line of code gives you one of three random numbers: -1, 0, or 1. This sets the direction for changing the column. If -1, the column moves left (C decreases), if 0, the column stays the same, if +1, the column moves right (C increases). After this, we make a similar random change to the row value (R). We make sure C is always between 1 and 80 and R is always between 1 and 25.

After this, we pick one of five colors (Yellow, Blue, Red, Green, Magenta, a light purple) at random. The color is assigned to the **BackgroundColor**. Then, we set the row and column values, and print a space (" ") at that location. The space character will draw a blank in the **BackgroundColor**.

Finally, we delay for 1/20th of a second 50 milliseconds), and then do it all over again. What happens if you set the delay to zero?

142

1. Use the **GetRandomNumber** method to write your name at random places in the text window. Make it write your name many times.

2. Use **CursorTop** and **CursorLeft** to write your name in a large "X" shape in the text window.

3. Write a program that makes a bird flap its wings and fly across the text window.

INSTRUCTOR NOTES 16   GRAPHICS WINDOW, DRAWING LINES

This lesson introduces the graphics window. It illustrates the **DrawPixel** and **DrawLine** methods.

Think of the graphics window as a grid with its origin at the upper left. The **X** value runs horizontally to the right from 0 to the window width – 1. The window width is set using **GraphicsWindow.Width** property. The Y direction runs vertically from 0 at the top to window height – 1 at the bottom. **GraphicWindow.Height** sets the window height. Both **DrawPixel** and **DrawLine** use the pair (X, Y) to refer to points.

DrawPixel colors a single point.

DrawLine needs two points, the start and the end. The line width is set by the **PenWidth** property and color is set by **PenColor**. A future lesson shows how to draw and fill shapes like rectangles, ellipses and triangles.

Small Basic does not object if part of a line or drawing is off the window. For example:

```
GraphicsWindow.DrawLine(-300, 200, 300, 200)
```

is acceptable. The portion of the line out of the window will not be seen.

QUESTIONS:

1. Where on the screen will `GraphicsWindow.SetPixel(160, 100, "Red")` put a dot?

2. What are the (X, Y) pairs for the four corners of the graphics window?

3. How do you draw a large X in the graphics window?

144

LESSON 16   GRAPHICS WINDOW, DRAWING LINES

We can do simple graphics with the text window. Let's look at some advanced graphics using the Small Basic **graphics window**. With this window, we can color points, draw lines, draw shapes, add text and build some simple games.

Start a **New** program. Type this simple program:

```
'graphics window
GraphicsWindow.Show()
```

Run the program. You will see an empty window like this:

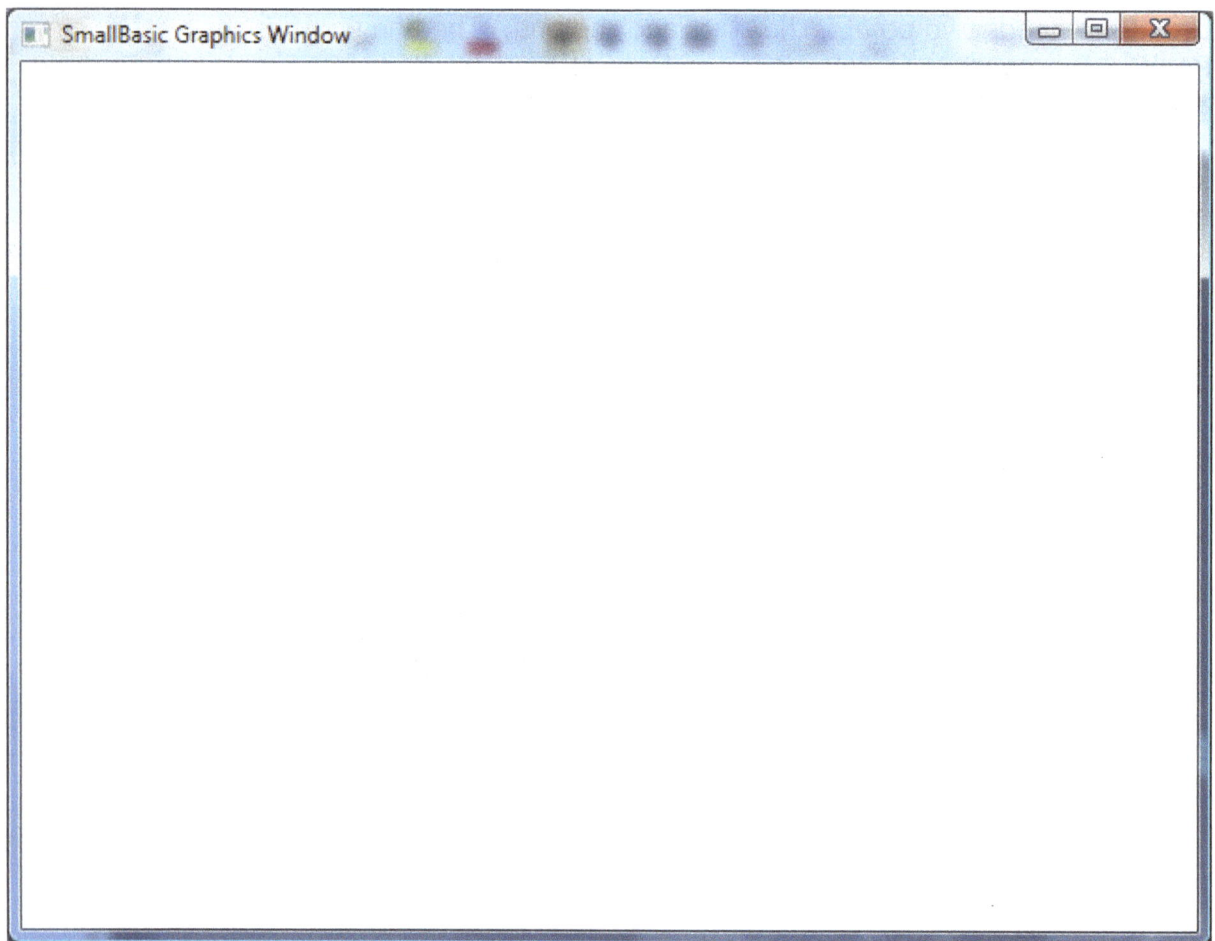

This is the **graphics window**. It has many **properties** that can change how it looks and has many **methods** that let us draw things.

BACKGROUND COLOR

Add one line to the program:

```
'graphics window
GraphicsWindow.Show()
GraphicsWindow.BackgroundColor = "Yellow"
```

Run the program and the graphics window will be yellow. The **BackgroundColor** property sets the color of the graphics window.

WIDTH AND HEIGHT

Change the code so it now reads:

```
'graphics window
GraphicsWindow.Show()
GraphicsWindow.BackgroundColor = "Yellow"
GraphicsWindow.Width = 300
GraphicsWindow.Height = 200
```

Run the program again. You see:

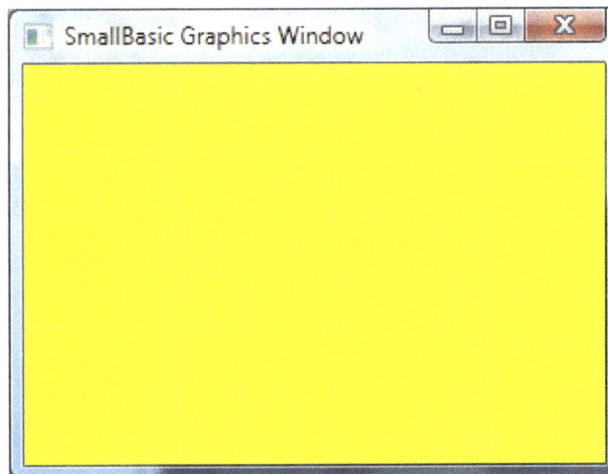

The **Width** property sets the width of the graphics window. The **Height** property sets the height. This window is 300 pixels wide by 200 pixels high. A **pixel** is simply a dot on the screen.

This window is like a sheet of graph paper with 300 pixels across and 200 pixels down. The pixels are numbered from 0 to 299 across and from 0 to 199 down. This numbering is like the columns and rows of the text window.

To refer to one point in the graphics window, you give the across value (we will call it **X**) and the down value (we call it **Y**). We call the two numbers together a "coordinate pair" (**X, Y**).

SETPIXEL METHOD

We can set the color of a single pixel using:

```
GraphicsWindow.SetPixel(X, Y, Color)
```

Where (**X, Y**) is the coordinate pair and **Color** is the desired color.

Change the program we have been using to:

```
'graphics window
GraphicsWindow.Show()
GraphicsWindow.BackgroundColor = "Yellow"
GraphicsWindow.Width = 300
GraphicsWindow.Height = 200
For X = 0 To 299
  For Y = 0 To 199
    C = GraphicsWindow.GetRandomColor()
    GraphicsWindow.SetPixel(X, Y, C)
  EndFor
EndFor
```

Run the program. Wait a bit a you will see:

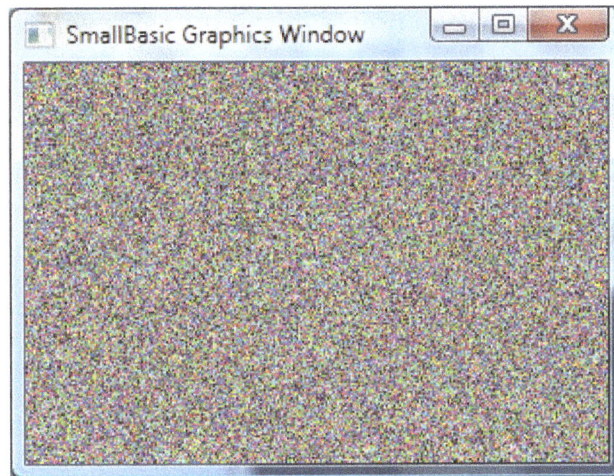

The program goes through every point in the window (using nested For loops) and assigns it a random color (using the **GetRandomColor** method of the graphics window).

DRAWLINE METHOD

The **DrawLine** method connects two points in the graphics window:

```
GraphicsWindow.DrawLine(X1, Y1, X2, Y2)
```

This statement draws a line between (**X1, Y1**) and (**X2, Y2**).

Start a **New** program. Use this code:

```
'draw Line
GraphicsWindow.Show()
GraphicsWindow.Width = 300
GraphicsWindow.Height = 200
GraphicsWindow.DrawLine(20, 150, 260, 10)
```

Run the program to see:

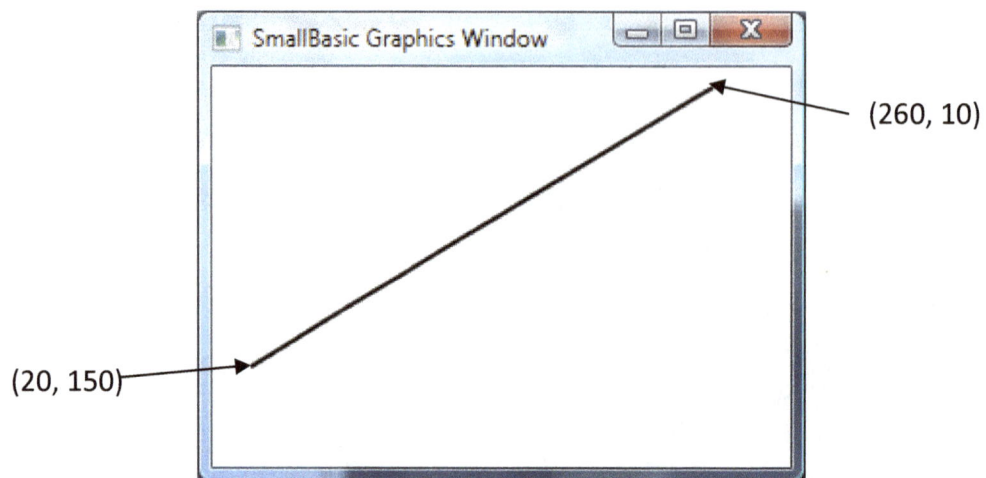

A line is drawn from (20, 150) to (260, 10).

Start another **New** program. Type this code:

```
'Splat
GraphicsWindow.Show()
GraphicsWindow.Width = 600
GraphicsWindow.Height = 400
For I = 1 To 100
  X = Math.GetRandomNumber(600) - 1
  Y = Math.GetRandomNumber(400) - 1
  GraphicsWindow.DrawLine(300, 200, X, Y)
EndFor
```

Run the program. Look at the pretty design.

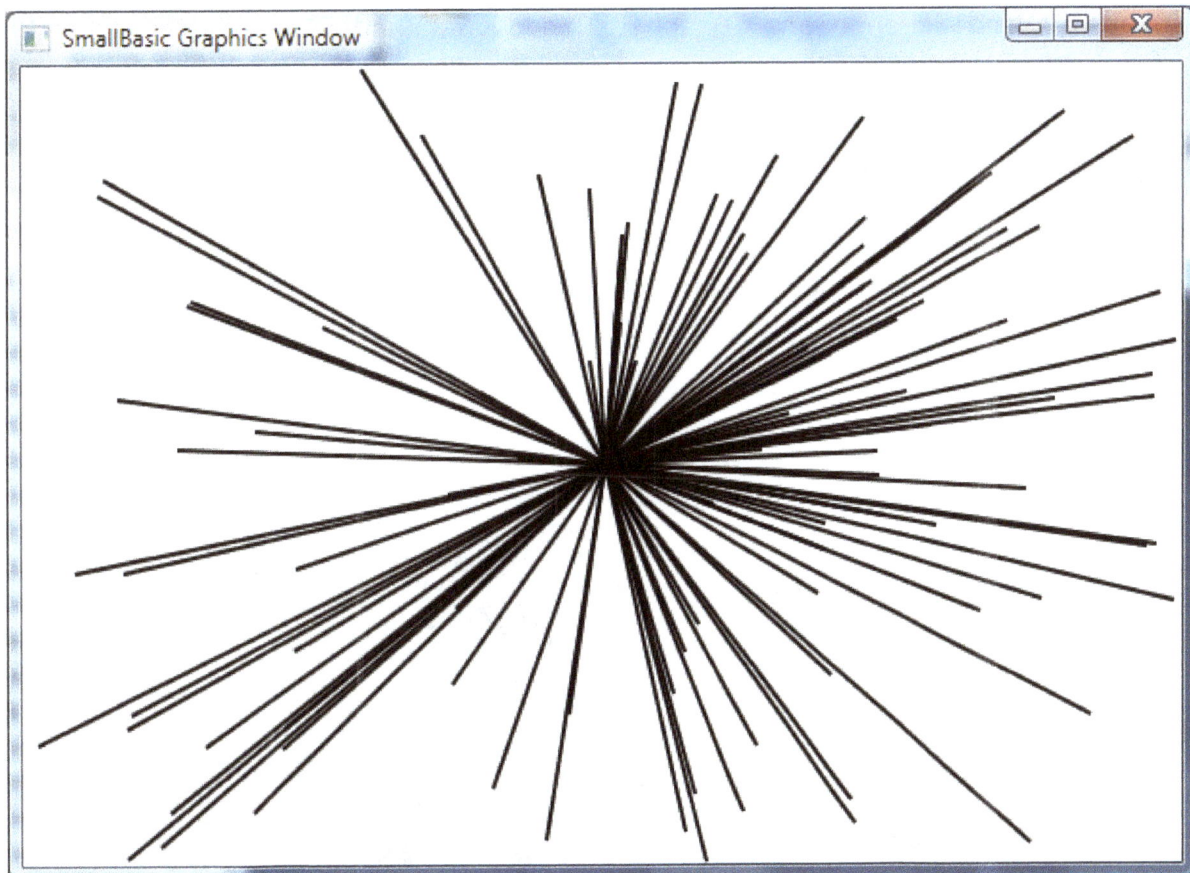

THE PEN

By default (making no changes), the **DrawLine** method draws a black line. We can change this using the graphics window **pen**. It is used to set the color and width of the drawn line.

Change the program you just wrote to include the two lines setting **PenWidth** (how wide the line is; 2 by default) and **PenColor** (the drawing color; black by default):

```
'Splat
GraphicsWindow.Show()
GraphicsWindow.Width = 600
GraphicsWindow.Height = 400
GraphicsWindow.PenWidth = 1
For I = 1 To 100
  GraphicsWindow.PenColor = GraphicsWindow.GetRandomColor()
  X = Math.GetRandomNumber(600) - 1
  Y = Math.GetRandomNumber(400) - 1
  GraphicsWindow.DrawLine(300, 200, X, Y)
EndFor
```

We again use the **GetRandomColor** method to assign a color. Once you change **PenWidth** and **PenColor**, they keep the changed values until changed again.

Run the program. I think you'll see you get a prettier result:

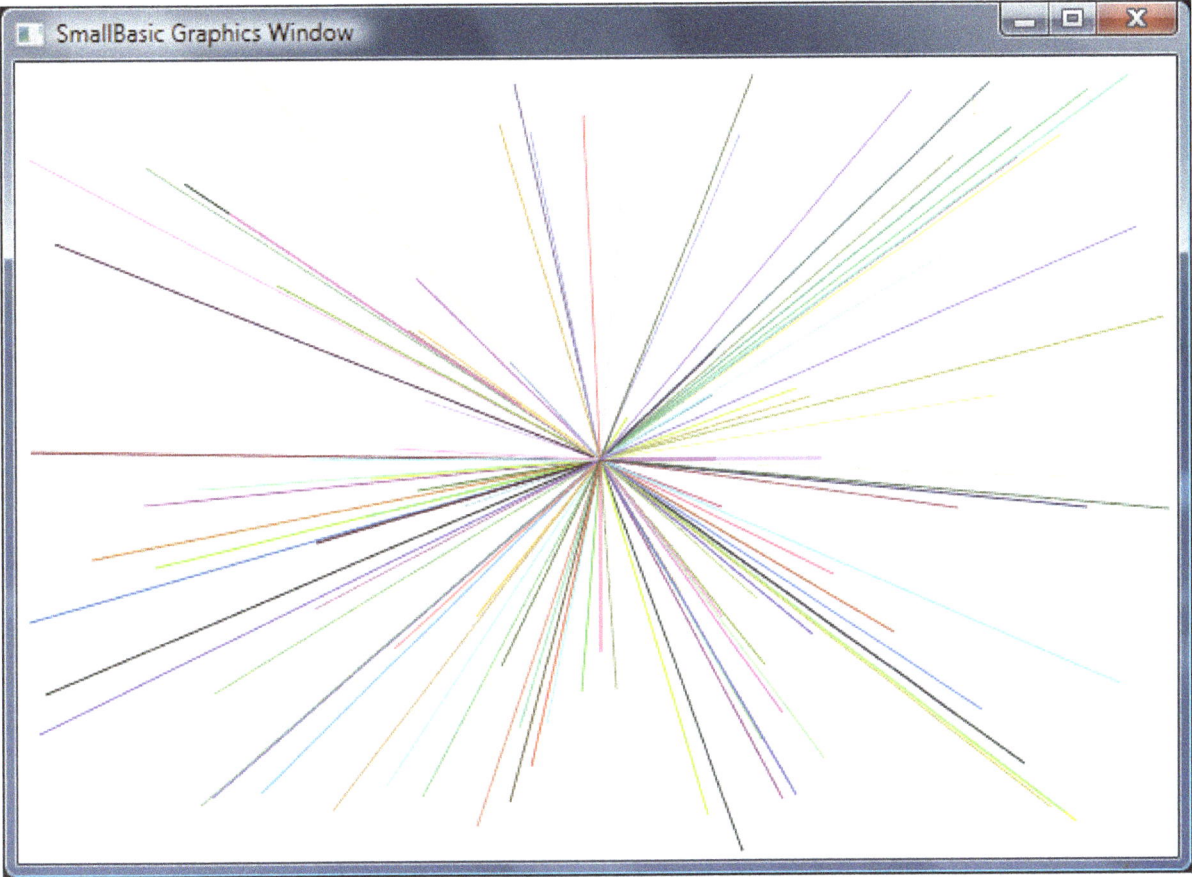

COLORS

We've used many colors in our programs. A fun method we have used to get a random color is:

```
GraphicsWindow.GetRandomColor()
```

We can use this for **BackgroundColor**, **PenColor** and, later, for something called **BrushColor**.

If you want a specific color, you give that color's name. We have used a few of these already like: **Yellow**, **Black**, **Red**, **Green**, **Magenta**, etc. A complete list of Small Basic colors is given in Appendix I. Look there whenever you need a cool color like **PeachPuff**!

1. Use the **DrawLine** method to draw a rectangle. Use a pen width of 10 and a pen color of Blue.

2. Use the **DrawLine** method to draw your school's initials. Make each letter a different color. Save your program.

INSTRUCTOR NOTES 17   DRAWING SHAPES

This lesson shows how to draw and fill three basic shapes (rectangle, ellipse, triangle) with color. Some explanation may be needed for students to understand how an ellipse is drawn in a "rectangle." Also explain a square ellipse is a circle. The six methods studied are:

```
GraphicsWindow.DrawRectangle
GraphicsWindow.FillRectangle
GraphicsWindow.DrawEllipse
GraphicsWindow.FillEllipse
GraphicsWindow.DrawTriangle
GraphicsWindow.FillTriangle
```

The border colors for the shapes are set by the **PenColor** and **PenWidth**.

The fill colors for the shapes are set by the **BrushColor**.

QUESTIONS:

1. How do you draw a rectangle with upper left corner at (30, 10), width 30 and height 100?

2. How do you draw a circle with the center in the middle of the window and the radius half of the window height? A little math is needed here.

3. How would you draw a "right triangle" with blue border and filled with red?

LESSON 17   DRAWING SHAPES

DRAWRECTANGLE METHOD

The **DrawRectangle** method draws a rectangle in the graphics window:

```
GraphicsWindow.DrawRectangle(X, Y, W, H)
```

This statement draws a rectangle with upper left corner at (**X, Y**). The rectangle is **W** pixels wide and **H** pixels high. It is drawn with the current pen width and current pen color.

Start a **New** program. Use this code:

```
'Rectangle
GraphicsWindow.Show()
GraphicsWindow.Width = 400
GraphicsWindow.Height = 300
GraphicsWindow.PenWidth = 3
GraphicsWindow.PenColor = "Blue"
GraphicsWindow.DrawRectangle(50, 50, 300, 200)
```

Run the program to see the blue rectangle that is 300 pixels wide by 200 pixels high:

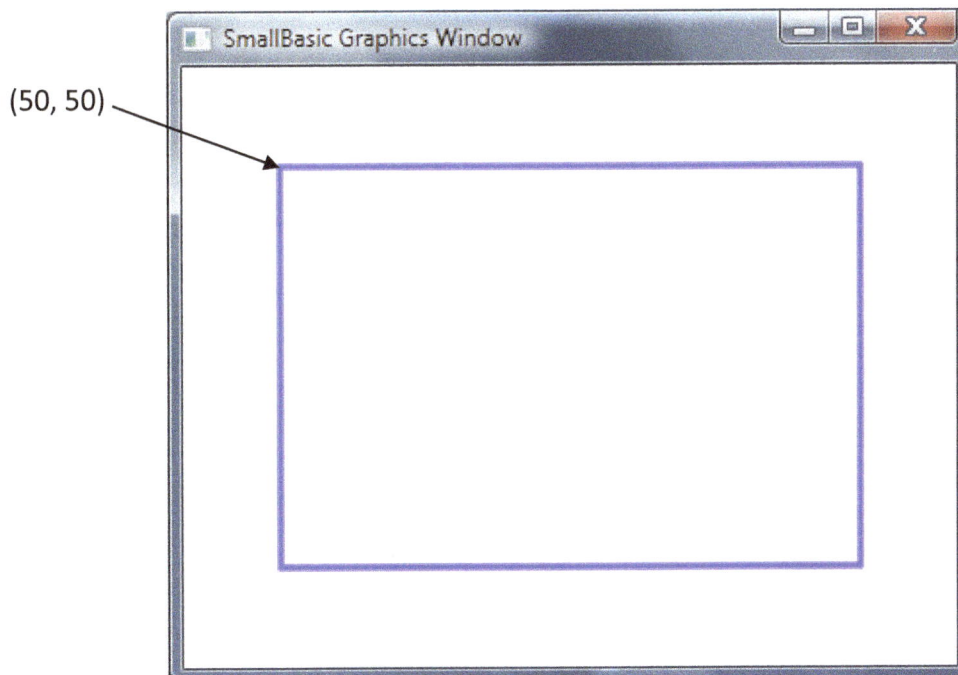

DRAWELLIPSE METHOD

The **DrawEllipse** method draws an ellipse in the graphics window:

GraphicsWindow.DrawEllipse(X, Y, W, H)

This statement draws an ellipse in a rectangle with upper left corner at (**X, Y**), width **W** and height **H**. It is drawn with the current pen width and current pen color. A "square" ellipse (width and height the same) is a circle.

Start a **New** program. Use this code:

```
'Ellipse
GraphicsWindow.Show()
GraphicsWindow.Width = 400
GraphicsWindow.Height = 300
GraphicsWindow.PenWidth = 3
GraphicsWindow.PenColor = "Red"
GraphicsWindow.DrawEllipse(125, 25, 150, 250)
```

Run the program to see the red ellipse in a rectangle that is 150 pixels wide by 250 pixels high:

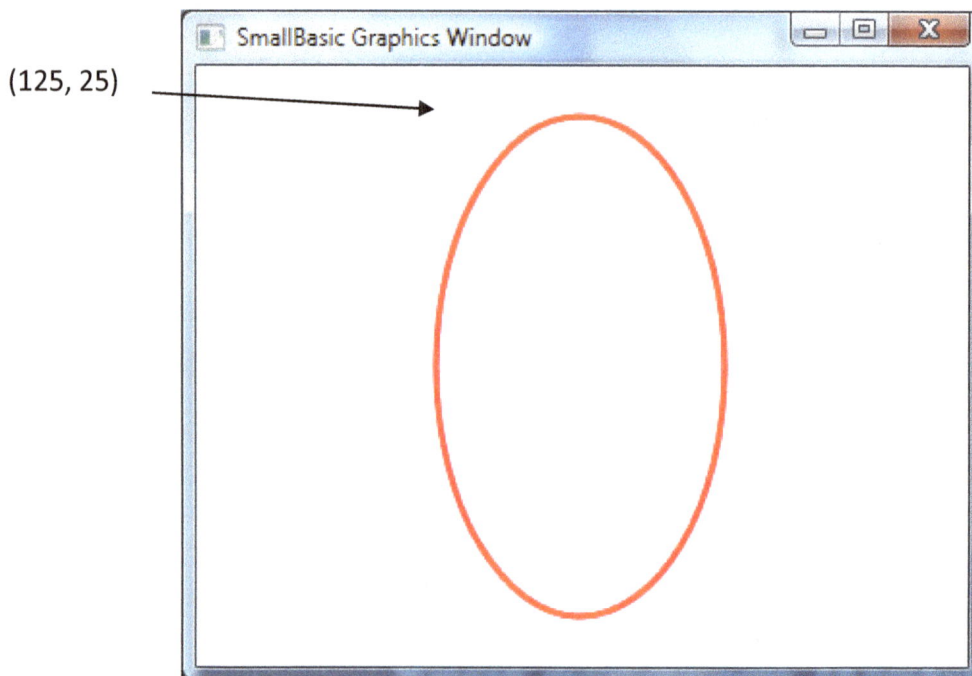

You don't see the rectangle that surrounds the ellipse – it is invisible.

DRAWTRIANGLE METHOD

The **DrawTriangle** method draws a triangle in the graphics window:

```
GraphicsWindow.DrawTriangle(X1, Y1, X2, Y2, X3, Y3)
```

This statement draws a triangle that connects the three coordinate pairs. It is drawn with the current pen width and current pen color.

Start a **New** program. Use this code:

```
'Triangle
GraphicsWindow.Show()
GraphicsWindow.Width = 400
GraphicsWindow.Height = 300
GraphicsWindow.PenWidth = 3
GraphicsWindow.PenColor = "Green"
GraphicsWindow.DrawTriangle(250, 50, 50, 200, 350, 250)
```

Run the program to see the green triangle:

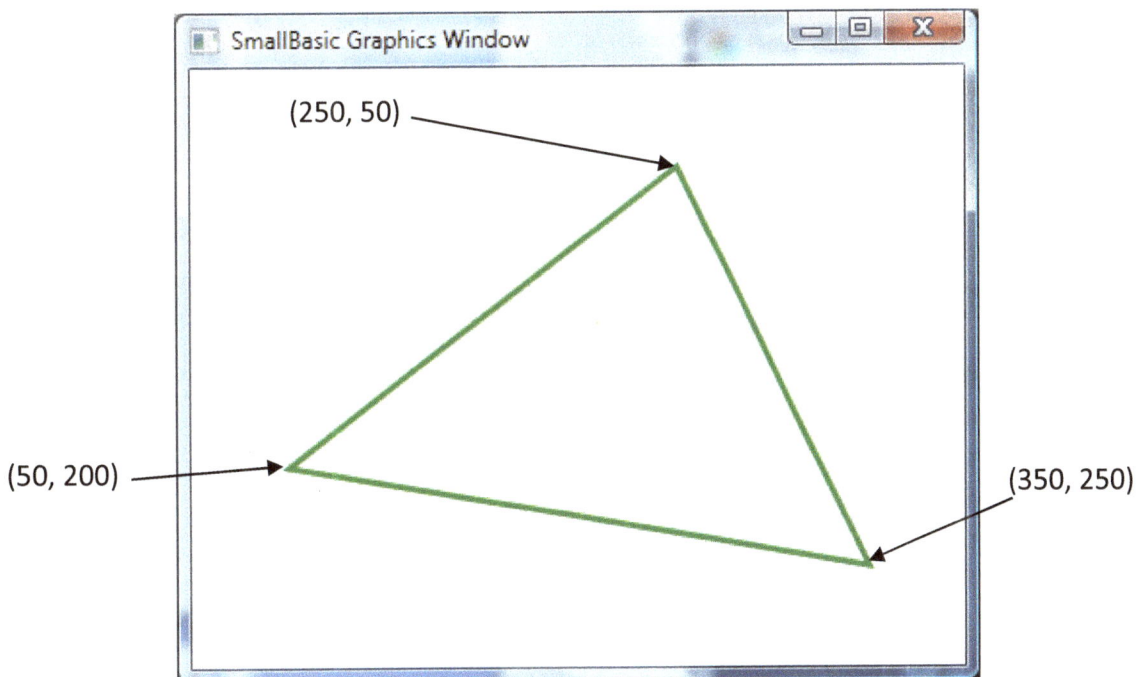

FILLING SHAPES WITH THE BRUSH

To fill a shape with color, you need a **brush**. Set the brush color using:

```
GraphicsWindow.BrushColor = Color
```

There are three methods for filling shapes. They use the same arguments as the corresponding draw methods:

```
GraphicsWindow.FillRectangle(X, Y, W, H)
GraphicsWindow.FillEllipse(X, Y, W, H)
GraphicsWindow.FillTriangle(X1, Y1, X2, Y2, X3, Y3)
```

Add these two lines at the end of the last little program:

```
GraphicsWindow.BrushColor = "Yellow"
GraphicsWindow.FillTriangle(250, 50, 50, 200, 350, 250)
```

Run the program and you get a green triangle filled with yellow:

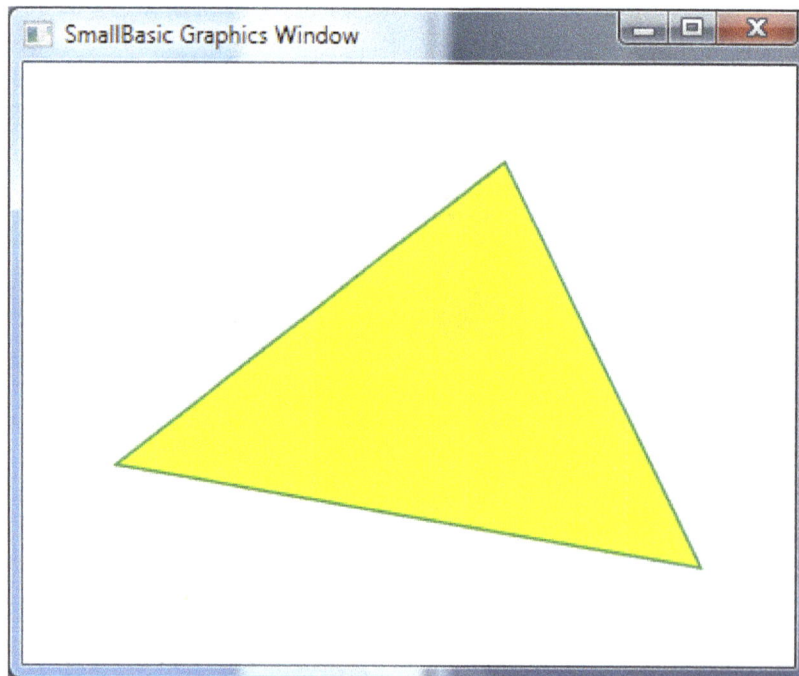

Assignment 17:

1. Draw a snowman using **DrawEllipse** for the body and head and **DrawLine** for his arms. How can you draw his face?

2. Draw a flag for a country you are doing a report for.

3. Write a program to draw "Sinbad's Magic Carpet." Have many colors in the rug.

INSTRUCTOR NOTES 18   DRAWING TEXT

Like shapes and lines, text is drawn to the graphic window using the **DrawText** method.

The text color is set by the **BrushColor**. Text properties include **FontBold**, **FontItalic**, and **FontSize**. There is also **FontName**, but we do not address this property.

Any string can be drawn as text. The (X, Y) position for the text is the upper left corner of where the text will draw.

QUESTIONS:

1. What values would you use to left justify text with **DrawText**?

2. How can you use **DrawText** to write more than one line of text?

3. How could you write a program that makes displayed text flash every second or so?

LESSON 18   DRAWING TEXT

The **Write** and **WriteLine** statements do not work in the graphics window. We have to "draw text" in a graphics window.

Start a **New** program. Use this code:

```
'drawing text
GraphicsWindow.Show()
GraphicsWindow.Width = 400
GraphicsWindow.Height = 150
GraphicsWindow.DrawText(50, 50, "Drawing text ...")
```

Run the program to see:

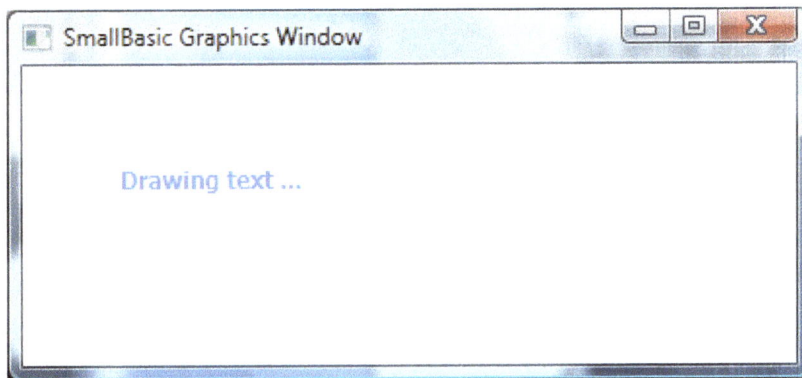

Look at the text drawn in the window. This was done by the **DrawText** statement. It is:

```
GraphicsWindow.DrawText(X, Y, String)
```

This statement draws the text **String** at the coordinate pair (**X, Y**).

COLORED TEXT

The color of text drawn to the graphics window is set by the **BrushColor** property.

Change the code above to make the text red:

```
'drawing text
GraphicsWindow.Show()
GraphicsWindow.Width = 400
GraphicsWindow.Height = 150
GraphicsWindow.BrushColor = "Red"
GraphicsWindow.DrawText(50, 50, "Drawing text ...")
```

Run the modified code to see the newly colored text:

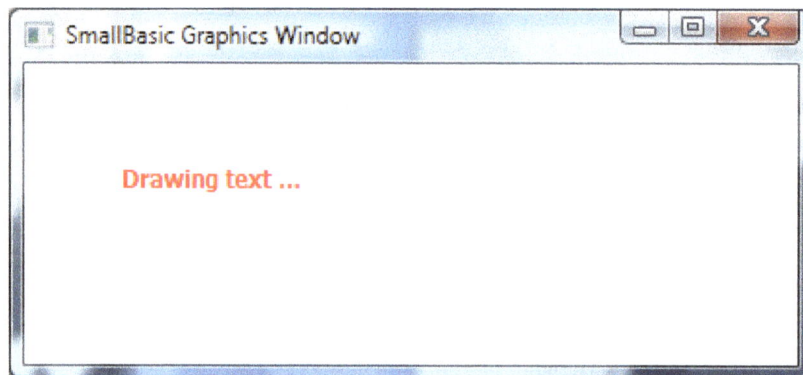

The size of text drawn to the graphics window is set by the **FontSize** property. Font size is measured in **points.**

Change the code above to make the text font larger (size is 24):

```
'drawing text
GraphicsWindow.Show()
GraphicsWindow.Width = 400
GraphicsWindow.Height = 150
GraphicsWindow.BrushColor = "Red"
GraphicsWindow.FontSize = 24
GraphicsWindow.DrawText(50, 50, "Drawing text ...")
```

Run the new code to see the bigger text:

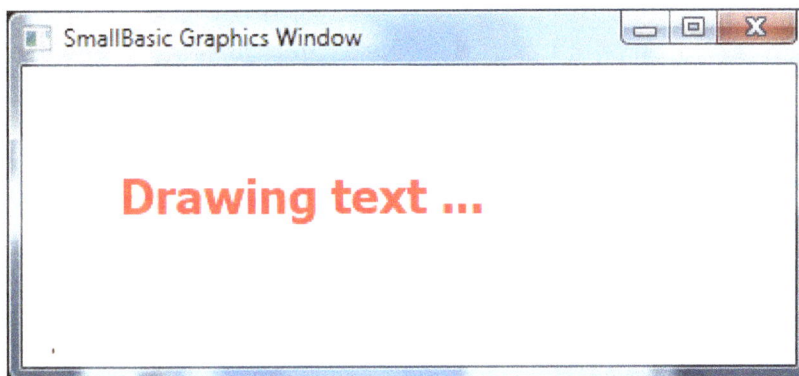

BOLD AND ITALIC TEXT

There are other things you can do to text drawn in the graphics window.

By default, the displayed text is in boldface. We can change this. Add the line setting the **FontBold** property to "false":

```
'drawing text
GraphicsWindow.Show()
GraphicsWindow.Width = 400
GraphicsWindow.Height = 150
GraphicsWindow.BrushColor = "Red"
GraphicsWindow.FontSize = 24
GraphicsWindow.FontBold = "false"
GraphicsWindow.DrawText(50, 50, "Drawing text ...")
```

Run the program to see the "thinner" text:

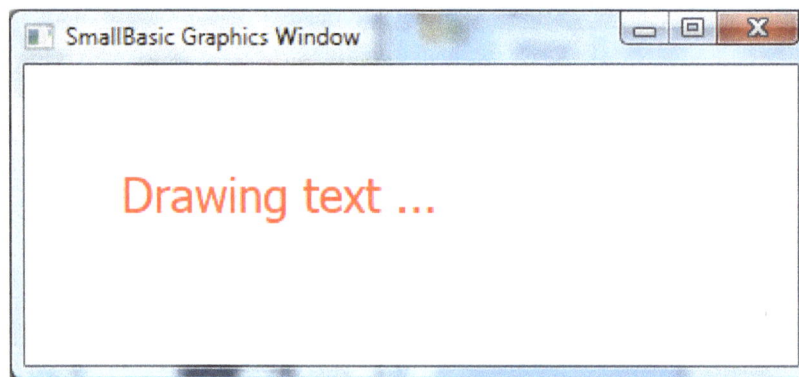

If you want italic text, set the **FontItalic** property to "true":

```
'drawing text
GraphicsWindow.Show()
GraphicsWindow.Width = 400
GraphicsWindow.Height = 150
GraphicsWindow.BrushColor = "Red"
GraphicsWindow.FontSize = 24
GraphicsWindow.FontBold = "false"
GraphicsWindow.FontItalic = "true"
GraphicsWindow.DrawText(50, 50, "Drawing text ...")
```

Now, **Run** this to see:

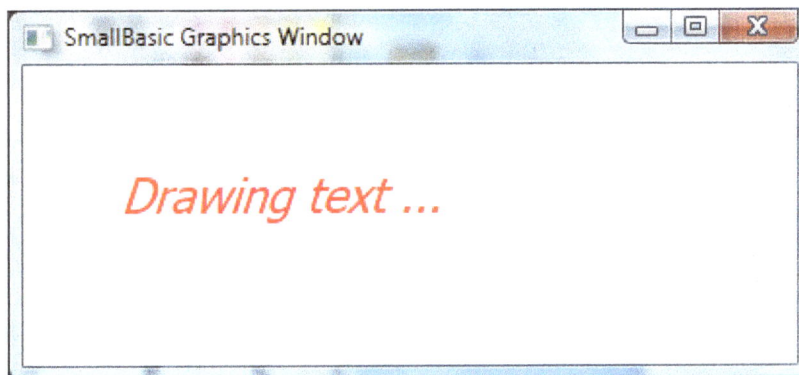

ERASING TEXT

In games, you might use **DrawText** to keep track of a score. When the score changes, you need to display a new score. To do this, you need to erase the old score first.

Start a **New** program. Enter this code:

```
'erasing text
GraphicsWindow.Show()
GraphicsWindow.Width = 400
GraphicsWindow.Height = 150
GraphicsWindow.BackgroundColor = "Blue"
GraphicsWindow.BrushColor = "Yellow"
GraphicsWindow.FontSize = 18
GraphicsWindow.DrawText(50, 50, "Score:")
Score = 0
For I = 1 To 20
  'erase space
  GraphicsWindow.BrushColor = "Blue"
  GraphicsWindow.FillRectangle(150, 50, 100, 30)
  ' draw score
  GraphicsWindow.BrushColor = "White"
  GraphicsWindow.DrawText(150, 50, Score)
  Program.Delay(1000)
  Score = Score + 5
EndFor
```

Run the program and watch:

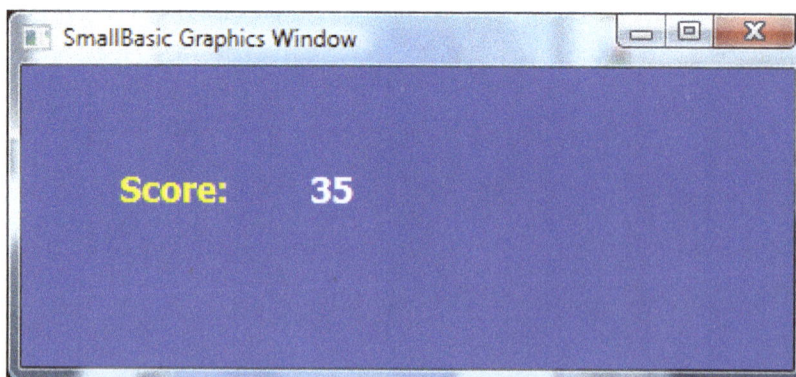

Every second, a new score is shown. The **FillRectangle** method erases the old score before the new one is displayed with **DrawText**. The arguments used in **FillRectangle** (that tell you how big an area to erase) are usually found by trial and error.

1. Write you name close to the center of the graphics window. Use colors and large font size.

2. Write a program that randomly displays the digits from 1 to 9 in the graphics window.

INSTRUCTOR NOTES 19   TURTLE GRAPHICS

In this lesson, we study the Small Basic turtle. Actually, the turtle has been around for a long time, being a critical part of the Logo programming language that was very popular in the 1980's.

A neat thing about turtle graphics is that even younger children can draw with it. There is no need to understand coordinate systems or even to know any Small Basic programming. Turtle graphics can be done without every worrying about an (X, Y) coordinate pair. There is a need to understand angles. Kids need to know that there are 360 degrees in a circle.

For more elaborate drawings, some programming skills are needed.

There are lots of examples of turtle graphics on the Internet. Be aware some are written using commands similar to, but not the same as, Small Basic. And, some are written in "pseudo-code." You, as the instructor, can help the student do the necessary conversions.

QUESTIONS:

1. What is the difference between the Small Basic DrawLine method and the turtle Move method?

2. How can you replicate the Small Basic **DrawRectangle** method with turtle graphics?

3. Can you think of how to fill a shape with color using turtle graphics?

4. Can you figure out how to draw a six point star with turtle graphics?

LESSON 19   TURTLE GRAPHICS

There's another way to draw in Small Basic. It uses a little turtle.

DRAW A LINE

Start a **New** program. Type this code:

```
'Draw Line
Turtle.Show()
Turtle.Move(100)
```

Run the program and you will see the turtle draw a line:

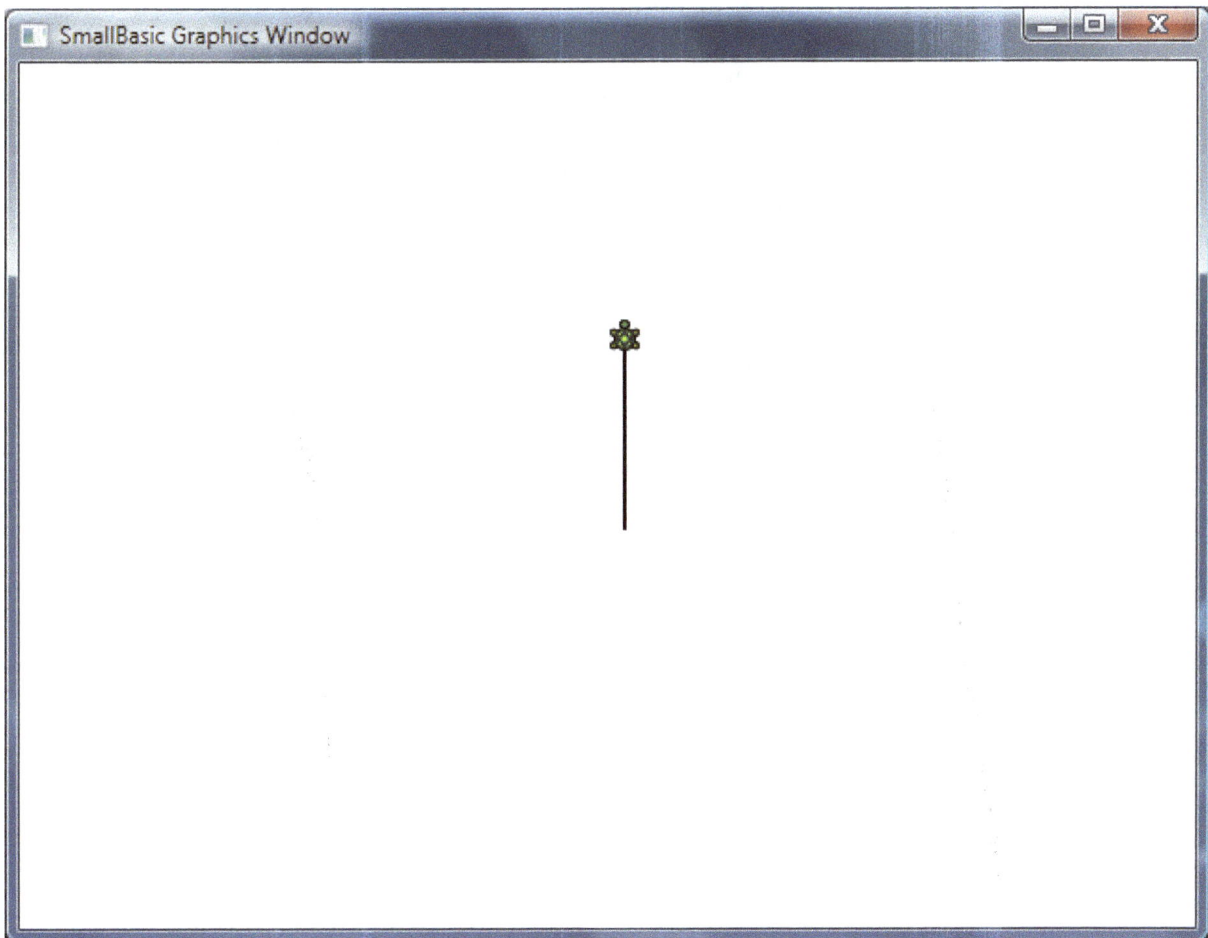

The first statement displays the turtle in the graphics window. He is pointing up.

The second statement:

`Turtle.Move(100)`

Tells the turtle to move 100 pixels in the direction he is pointing.

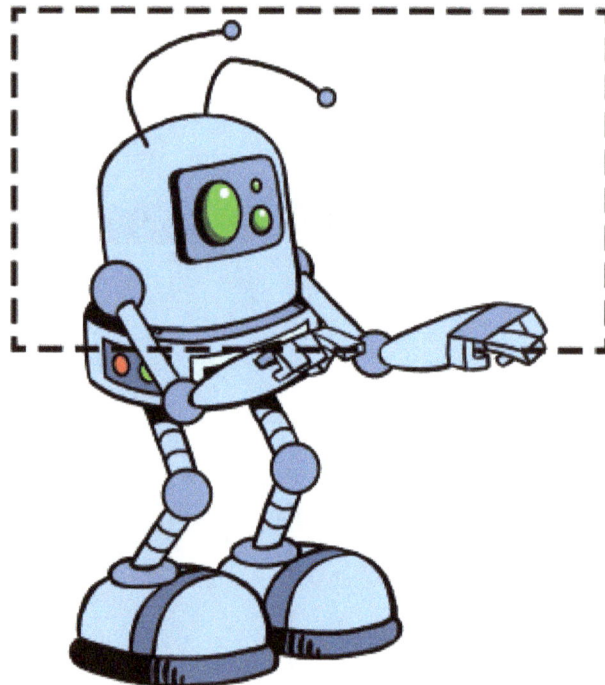

TURNING THE TURTLE

Start a **New** program. Use this code:

```
'Draw square
Turtle.Show()
For I = 1 To 4
  Turtle.Move(150)
  Turtle.TurnRight()
EndFor
```

Run the program. The turtle draws a square:

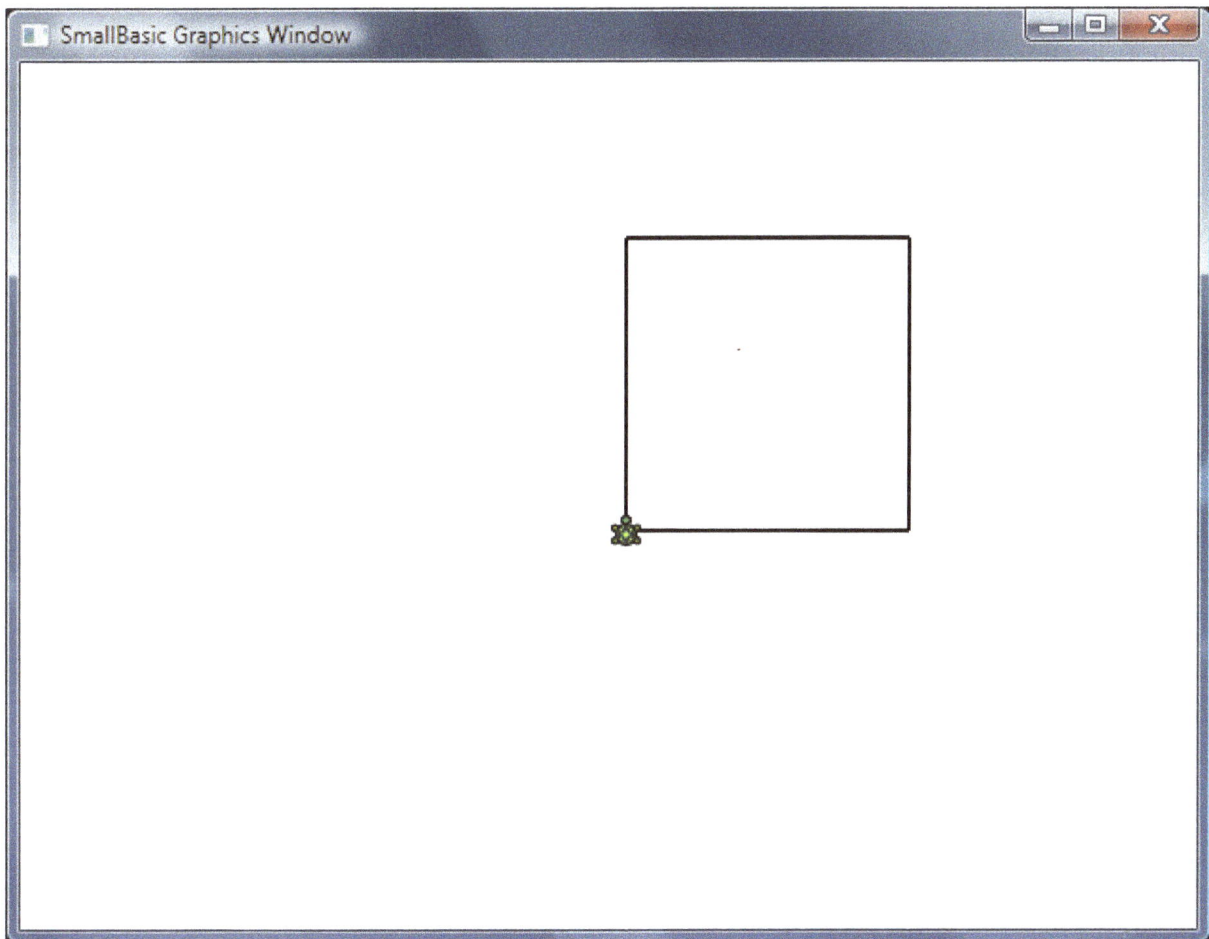

The **TurnRight** statement makes the turtle change direction by 90 degrees to the right. There is also a **TurnLeft** statement that makes the turtle change dirction by 90 degrees to the left. We can use any Small Basic statements with turtle graphics too. We used a **For** loop to draw each side of the square.

TURTLE PEN

The turtle draws with the graphics window pen. So, to change pen width, use the PenWidth property. To change pen color, use the PenColor property.

Change the code drawing the square to this:

```
'Draw square
Turtle.Show()
GraphicsWindow.PenWidth = 10
GraphicsWindow.PenColor = "Red"
For I = 1 To 4
  Turtle.Move(150)
  Turtle.TurnRight()
EndFor
```

Run the program to see a red square with 'fat' sides:

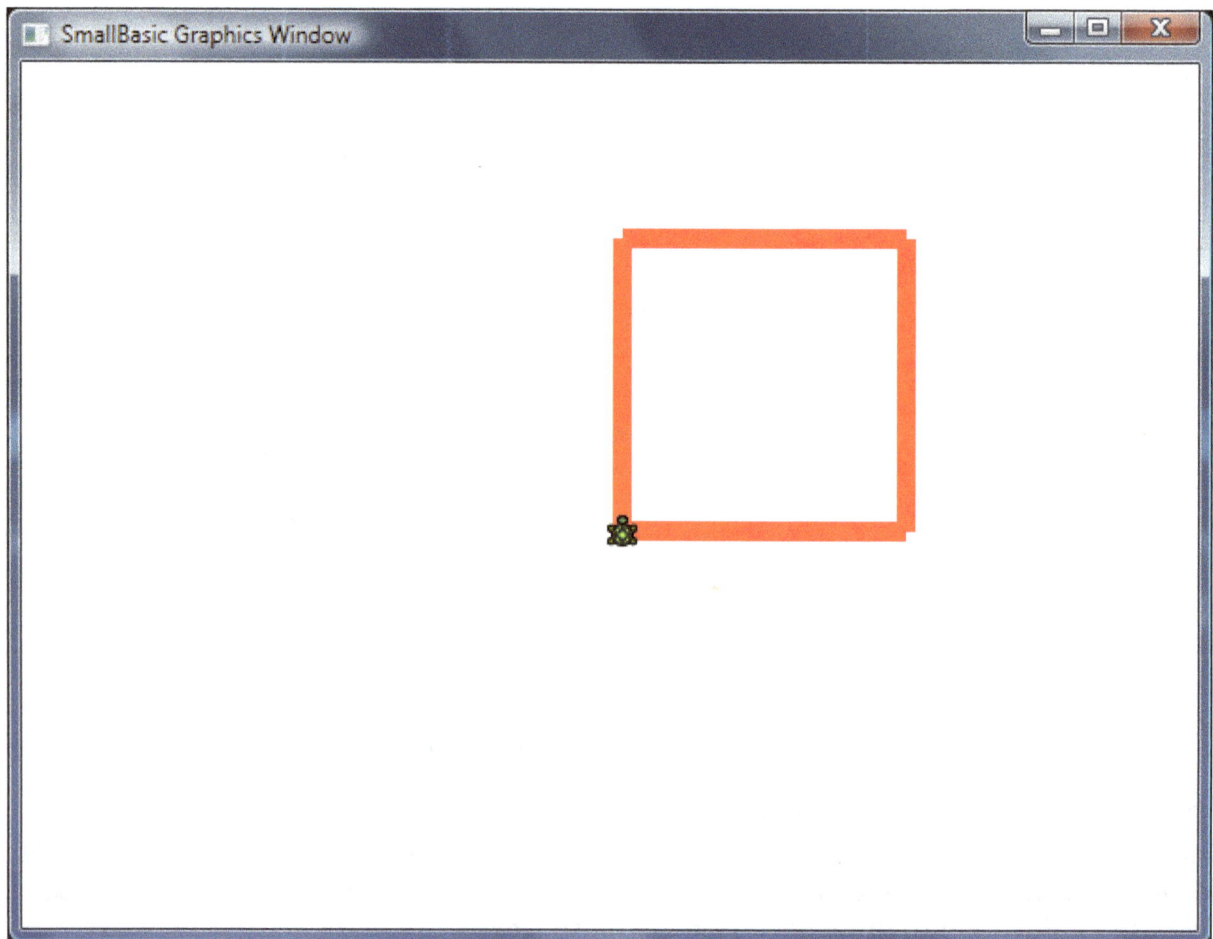

TURTLE SPEED

The turtle can move at different speeds. The speed is set by the **Speed** property. It can range from 1 to 10. When you first start, his speed is 5. When you set the speed to 10, turns are made quickly, and lines are drawn quickly.

Change the square program, adding one line setting **Speed** to 10:

```
'Draw square
Turtle.Show()
GraphicsWindow.PenWidth = 10
GraphicsWindow.PenColor = "Red"
Turtle.Speed = 10
For I = 1 To 4
  Turtle.Move(150)
  Turtle.TurnRight()
EndFor
```

Run the program. You see the same square, but it is drawn very quickly.

For complex drawings, we often use faster speeds.

ANOTHER WAY TO TURN

TurnRight and **TurnLeft** make 90 degree turns. The **Turn** statement is used to turn any number of degrees you specify. A positive value is a clockwise turn. A negative value is counterclockwise.

Start a **New** program. Type this code:

```
'Draw triangle
Turtle.Show()
Turtle.Turn(30)
Turtle.Move(150)
Turtle.Turn(120)
Turtle.Move(150)
Turtle.Turn(120)
Turtle.Move(150)
```

Run the program to see a triangle:

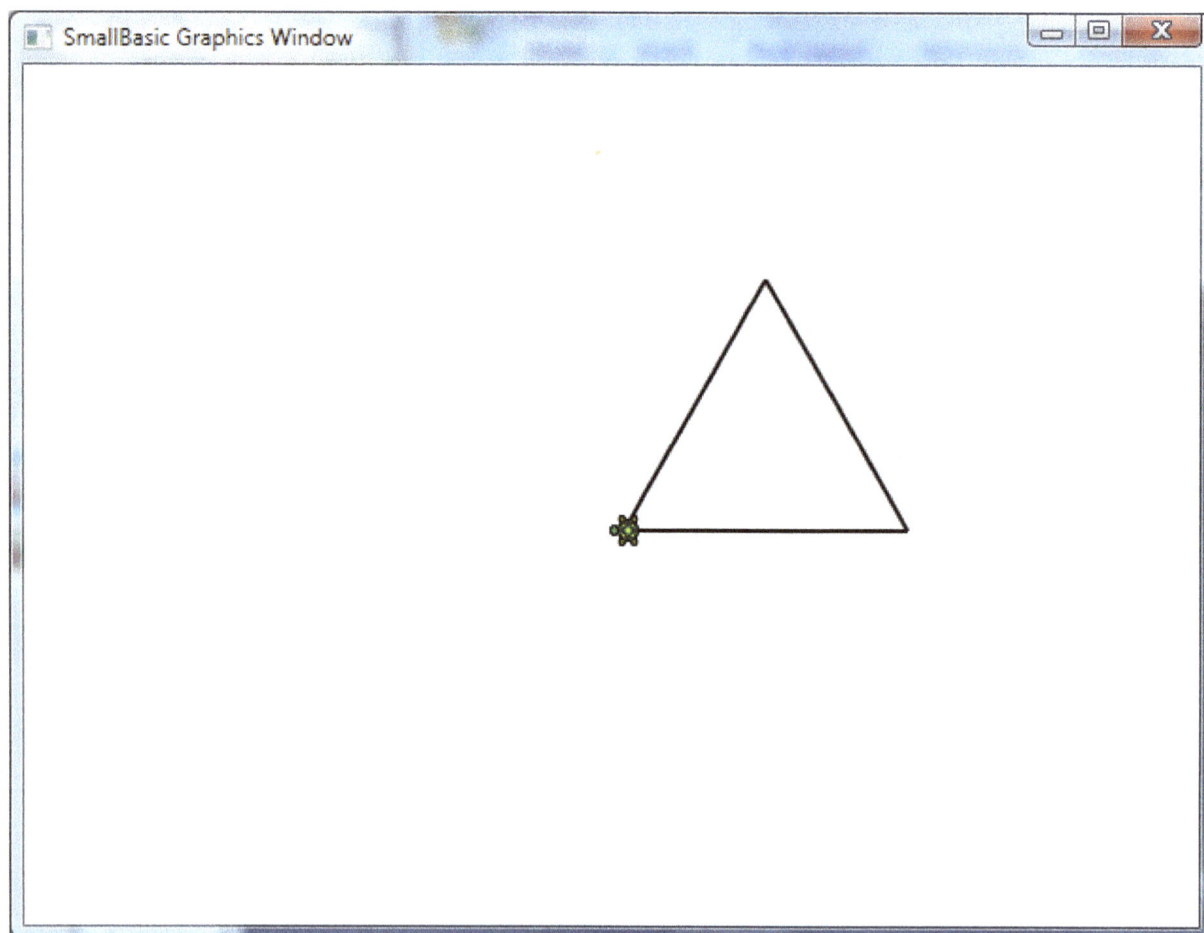

If you need help understanding turning angles, ask for it. It's not too hard.

DRAWING MANY SIDED SHAPES

A many sided shape is called a **polygon**. Let's write a program that can draw a shape with any number of sides we want.

Start a **New** program. Write this code:

```
'Draw polygon
'you can change these numbers
N = 5
P = 500
'draw shape
S = P / N
A = 360 / N
For I = 1 To N
  Turtle.Move(S)
  Turtle.Turn(A)
EndFor
```

Run the program to see a pentagon:

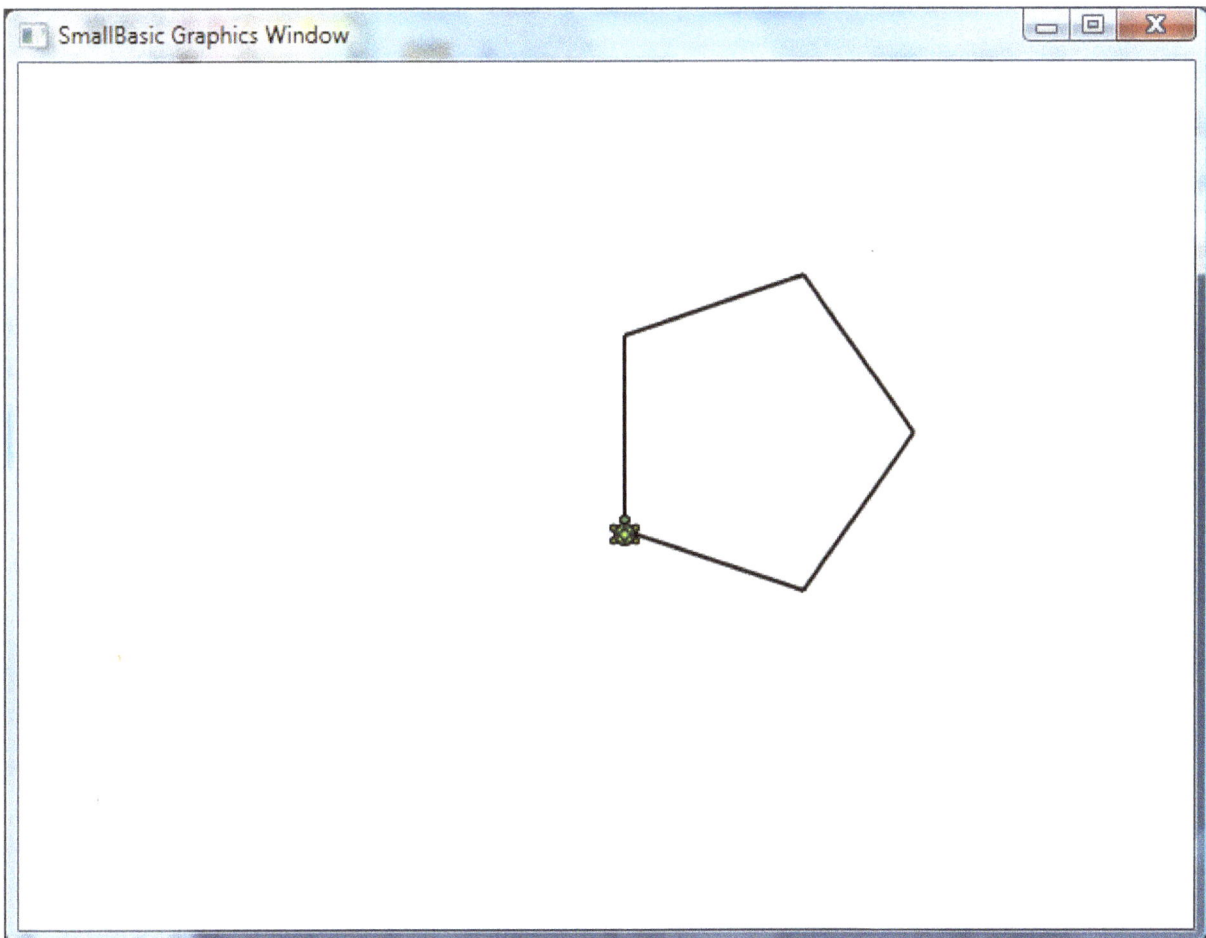

In this program, you can change the **N** (the number of sides). With **N** equal to **5**, we get a pentagon. You can also change **P** - this sets the perimeter (distance around) of the shape.

Let's draw a blue octagon (**N = 8**):

```
'Draw polygon
'you can change these numbers
N = 8
P = 500
GraphicsWindow.PenColor = "Blue"
'draw shape
S = P / N
A = 360 / N
For I = 1 To N
  Turtle.Move(S)
  Turtle.Turn(A)
EndFor
```

Run the program to see the new shape:

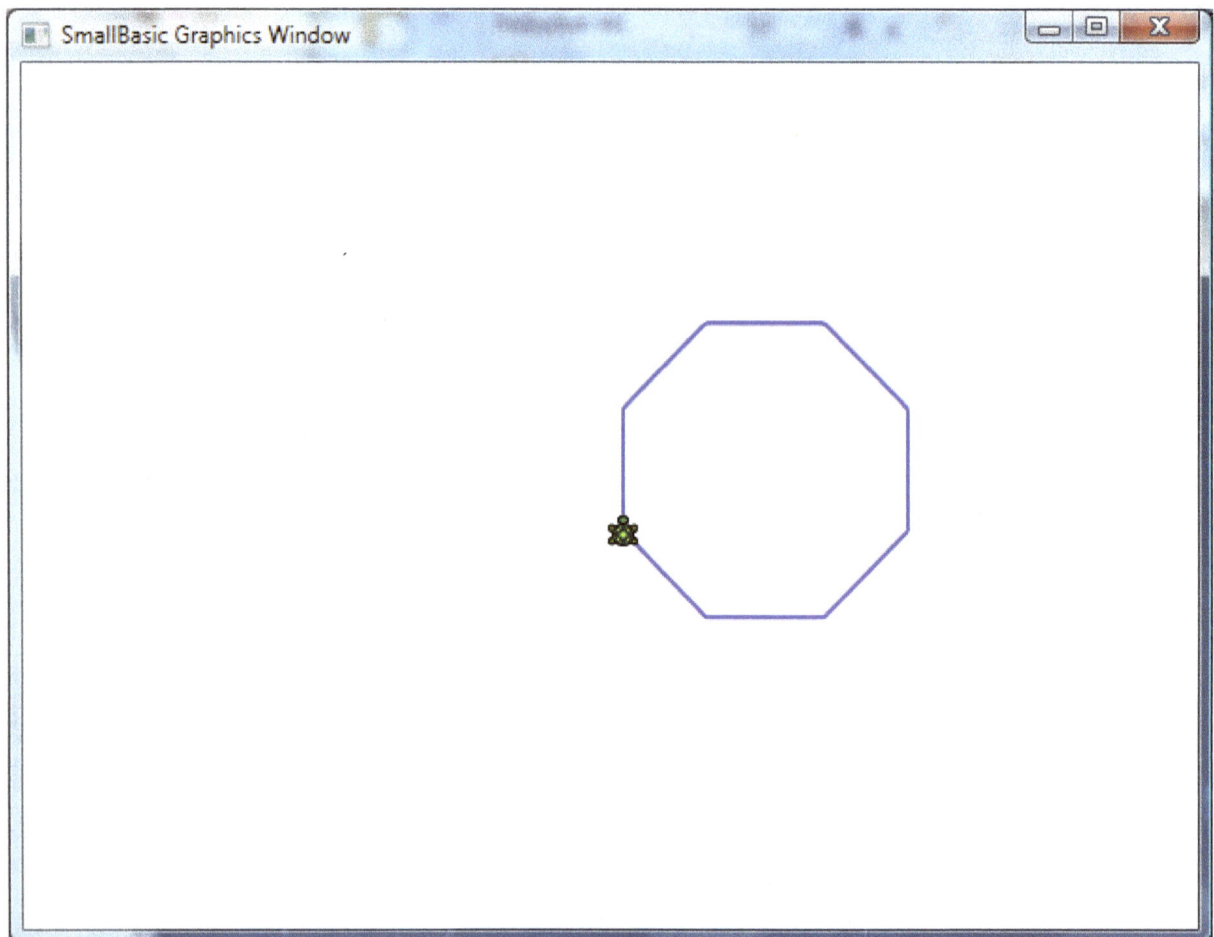

Set **N** to **30** and **Run** the program again.

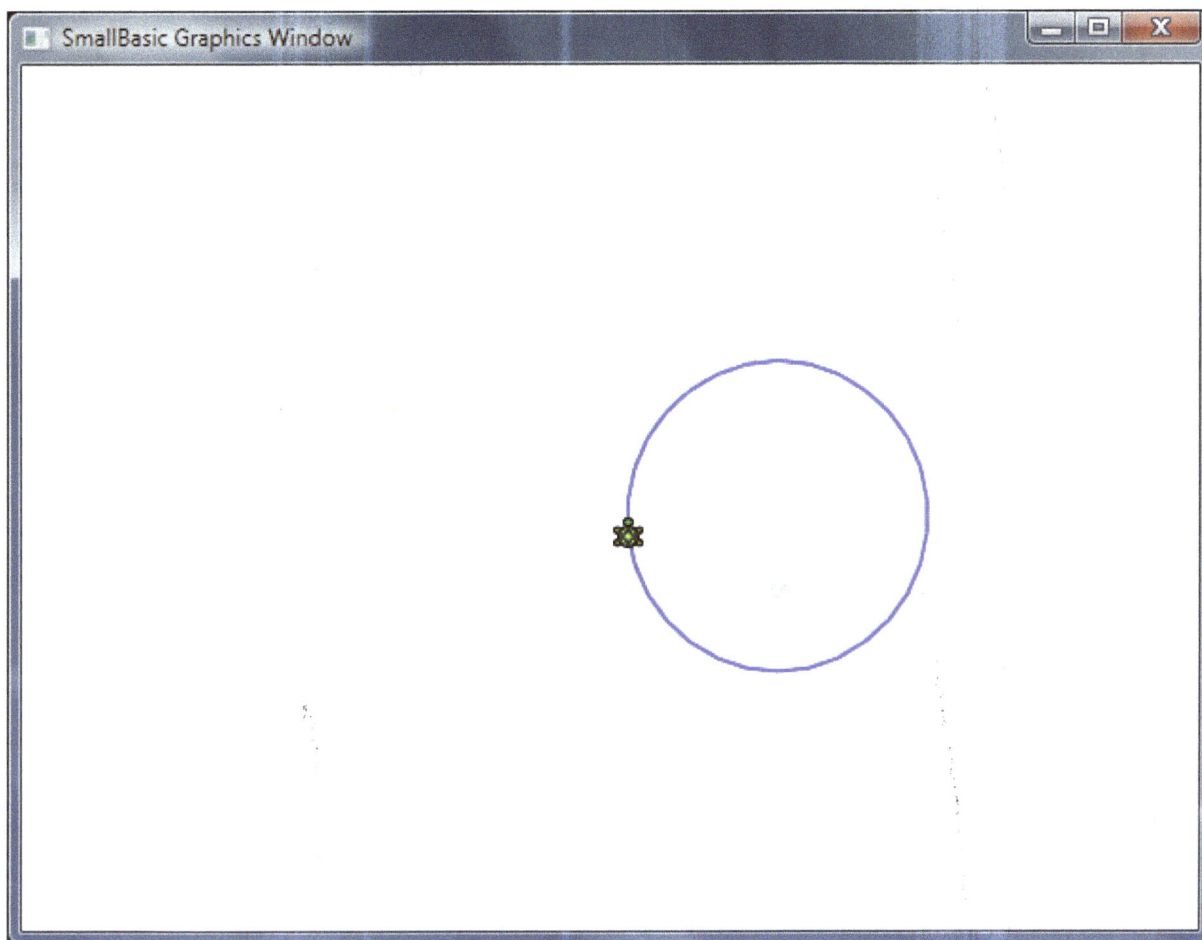

A polygon with many sides looks much like a circle!

FANCY GRAPHICS

A fun part of turtle graphics is to use Small Basic programming to generate some beautiful pictures. We will do that with our little circle program.

Start a **New** program. Use this code (it adds some code to the circle program):

```
'Draw many multi-colored shapes
'you can change these numbers
N = 30
P = 500
M = 50
'draw shape
S = P / N
A = 360 / N
D = 360 / M
Turtle.Speed = 10
For J = 1 To M
  GraphicsWindow.PenColor = GraphicsWindow.GetRandomColor()
  For I = 1 To N
    Turtle.Move(S)
    Turtle.Turn(A)
  EndFor
  Turtle.Turn(D)
EndFor
```

This program draws **M** randomly colored circles, turning a little (**D** degrees) after drawing each one. We use a **Speed** of 10 to make things go faster.

Run the program. Look at the beauty!

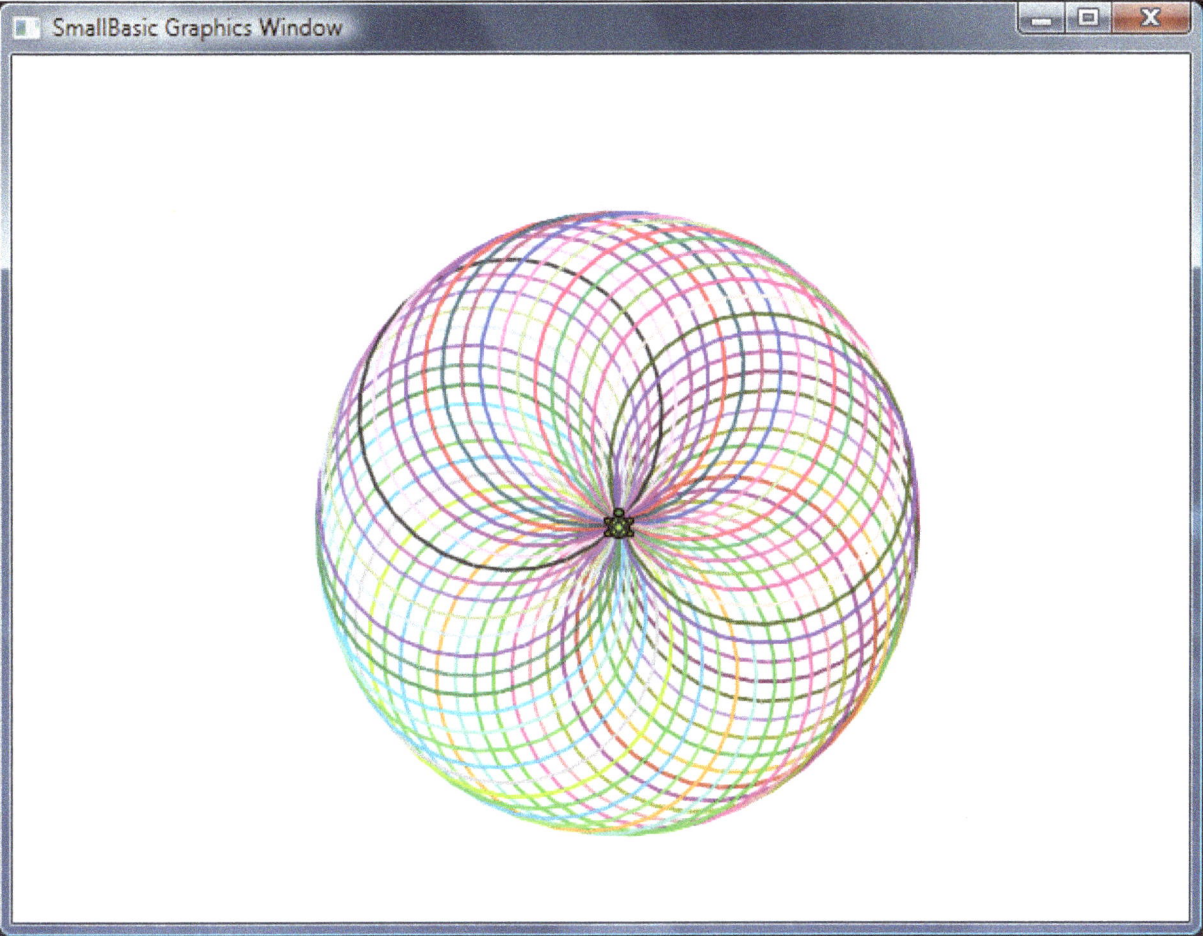

NOT DRAWING

Sometimes you want to move the turtle without drawing a line. The **PenUp** statement "lifts" the drawing pen. Then you can move somewhere else in the graphics window. To continue drawing, use the **PenDown** statement.

Start a **New** program. Write this code to draw the "Olympic Rings". There's lots of repeated code – you might like to use lots of copy and paste:

```
'Draw olympic rings
'you can change these numbers
N = 30
P = 500
GraphicsWindow.BackgroundColor = "LightBlue"
'draw shape
S = P / N
A = 360 / N
Turtle.Speed = 10
GraphicsWindow.PenWidth = 10
'center top ring
Turtle.TurnLeft()
GraphicsWindow.PenColor = "Black"
For I = 1 To N
  Turtle.Move(S)
  Turtle.Turn(A)
EndFor
'left top ring
Turtle.PenUp()
Turtle.Move(200)
Turtle.PenDown()
GraphicsWindow.PenColor = "Blue"
For I = 1 To N
  Turtle.Move(S)
  Turtle.Turn(A)
EndFor
'right top ring
Turtle.Turn(180)
Turtle.PenUp()
Turtle.Move(400)
Turtle.Turn(180)
Turtle.PenDown()
GraphicsWindow.PenColor = "Red"
For I = 1 To N
  Turtle.Move(S)
  Turtle.Turn(A)
EndFor
```

```
'right bottom ring
Turtle.PenUp()
Turtle.Move(100)
Turtle.TurnLeft()
Turtle.Move(100)
Turtle.TurnRight()
Turtle.PenDown()
GraphicsWindow.PenColor = "Green"
For I = 1 To N
  Turtle.Move(S)
  Turtle.Turn(A)
EndFor
'left bottom ring
Turtle.PenUp()
Turtle.Move(200)
Turtle.PenDown()
GraphicsWindow.PenColor = "Yellow"
For I = 1 To N
  Turtle.Move(S)
  Turtle.Turn(A)
EndFor
```

Run the program to see:

Too bad we can't play the Olympic theme music. Well, actually we can do that in Small Basic and we show you how in the next lesson!

FINDING OTHER TURTLE GRAPHICS

Turtle graphics have been around for many years. If you search the Internet, you can find lots of examples. There are some pretty neat things out there. Let's look at a few examples.

Want to draw a flower? Start a **New** program. Type in this code:

```
'flower
'move down a bit
Turtle.Speed = 10
Turtle.PenUp()
Turtle.Turn(180)
Turtle.Move(50)
Turtle.Turn(180)
'ground
Turtle.PenDown()
GraphicsWindow.PenColor = "Orange"
Turtle.Turn(90)
Turtle.Move(150)
Turtle.Turn(180)
Turtle.Move(300)
Turtle.Turn(180)
Turtle.Move(150)
Turtle.Turn(-90)
'draw plant body
GraphicsWindow.PenColor = "Green"
Turtle.Turn(-10)
For I =1 To 3
  Turtle.Move(100)
  Turtle.Turn(180)
  Turtle.Move(100)
  Turtle.Turn(190)
EndFor
'Draw stem
Turtle.Turn(-20)
Turtle.Move(120)
'Draw flower petals
GraphicsWindow.PenColor = "Red"
Turtle.Turn(-90)
For I =1 To 10
  Turtle.Move(20)
  For J =1 To 10
    Turtle.Turn(20)
    Turtle.Move(2)
  EndFor
```

```
    Turtle.Move(20)
EndFor
'flower center
GraphicsWindow.PenWidth = 3
GraphicsWindow.PenColor = "Yellow"
Turtle.PenUp()
Turtle.Move(-2)
Turtle.PenDown()
For I =1 To 18
  Turtle.Move(1)
  Turtle.Turn(20)
EndFor
'get turtle out of way
Turtle.PenUp()
Turtle.Move(100)
```

Run the program to see:

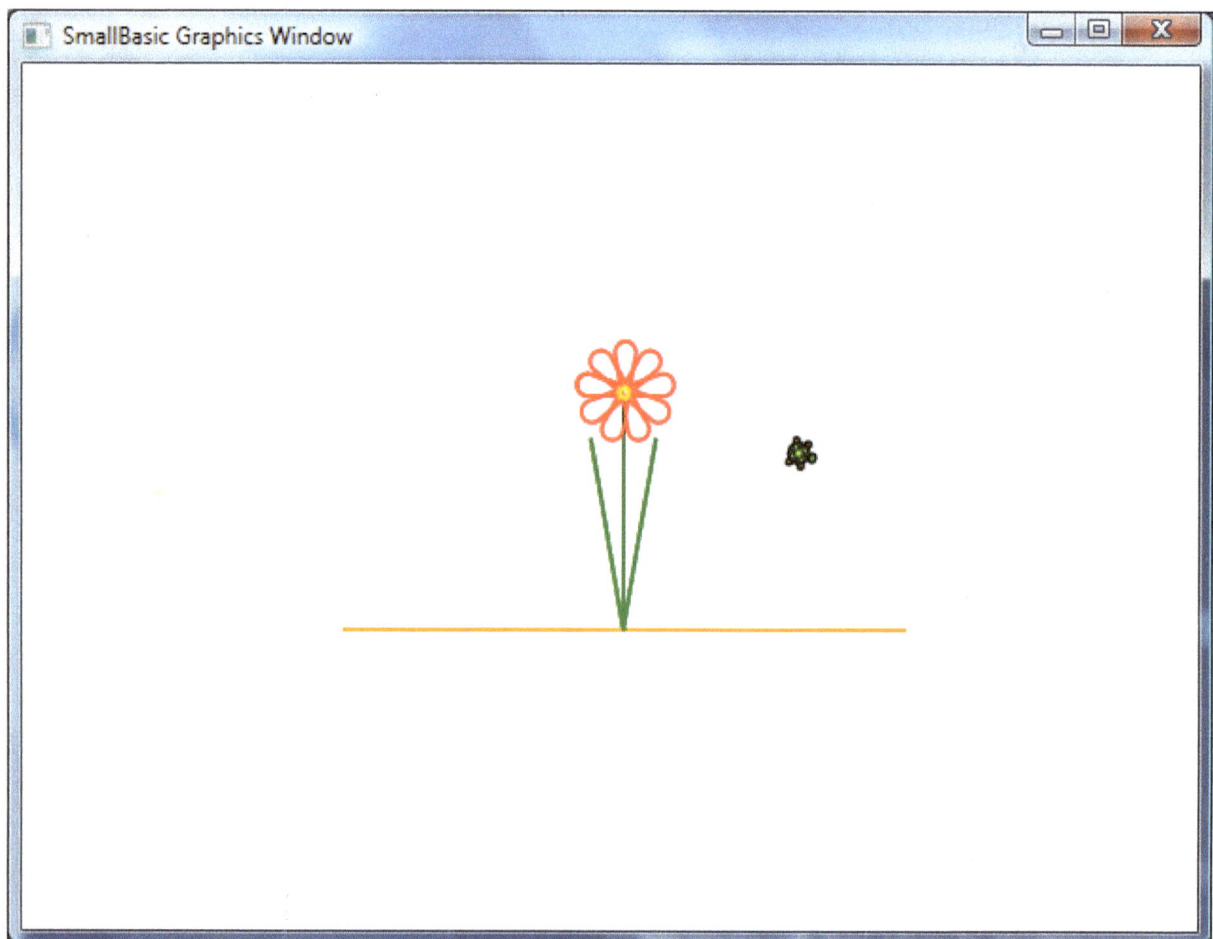

How about a patriotic pinwheel effect? Start a **New** program and use this code:

```
'patriotic pinwheel
GraphicsWindow.BackgroundColor = "Black"
Turtle.Speed = 10
For I = 1 To 10
  For J = 1 To 18
    If (Math.Remainder(J, 3) = 0) Then
      GraphicsWindow.PenColor = "Red"
    EndIf
    If (Math.Remainder(J, 3) = 1) Then
      GraphicsWindow.PenColor = "White"
    EndIf
    If (Math.Remainder(J, 3) = 2) Then
      GraphicsWindow.PenColor = "Blue"
    EndIf
    For K =1 To 2
      Turtle.Move(200)
      Turtle.Turn(200)
    EndFor
  EndFor
  Turtle.Turn(36)
EndFor
```

Run the program. Pretty neat heh?

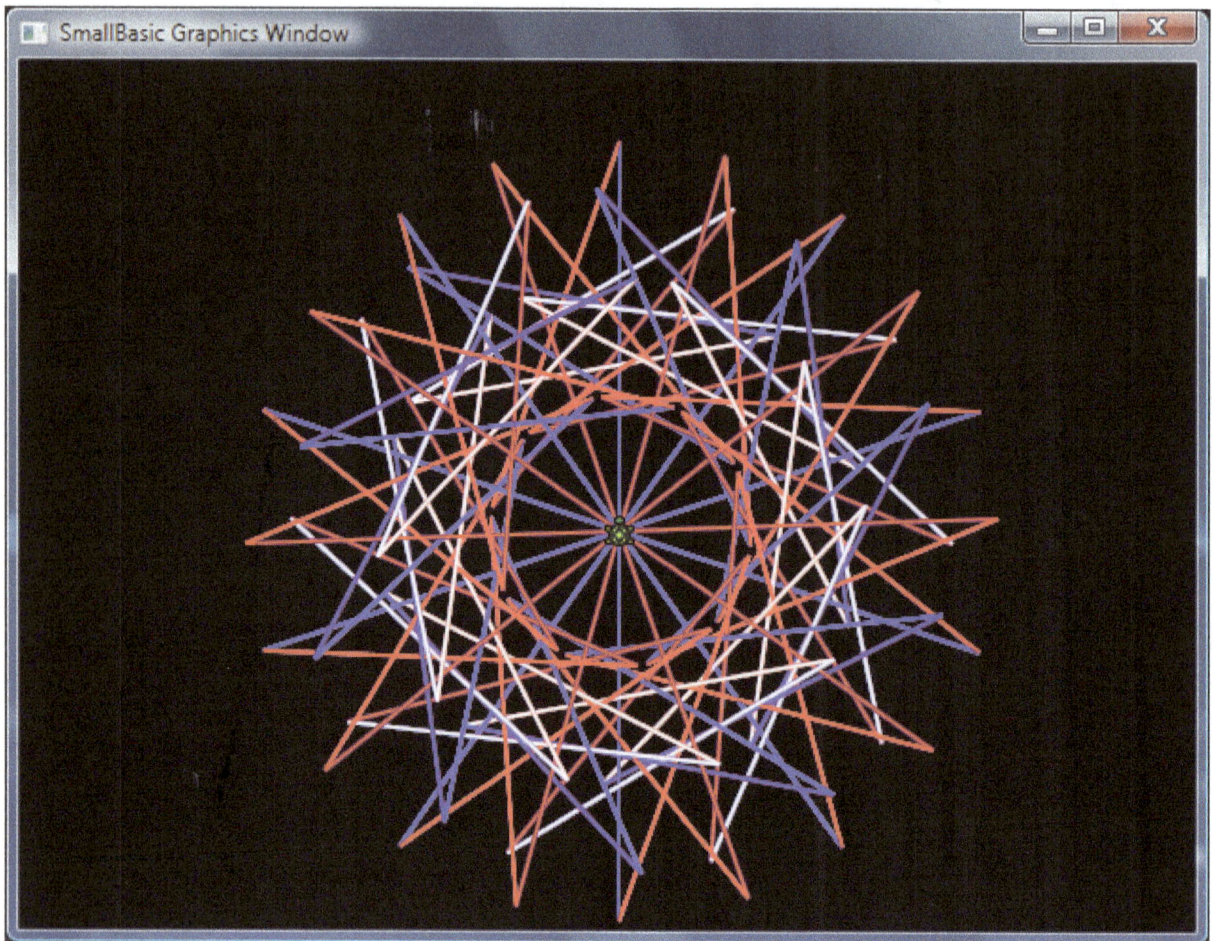

Finally, let's see a really cool spiral effect. Start a **New** program again. Use this code:

```
'spiral
D = 0.01
A = 89.5
X = 0.01
S = 250
Turtle.Turn(90)
Turtle.Speed = 10
GraphicsWindow.PenColor = "Blue"
For I = 1 To S
  Turtle.Move(D * 0.5 * GraphicsWindow.Width)
  Turtle.Turn(A)
  D = D + X
EndFor
```

Run the program. Kind of hypnotizing?

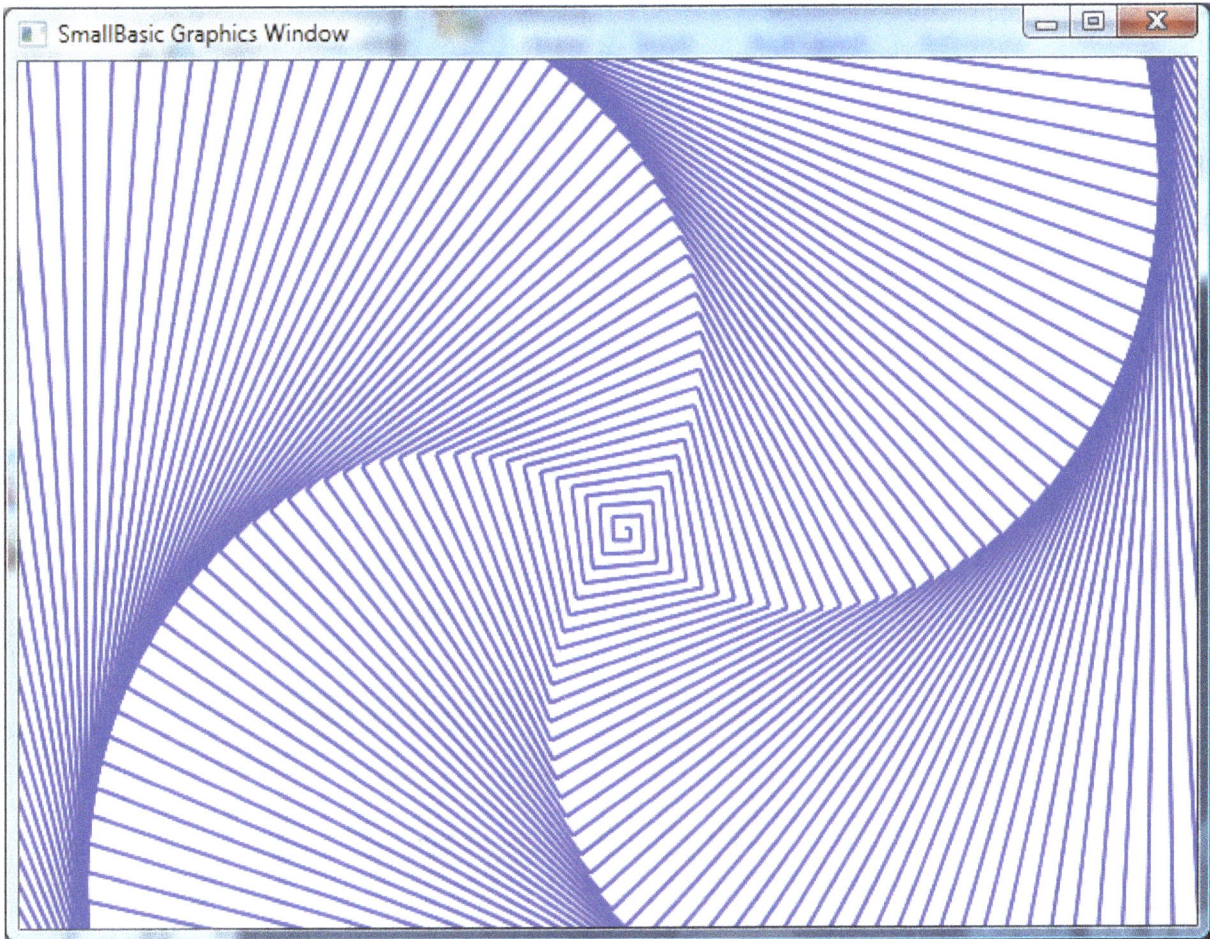

1. Draw a green rectangle using the turtle.

2. Draw a Tic-Tac-Toe grid using the turtle.

3. Search the Internet for Small Basic turtle graphics examples. Type some of them and try them. Make changes to the programs to add color and other effects.

ADVANCED PROGRAMMING AND GAMES

INSTRUCTOR NOTES 20   MUSIC

The **PlayMusic** method of the **Sound** object reads notes and other instructions from a string and plays music over the computer speakers.

PlayMusic has two modes: MF (foreground mode) in which the execution of the program pauses while the music plays, and MB (background mode) in which the computer goes on executing statements.

Only the notes that are white and black keys on a piano are accepted by the **PlayMusic** method. For example, B# is okay, but B flat is not. The octave symbol (**O**) sets the octave (1 to 7) from which notes are chosen. An octave starts at C. Middle C is the lowest note in octave 3.

The lengths of notes are set by numbers following the note. A table of values for traditional note names, such as "quarter note" is given. This method also allows for "triplets" where three notes are played in the same time as two are ordinarily.

Rests are signified by a **P**, followed by a length value (same lengths used for notes).

The overall tempo is set (or changed) by **TEMPO** symbols in the string.

QUESTIONS:

1. Where does the **PlayMusic** method get the notes it plays?

2. What does "B#" mean in a **PlayMusic** string?

3. What does "ML" mean in a **PlayMusic** string?

4. What is a "triplet" of quarter notes? How do you tell the computer to play them?

5. What is the difference between "background" and "foreground" for the **PlayMusic** method?

191

LESSON 20   MUSIC

ROW, ROW, ROW YOUR BOAT

Start a **New** program. Type in this very long line of code:

```
Sound.PlayMusic("T100 O3 C4 C4 C6 D16 E4 E6 D16 E6 F16 G2 O4 C12 C12
C12 O3 G12 G12 G12 E12 E12 E12 C12 C12 C12 G8 F8 E8 D8 C2")
```

Run the program. You will hear a piano playing "Row, Row, Row Your Boat" over your computer's speakers.

The computer can play a whole tune with just one statement **Sound.PlayMusic**.

But first you have to put all the notes of the tune in a string where the **PlayMusic** statement can find them.

It can play the tune while it is doing something else, like moving graphics in a game.

WHAT GOES IN THE PLAYMUSIC STRING?

You have to put in a symbol in for each note and rest.

NOTES	A	B	C	D	E	F	G	(natural notes)
	A#		C#	D#		F#	G#	(sharp notes)
	A-	B-		D-	E-		G-	(flat notes)

Each note is followed by a number indicating length.

LENGTH		
	full note	1
	half note	2
	"triplet half"	3
	quarter note	4
	"triplet quarter"	6
	eighth note	8
	"triplet eighth"	12
	sixteenth note	16
	"triplet sixteenth"	24

You use similar symbols for rest (**P** for pause).

REST		
	full note rest	P1
	half note rest	P2
	"triplet half"	P3
	quarter note rest	P4
	"triplet quarter"	P6
	eighth note rest	P8
	"triplet eighth"	P12
	sixteenth note rest	P16
	"triplet sixteenth"	P24

Put in the following symbols just once and they hold the "notes" for the music from the time you put the symbols in, until you change by putting in a new symbol.

OCTAVE   O1   O2   O3   O4   O5   O6   O7
Octave O1 is the lowest
Octave O3 starts with the note "middle C"
Octave O7 is the highest

TEMPO			
	T32 to T39	very slow	larghissimo
	T40 to T59		largo
	T60 to T65		larghetto
	T66 to T75		adagio
	T76 to T107	slow	andante
	T108 to T119	medium	moderato
	T120 to T167	fast	allegro
	T168 to T208		presto
	T208 to T255		prestissimo

MF	Foreground	The program stops while the music plays
MB	Background	The program continues to run while the music plays.
MN	Normal	Not legato or staccato
ML	Legato	Ties each note to next
MS	Staccato	Notes clipped off

Assignment 20:

1. Change the string in "Row, Row, Row Your Boat" program so that it plays very fast, very slow, an octave higher, an octave lower, staccato, legato.

2. Play some other tune with **PlayMusic**.

3. Crossing friends. While music plays, make your name move down the screen while a friend's name move along the screen. Use the MB symbol in the string. The names cross in the middle.

Explaining subroutines is the main purpose of this lesson. Subroutines are useful for making modules in a program, "chunking" a task into sections leads to clarity.

Subroutines are placed after the main program. They have the form:

```
Sub SubName
       (Here you place the statements of the subroutine)
EndSub
```

SubName is the name you choose for the subroutine. This subroutine is "called" by simply using its name:

```
SubName()
```

Like a **Goto**, calling a subroutine causes the program to move to another place in the program. The only difference is that in a subroutine, control returns to the statement line after the calling line when the subroutine is done executing.

Small Basic uses subroutines for making modules. This lesson shows modular construction in a graphics program. The subroutine draws a moving submarine boat.

QUESTIONS:

1. How is a subroutine different from using a **Goto** statement?

2. What does "call the subroutine" mean?

3. Why do you want to have subroutines in your program?

Start a **New** program. Type in this code and save the program:

```
' Take a trip
TextWindow.WriteLine("Hop to the subroutine")
TakeTrip()
TextWindow.WriteLine("Back from subroutine")
Program.Delay(1000)
TextWindow.WriteLine("")
TextWindow.WriteLine("Hop again")
TakeTrip()
TextWindow.WriteLine("Home for good")
Program.Delay(1000)
Program.End()

Sub TakeTrip
  'subroutine
  TextWindow.WriteLine("Got here okay")
  Program.Delay(1000)
  TextWindow.WriteLine("Pack your bags, back we go")
  Program.Delay(1000)
EndSub
```

Run the program. Here is what you see before the text window disappears - no "Press any key to continue ..." message appears:

This is the skeleton of a long program. The 'main' program starts at the top and continues to this line:

```
Program.End()
```

Where there are **WriteLine** statements, you may put in many more program lines.

After the main program is this code:

```
Sub TakeTrip
  'subroutine
  TextWindow.WriteLine("Got here okay")
  Program.Delay(1000)
  TextWindow.WriteLine("Pack your bags, back we go")
  Program.Delay(1000)
EndSub
```

This is a **subroutine**. It is a self-contained section of code that can be "called" from anywhere in the main program. A subroutine starts with the **Sub** keyword, followed by the name of the subroutine. The name of this subroutine is **TakeTrip**. The subroutine ends with the **EndSub** keyword.

In this example, the subroutine is "called" twice in the main program using the line:

```
TakeTrip()
```

This statement is like a **Goto TakeTrip** statement, except the computer remembers where it was called from so that it can go back there again. Go through the code to see how the subroutine works.

WHAT GOOD IS A SUBROUTINE?

In a short program, perhaps not much.

In a long program, it does two things:

1. It can save you work and saves space in memory. You do not have to repeat the same program lines in different parts of the program.

2. It makes the program easier to understand and faster to write and can help uncover errors (debugging). By an error, we mean the program did what you told it to do, but not what you actually wanted it to do.

THE END STATEMENT

A program may have zero, one or many **End** statements:

```
Program.End()
```

This tells the computer to stop running the program and return to Small Basic edit mode. You won't see the "Press any key to continue …" message in the text window.

That is really all it does. You can put an **End** statement anywhere in the program: for example after **Then** in an **If** statement.

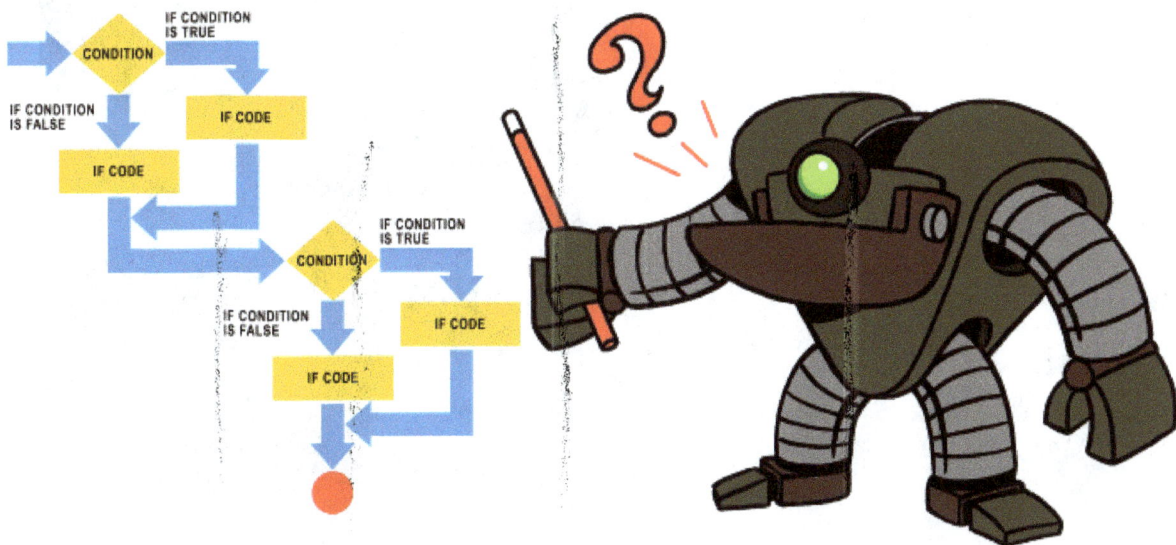

MULTIPLE SUBROUTINES

A program can have many subroutines. And, variables used in the main program and other subroutines can be accessed from any subroutine.

Start a **New** program. Type this simple example:

```
'two subroutines
J = 0
For I = 1 To 10
  J = J + 1
  FirstSub()
  J = J + 1
  SecondSub()
EndFor

Sub FirstSub
  TextWindow.WriteLine("In first subroutine, J is " + J)
EndSub

Sub SecondSub
  TextWindow.WriteLine("In second subroutine, J is " + J)
EndSub
```

Run the program. Notice how J changes with each subroutine call.

```
C:\Users\Lou\AppData\Local\Temp\tmp8C4E.tmp.exe
In first subroutine, J is 1
In second subroutine, J is 2
In first subroutine, J is 3
In second subroutine, J is 4
In first subroutine, J is 5
In second subroutine, J is 6
In first subroutine, J is 7
In second subroutine, J is 8
In first subroutine, J is 9
In second subroutine, J is 10
In first subroutine, J is 11
In second subroutine, J is 12
In first subroutine, J is 13
In second subroutine, J is 14
In first subroutine, J is 15
In second subroutine, J is 16
In first subroutine, J is 17
In second subroutine, J is 18
In first subroutine, J is 19
In second subroutine, J is 20
Press any key to continue...
```

SUBMARINE

Start a **New** program. Use this code (notice how "clean" the program looks). In the first part, some necessary values are set. Next, in the **For** loops, the main action is outlined: moving the submarine repeatedly. The third part is the subroutine, which takes are of moving the submarine one step.

```
'Moving submarine
GraphicsWindow.Show()
GraphicsWindow.Width = 600
GraphicsWindow.Height = 100
GraphicsWindow.BackgroundColor = "Black"
X = 0
Y = 25
D = 10
For I = 1 To 20
  For J = 1 To 43
    MoveSubmarine()
  EndFor
  'at end of window change direction
  D = -D
EndFor

Sub MoveSubmarine
  'erase
  GraphicsWindow.BrushColor = GraphicsWindow.BackgroundColor
  GraphicsWindow.FillRectangle(X, Y, 175, 50)
  'move by D
  X = X + D
  ' draw body
  GraphicsWindow.BrushColor = "Red"
  GraphicsWindow.FillEllipse(X, Y, 150, 50)
  'draw fin
  GraphicsWindow.BrushColor = "Silver"
  GraphicsWindow.FillTriangle(X + 150, Y + 25, X + 170, Y, X + 170, Y + 50)
  Program.Delay(100)
EndSub
```

Notice the **FillTriangle** line is displayed on two lines due to margin restrictions. Make sure this is typed on one line in the code editor.

Run the program. Watch the little submarine go back and forth across the graphics window:

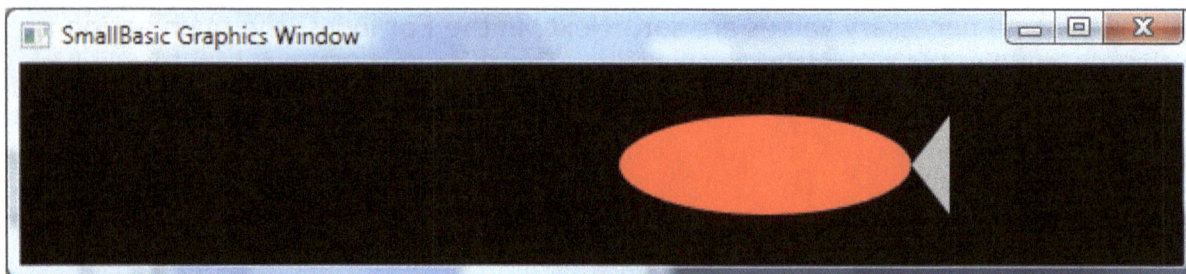

In the **MoveSubmarine** subroutine, the submarine is first erased (**BrushColor** is the window **BackgroundColor**) at its current location using **FillRectangle**. Then, it is redrawn at its new location.

Assignment 21:

1. Go back to the coin flip game in Assignment 11. Clean up the main program by using subroutines. Use a subroutine to flip the coin, one to check the results and one to display the score.

2. Change the moving submarine program. Make the graphics window taller. Then, make the submarine move from the lower right corner to the upper left corner. This makes it look like the sub is surfacing.

This lesson teaches about the **KeyDown** event and intercepting key presses using the graphics window. It is event-driven program without mentioning that's what we're doing.

Using **KeyDown** requires most of the program move to the assigned subroutine. Emphasize the main program is used for initialization. Everything else goes on in the subroutine.

With **KeyDown**, there is no window display at all. No prompt or cursor is displayed and the keystroke is not echoed to the screen. This is an advantage if entering a secret code or password. If you need to display the key presses, use **DrawText**.

QUESTIONS:

1. Compare **Read**/**ReadNumber** with **KeyDown**. For each item below, which does which?

    One gets one character at a time, the other gets whole strings or numbers
    One has a cursor, one does not
    One writes in the window, one does not
    One needs the **Enter** key, one does not

2. What is needed to make sure the **KeyDown** event works properly?

3. When using **KeyDown**, where is most of the program logic located/

LESSON 22   GRAPHICS WINDOW INPUT

READ AND READNUMBER STATEMENTS

We use the **Read** and **ReadNumber** methods with the text window to get inputs.

With both methods, the computer waits for you to type a word, sentence or number. Then, you press the **Enter** key to tell the computer you are done entering. Everything you type shows up in the text window.

GRAPHICS WINDOW INPUT

There are no **Read** or **ReadNumber** methods to use with the graphics window. But, we can still get keyboard input. It's just a litle tricky.

The graphics window is always secretly waiting to see if you press a key. If you do, the window generates what is called a **KeyDown** event.

To see what is typed, we assign a subroutine to the **KeyDown** event. Small Basic will automatically "call" this subroutine whenever a key is pressed. Then, in the subroutine, we can look at the graphics window **LastKey** property to see what key was pressed.

The graphics window will not display the pressed key. If you want to display the pressed key, you need to use the **DrawText** method.

Start a **New** program. Type this code:

```
'Secret input
GraphicsWindow.Show()
GraphicsWindow.Width = 300
GraphicsWindow.Height = 200
GraphicsWindow.KeyDown = KeyDownSub

Sub KeyDownSub
  'clear window
  GraphicsWindow.Clear()
  GraphicsWindow.FontSize = 36
  GraphicsWindow.DrawText(120, 50, GraphicsWindow.LastKey)
EndSub
```

Run the program. Press any key on the keyboard. The key you pressed will be displayed in the graphics window. Here's what I see when I press the **Space** bar:

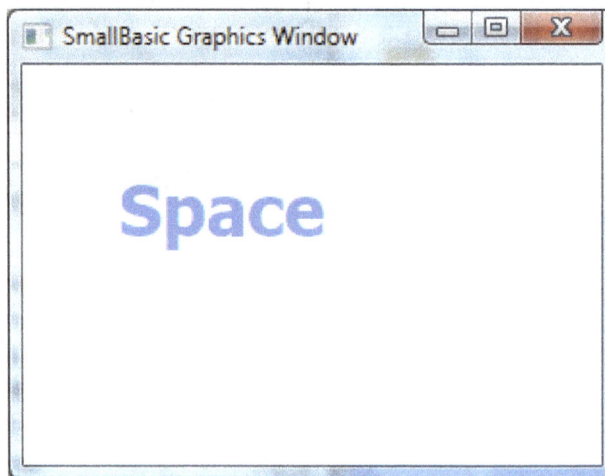

Press lots of letters, numbers, cursor arrows, function keys, etc., to see what is displayed.

In the code, we set the dimensions of the graphics window, then assign the subroutine **KeyDownSub** to the **KeyDown** event:

```
GraphicsWindow.KeyDown = KeyDownSub
```

In this subroutine (called automatically when a key is pressed), the window is cleared and the pressed key (`GraphicsWindow.LastKey`) is shown.

USING THE KEYDOWN EVENT

We need to program a little differently when using the **KeyDown** event.

The main program is used to get everything in the program setup – set graphics window size and color, initialize variables, etc. Then, the final line of the main program assigns the subroutine to the **KeyDown** event. From that point on, all of the program steps go on in that subroutine, and perhaps others called by the **KeyDown** subroutine.

Typical things to do in the **KeyDown** event subroutine:

Find out what key was pressed using the **LastKey** property.
Display the pressed key.
Save the pressed key and build up a string until the **Enter** key (**LastKey** uses "**Return**" for this key) is detected.
Perform some function based on the pressed key.

Remember the **KeyDown** event subroutine is called <u>every</u> <u>time</u> a key is pressed, so keystrokes could start flying into that subroutine.

VALUES RETURNED BY LASTKEY

As we saw, the **LastKey** property returns values for the key pressed. Some of those values are:

Letter and Number Keys

Key	Value	Key	Value	Key	Value	Key	Value
A	"A"	J	"J"	S	"S"	1	"D1"
B	"B"	K	"K"	T	"T"	2	"D2"
C	"C"	L	"L"	U	"U"	3	"D3"
D	"D"	M	"M"	V	"V"	4	"D4"
E	"E"	N	"N"	W	"W"	5	"D5"
F	"F"	O	"O"	X	"X"	6	"D6"
G	"G"	P	"P"	Y	"Y"	7	"D7"
H	"H"	Q	"Q"	Z	"Z"	8	"D8"
I	"I"	R	"R"	0	"D0"	9	"D9"

Numeric Keypad Keys

Key	Value	Key	Value
0	"NumPad0"	8	"NumPad8"
1	"NumPad1"	9	"NumPad9"
2	"NumPad2"	/	"Divide"
3	"NumPad3"	*	"Multiply"
4	"NumPad4"	-	"Subtract"
5	"NumPad5"	+	"Add"
6	"NumPad6"	Enter	"Return"
7	"NumPad7"	.	"Decimal"

Cursor Control Keys

Key	Value	Key	Value
Left arrow	"Left"	Delete	"Delete"
Right arrow	"Right"	Home	"Home"
Up arrow	"Up"	End	"End"
Down arrow	"Down"	Page Up	"PageUp"
Insert	"Insert"	Page Down	"Next"

207

BACKWARDS WORD

Start a **New** program. Type in this code:

```
'Backwards word
GraphicsWindow.Show()
GraphicsWindow.Width = 300
GraphicsWindow.Height = 150
N = 0
W = ""
B = ""
GraphicsWindow.FontSize = 36
GraphicsWindow.KeyDown = KeyDownSub

Sub KeyDownSub
  If (N < 5) Then
    K = GraphicsWindow.LastKey
    N = N + 1
    W = W + K
    B = K + B
    GraphicsWindow.DrawText(30, 30, W)
  EndIf
  If (N = 5) Then
    GraphicsWindow.DrawText(30, 80, B)
  EndIf
EndSub
```

Run the program. Type a five letter word. The computer will show you what you typed and then show you the word in reverse. Here's my result for **BASIC**:

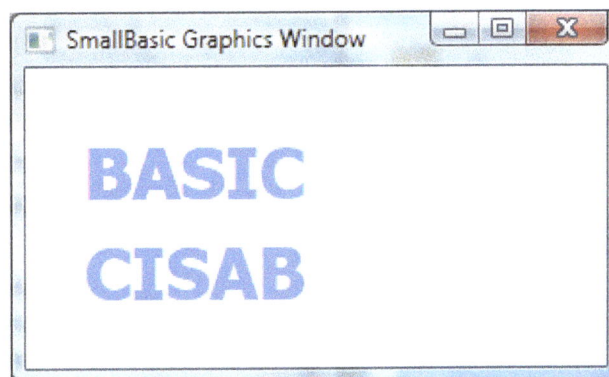

With each entered letter, the forward (**W**) and backward (**B**) words are formed. The backward word is displayed once five letters are entered.

MAKING WORDS OUT OF LETTERS

Start a **New** program. Type in this code:

```
'Backwards word
GraphicsWindow.Show()
GraphicsWindow.Width = 450
GraphicsWindow.Height = 250
W = ""
GraphicsWindow.FontSize = 24
GraphicsWindow.BrushColor = "Blue"
GraphicsWindow.DrawText(30, 30, "Type a word, then press Enter")
GraphicsWindow.KeyDown = KeyDownSub

Sub KeyDownSub
  K = GraphicsWindow.LastKey
  If (K <> "Return") Then
    W = W + K
    GraphicsWindow.BrushColor = "Black"
    GraphicsWindow.DrawText(30, 80, W)
  EndIf
  If (K = "Return") Then
    GraphicsWindow.BrushColor = "Blue"
    GraphicsWindow.DrawText(30, 130, "Word is entered")
  EndIf
EndSub
```

Run the program. You'll see:

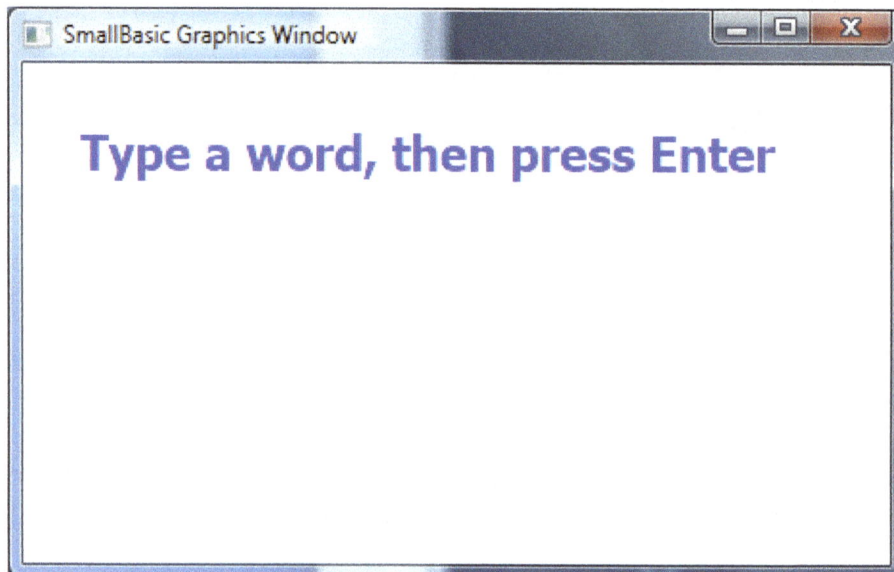

Type a word, then press **Enter**. Here's what I got:

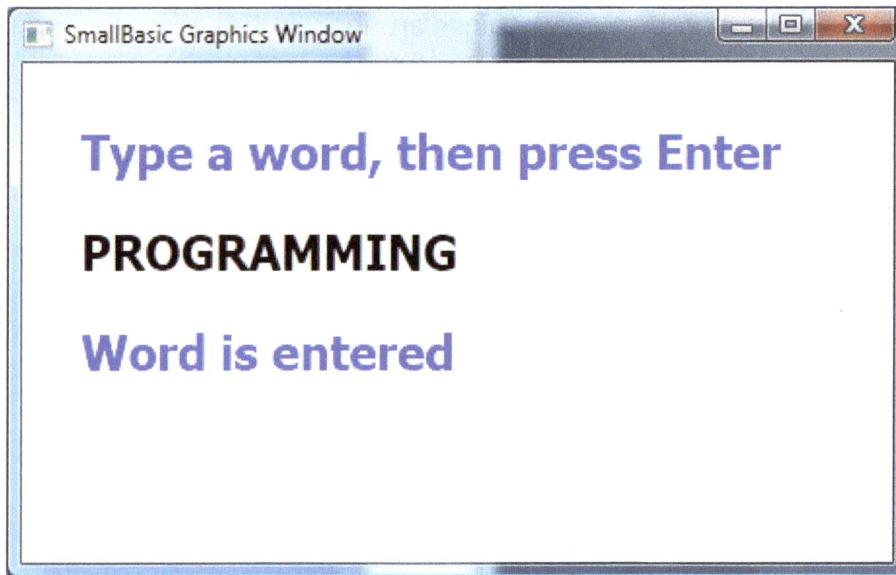

How did the computer know when the word was all typed in? In the **KeyDownSub** subroutine, we looked for the **LastKey** value of "**Return**" to tell us the word was complete.

SECRET NUMBERS

If you want to enter a secret number from the keyboard, you could use the **KeyDown** event to enter digits from 0 to 9, and glue them into a string.

GAME PLAY

Many games use the keyboard to move things around. In this program, we use the left and right arrow keys to move the submarine from the last lesson.

Start a **New** Program. Enter this code:

```
'Moving submarine with keys
GraphicsWindow.Show()
GraphicsWindow.Width = 600
GraphicsWindow.Height = 100
GraphicsWindow.BackgroundColor = "Black"
X = 275
Y = 25
D = 0
MoveSubmarine()
GraphicsWindow.KeyDown = KeyDownSub

Sub KeyDownSub
  K = GraphicsWindow.LastKey
  D = 0
  If (K = "Left") Then
    D = -10
  EndIf
  If (K = "Right") Then
    D = 10
  EndIf
  MoveSubmarine()
EndSub

Sub MoveSubmarine
  'erase
  GraphicsWindow.BrushColor = GraphicsWindow.BackgroundColor
  GraphicsWindow.FillRectangle(X, Y, 175, 50)
  'move by D
  X = X + D
  ' draw body
  GraphicsWindow.BrushColor = "Red"
  GraphicsWindow.FillEllipse(X, Y, 150, 50)
  'draw fin
  GraphicsWindow.BrushColor = "Silver"
  GraphicsWindow.FillTriangle(X + 150, Y + 25, X + 170, Y, X + 170, Y
+ 50)
EndSub
```

In addition to the **KeyDownSub** subroutine, this uses the **MoveCircle** subroutine (without the **Delay** statement; waiting for a key puts in needed delay) from the last lesson. This is another advantage of subroutines – you can reuse program code you have already written.

Run the program. The submarine will be near the center of the window. Press the left and right arrow keys to move the submarine. Note you can even move it off the ends of the window. Here it is about to go off the left end:

Assignment 22:

1. Write a program where the user can change the graphics window color by pressing a key. Use R for red, G for green, B for blue, etc.

2. Write a program where the user enters a password. Have the program form the password from the entered keys, but display asterisks (*) in the graphics window.

3. For the moving submarine program, can you make the fin change sides when the direction changes?

INSTRUCTOR NOTES 23   SNIPPING STRINGS

In this lesson, we describe the use of three text functions: **GetSubText**, **GetSubTextToEnd** and **GetLength**.

These functions, together with the concatenation operation "+", allow complete freedom to cut up strings and glue them back together in any order.

The main characteristics of the functions are demonstrated. If the student experiences difficulty, an experienced programmer or adult should clear up the problem.

QUESTIONS:

1. If you want to save STAR from STARS AND STRIPES, what function would you use? What arguments?

2. If you want to save AND from the same string, what function and what arguments?

3. If you want to count the number of characters in the string P, what function do you use? What arguments?

4. What two arguments does the **GetSubTextToEnd** function need?

5. What statement will clip the third and fourth letters out of a word?

6. Write a short program that takes the word COMPUTER and makes it into PUTERCOM.

LESSON 23   SNIPPING STRINGS

GLUING STRINGS

You already know how to glue strings together. Try running this code:

```
A = "con" + "cat" + "en" + "ation"
TextWindow.WriteLine(A)
```

And you'll see:

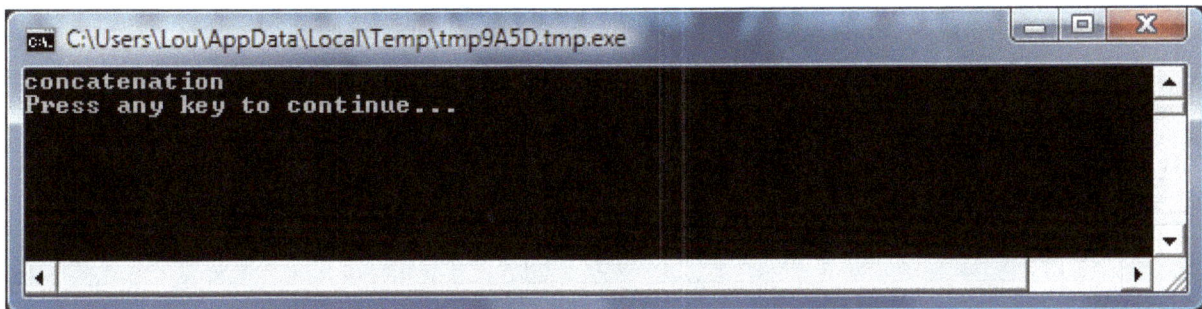

The real name for "gluing" is "concatentation."

Concatenation means make a chain. Maybe we should call them chains instead of strings.

SNIPPING STRINGS

Let's cut off a piece of a string. Start a **New** program. Type this code:

```
'Scissors
N = "123456789"
Q = Text.GetSubText(N, 1, 4)
TextWindow.WriteLine(N)
TextWindow.WriteLine(Q)
```

Run the program. You will see:

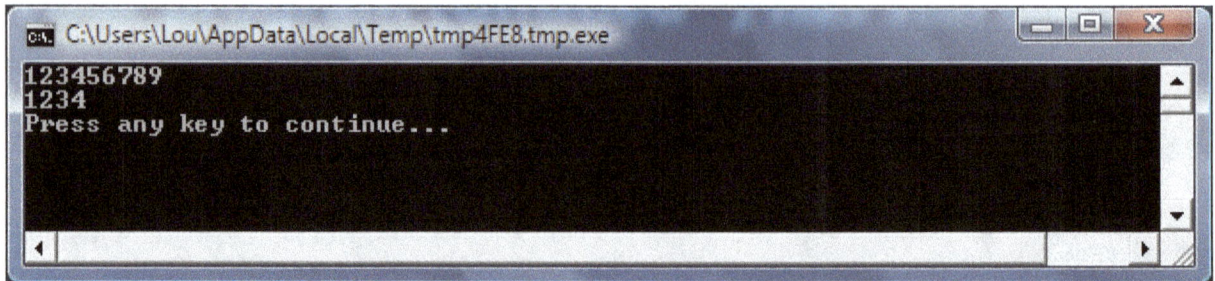

The **GetSubText** function snipped off the left end of the string. The snipped piece can be put in a box or written to the window or whatever.

RULE: The **GetSubText** function needs three things (arguments) inside the parentheses:

1. The string you want to snip
2. The character you want to start at (1 if you want the left end)
3. The number of characters you want to keep

Let's try another. Change the code (the line snipping the string has changed) to:

```
'Scissors
N = "123456789"
Q = Text.GetSubTextToEnd(N, 7)
TextWindow.WriteLine(N)
TextWindow.WriteLine(Q)
```

Run the program to see:

The **GetSubTextToEnd** function snipped off the right end of the string.

RULE: The **GetSubTextToEnd** function needs two things (arguments) inside the parentheses:

1. The string you want to snip
2. The character you want to start at

MORE SNIPPING AND GLUING

Start a **New** program. Type in this code:

```
'Scissors and glue
N = "123456789"
For I = 1 To 9
  L = Text.GetSubText(N, 1, I)
  R = Text.GetSubTextToEnd(N, 10 - I)
  TextWindow.WriteLine(I + " character(s) - " + L + " : " + R)
EndFor
```

Run the program to see:

```
C:\Users\Lou\AppData\Local\Temp\tmp3A51.tmp.exe
1 character(s) - 1 : 9
2 character(s) - 12 : 89
3 character(s) - 123 : 789
4 character(s) - 1234 : 6789
5 character(s) - 12345 : 56789
6 character(s) - 123456 : 456789
7 character(s) - 1234567 : 3456789
8 character(s) - 12345678 : 23456789
9 character(s) - 123456789 : 123456789
Press any key to continue...
```

The program prints out 1 character from the left and right, then 2 characters from the left and right, and continues until it prints all the characters. Notice how we had to do a little math in **GetSubTextToEnd** to figure out how many characters to write.

HOW LONG IS THE STRING?

Start a **New** program. Use this code:

```
'Long rope
GetString:
TextWindow.WriteLine("")
TextWindow.Write("Give me a string: ")
N = TextWindow.Read()
L = Text.GetLength(N)
TextWindow.WriteLine("The string: '" + N + "'")
TextWindow.WriteLine("is " + L +" characters long")
Goto GetString
```

Run the program and enter a string. The program will tell count the characters in your string. Here's my result:

```
C:\Users\Lou\AppData\Local\Temp\tmpAA15.tmp.exe

Give me a string: I like small basic
The string: 'I like small basic'
is 18 characters long

Give me a string: computer
The string: 'computer'
is 8 characters long

Give me a string: _
```

The **GetLength** function returns the number of characters in a string; it counts everything in the string, even the spaces.

CUTTING A PIECE OUT OF THE MIDDLE

The **GetSubText** function can also cut a piece out of the middle of a string.

Start a **New** program. Type this code:

```
'Middle
N = "123456789"
P = Text.GetSubText(N, 3, 4)
TextWindow.WriteLine(P)
```

Run the program to see:

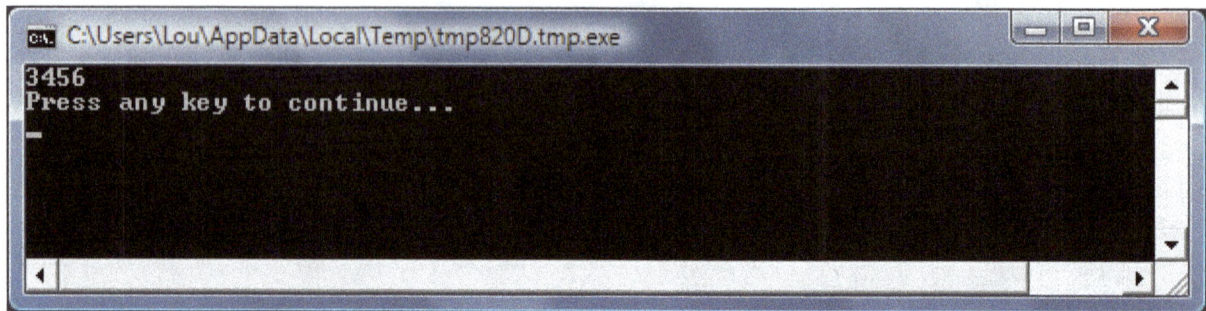

```
C:\Users\Lou\AppData\Local\Temp\tmp820D.tmp.exe
3456
Press any key to continue...
```

This line:

```
P = Text.GetSubText(N, 3, 4)
```

Means:

> Get the string from box N
> Count over three characters
> Save four characters into box P

LOOK MA, NO SPACES

Start a **New** program. Use this code:

```
'No spaces
GetSentence:
TextWindow.WriteLine("Give me a long sentence:")
S = TextWindow.Read()
L = Text.GetLength(S)
T = ""
For I = 1 To L
  'Look at each character - don't save spaces
  C = Text.GetSubText(S, I, 1)
  If (C <> " ") Then
    T = T + C
  EndIf
EndFor
TextWindow.WriteLine("")
TextWindow.WriteLine(T)
TextWindow.WriteLine("")
Goto GetSentence
```

Run the program and type in a sentence. The spaces will be removed:

```
C:\Users\Lou\AppData\Local\Temp\tmpBF00.tmp.exe

Give me a long sentence:
I enjoy working with Small Basic

IenjoyworkingwithSmallBasic

Give me a long sentence:
I hope you like Small Basic and kids

IhopeyoulikeSmallBasicandkids

Give me a long sentence:
```

1. Write a secret cipher making program. You give it a sentence and it finds out how long the sentence is, then switches the first letter with the second, third with the fourth, etc. Example:

   THIS IS A DRAGON

   Becomes

   HTSII S ARDGANO

2. Write a question answering program? You give it a question starting with a verb and it reverses verb and noun to answer the question. Example:

   ARE YOU A TURKEY?
   YOU ARE A TURKEY.

3. Write a pig latin program. It asks for a word. Then it takes all the letters up to the first vowel and puts them on the back of the word, followed by AY. If the word starts with a vowel, it only adds AY. Examples:

   BOX becomes OXBAY
   APPLE becomes APPLEAY

INSTRUCTOR NOTES 24   MORE LOGIC

This lesson treats the **And** and **Or** logical operators and the Boolean values of "true" and "false". Note Small Basic does not currently have a **Not** operator.

Give examples of each and the concept should be pretty clear to the student. Have them say the conditions out loud to understand how they work. Present these logic tables if they help:

And operator:

X	Y	X And Y
"true"	"true"	"true"
"true"	"false"	"false"
"false"	"true"	"false"
"false"	"false"	"false"

Or operator:

X	Y	X Or Y
"true"	"true"	"true"
"true"	"false"	"true"
"false"	"true"	"true"
"false"	"false"	"false"

1. Is each expression "true" or "false"?

   3 = 3
   3 = 3 Or 0 = 2
   3 = 3 And 0 = 2
   "A" = "B"

2. For given values for A and B, what is the value for the logical expression:

   A = "true", B = "true" A And B
   A = "false", B = "true" A And B
   A = "false", B = "false"A And B
   A = "false", B = "true" A Or B
   A = "false", B = "false"A or B

LESSON 24   MORE LOGIC

ANOTHER TEENAGE PROGRAM

Start a **New** program. Type in this code:

```
'AND OR LOGIC
TextWindow.Write("Your first name? ")
N = TextWindow.Read()
TextWindow.Write("Your age? ")
A = TextWindow.ReadNumber()
TextWindow.WriteLine("")
TextWindow.Write(N)
If (A > 12 And A < 20) Then
  TextWindow.WriteLine(" is a teenager")
EndIf
If (A <= 12 Or A >= 20) Then
  TextWindow.WriteLine(" is not a teenager")
EndIf
If (A = 16) Then
  TextWindow.WriteLine("and is sweet sixteen")
EndIf
If (A = 12 Or A = 20) Then
  TextWindow.WriteLine("and just missed")
EndIf
```

Run the program. When asked, enter your name and age (or someone else's name and age). Here's my run for my son:

See what messages print when you use an age of 11, 12, 16, 20, 22.

WHAT DOES "AND" MEAN?

Two things are true about teenagers: They are over 12 years old and they are less than 20 years old. Look at this **If** statement:

```
If (A > 12 And A < 20) Then
   TextWindow.WriteLine(" is a teenager")
EndIf
```

This statement reads "if you are over 12 <u>and</u> you are less than 20, then you are a teenager."

And is a **logical operator**. It compares two expressions. If both expressions are "true", then **And** returns "true". If either expression is "false", then **And** returns "false".

WHAT DOES "OR" MEAN?

Look at this **If** statement in the teenager program:

```
If (A <= 12 Or A >= 20) Then
   TextWindow.WriteLine(" is not a teenager")
EndIf
```

This statement reads "if you are 12 <u>or</u> younger or you are 20 or older, then you are not a teenager."

Or is another logical operator. It compares two expressions. If either expression is "true", then **Or** returns "true". If both expressions are "false", then **Or** returns "false".

PUTTING TRUE AND FALSE IN BOXES

The words "true" and "false" are reserved words in Small Basic. They are used to evaluate logical expressions. These values can be stored in named boxes (variables) like numeric and string data.

Start a **New** program. Type this simple program:

```
A = "true"
If (A) Then
   TextWindow.WriteLine("A is true!")
EndIf
```

Run the program to see:

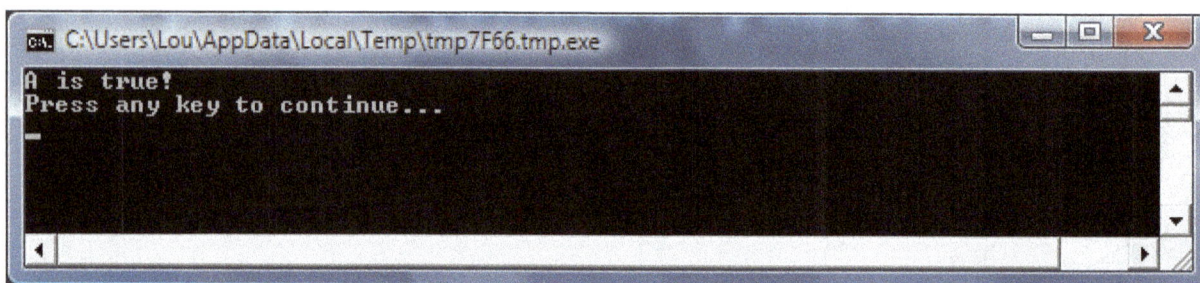

What happens if you change A to "false"?

THE LOGICAL SIGNS

We can use these six symbols in expressions in the **If** statement:

=	equal
<>	not equal
<	less than
>	greater than
<=	less than or equal
>=	greater than or equal

You have to press two keys to make the <> sign and the <= and >= signs.

The last two are new, look at this example to see the difference between < and <=:

2 <= 3 is "true"	2 < 3 is "true"
3 <= 3 is "true"	3 < 3 is "false"
4 <= 3 is "false"	4 < 3 is "false"

These two expressions mean the same thing:

2 <= Q   (2 < Q or 2 = Q)

TEST GRADING

The **And** and **Or** operators can be used to make elaborate decisions using **If** statements.

What if you want to check if you see what letter grade you got on a test. Start a **New** program. Type this code:

```
'grade
GetGrade:
TextWindow.Write("What is your score (0 - 100)? ")
S = TextWindow.ReadNumber()
If (S = 99 Or S = 100) Then
  TextWindow.WriteLine("A+ - Great Job!")
EndIf
If (S >= 90 And S < 99) Then
  TextWindow.WriteLine("You got an A!")
EndIf
If (S >= 80 And S < 90) Then
  TextWindow.WriteLine("It's a B.")
EndIf
If (S >= 70 And S < 80) Then
  TextWindow.WriteLine("It's a C.")
EndIf
If (S >= 60 And S < 70) Then
  TextWindow.WriteLine("It's a D.")
EndIf
If (S < 60) Then
  TextWindow.WriteLine("Sorry, you failed with an F.")
EndIf
Goto GetGrade
```

Run the program. Enter scores and see what grades you would get. Here's what I got:

```
C:\Users\Lou\AppData\Local\Temp\tmp6A27.tmp.exe

What is your score (0 - 100)? 55
Sorry, you failed with an F.
What is your score (0 - 100)? 100
A+ - Great Job!
What is your score (0 - 100)? 94
You got an A!
What is your score (0 - 100)? 82
It's a B.
What is your score (0 - 100)? 80
It's a B.
What is your score (0 - 100)? 79
It's a C.
What is your score (0 - 100)? _
```

Assignment 24:

1. Tell whether each expression is "true" or "false":

   4 = 3
   "G" <> "S"
   5 > 7
   3 > 2 And 3 < 2
   4 = 3 Or 4 = 4
   5 >= 4

2. For this **If** statement:

```
If (Condition) Then
    TextWindow.WriteLine("Jellybean")
EndIf
```

   Tell if the word Jellybean will be printed for these **Condition** expressions:

   "false"
   "true"
   3 <> 0
   "true" And "true"
   "false" Or "true"
   "A" = "Z"
   4 <= 5

230

This lesson shows how to write clear program which interact with th euser in a "friendly" way.

The "spaghetti" program should be discouraged. A format for writing programs is presented in this lesson. While method of imposing order on the task are largely a matter of taste, the methods used in this lesson can serve to introduce the ideas. Be aware there are different approaches depending if you are using the text window or the graphics window. This is especially true when using the **KeyDown** event in the graphics window where most of the programming occurs in the subroutine waiting for keystrokes.

"User friendly" means the window displays are easy to read, input is simple and errors are "trapped." Ask if entries are okay. If not, give the user an opportunity to fix things.

Instructions and help shuold be available. Prompts should be given. Beginners need complete prompts, but experienced users would rather have short prompts.

It is hard to teach the writing of "user friendly" programs. Success depends mostly on the attitude of the programmer. The best advice is to "turn up your annoyance detectors to high" as you write and debug your program.

Most young students will not progress very far toward fully "friendly" programming. To be acquainted with the desirability of "friendly" programming and to use some simple techniques toward accomplishing it are satisfactory achievements.

QUESTIONS:

1. Should your program give instructions whether your user wants them or not?

2. What is a "prompt"?

3. What is "scrolling"? How can you write to a text window without scrolling?

4. What are the rules for naming variables?

5. What is an "error trap"? How would you trap erros if you asked you user to enter a number from 1 to 5?

LESSON 25   USER-FRIENDLY PROGRAMS

There are two kinds of people who will want your programs:

1. Most want to run the program. We call them "users." They need:

> Instructions
> Prompts
> Clear writing in the window (text or graphics)
> No clutter on the window
> Clearing old stuff from the window
> Not too much key pressing
> Protection from their own stupid errors

2. Some want to change the program. We call them "programmers." They need:

> A program made in parts or modules
> Each part cleared labeled
> Lots of comments with explanations

Don't forget you too are a user of your own program, too! Be kind to yourself!

232

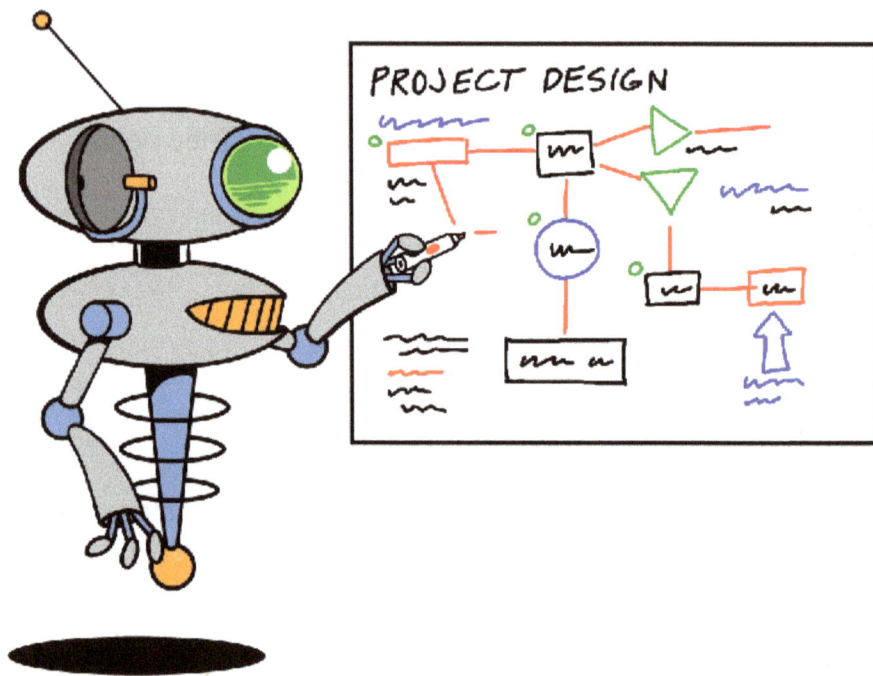

There is **starting stuff** at the beginning of the program:

      Give instructions to the user
      Draw in the initial window
      Set variables to their starting values
      Ask the user for starting information

There is the **main program** loop:

      Controls the order in which tasks are done (including the starting stuff)
      Calls subroutines to do the tasks.

Lastly there are **subroutines** that do the different parts of the program. Programs work best with subroutines. This way you can easily test your program in parts and it makes it easier to change.

PROGRAM OUTLINE

First, make an outline. You can do this on paper or right in the Small Basic editor. If you have trouble deciding what to do, first work though the program steps on paper and keep track of what happens. Then the program has to do the same things.

A program outline could be:

```
'Program Name
'give a description of the program
'Starting stuff
'initialize screen
'initialize variables
'give instructions

'main program
StartLoop:
'control program flow
'call subroutines
Goto StartLoop

'Subroutines go at end
'First subroutine
'Second subroutine
```

After making the outline, fill in the details, like subroutine names.

VARIABLE NAMES

As your programs get longer and more detailed, the one letter variable names we have been using can get confusing.

Start giving your variables names that mean something and are clear to someone looking at your program. For example, if you want to know how much you pay for 20 bananas at $0.30 each, you could write:

```
N = 20
C = 0.30
T = N * C
```

Or, you could write:

```
NumberBananas = 20
CostPerBanana = 0.30
TotalCost = NumberBananas * CostPerBanana
```

Which is clearer?

Small Basic variables can have very long names. Variable names must start with a letter and can use letters, numbers or the underscore (_) character.

One exception to the rule for meaningful names is for temporary variables or the counter variables in **For** loops. These are usually be kept short.

INFORMATION PLEASE

You can ask the user if they want instuctions with questions like:

Do you want instructions <Y/N>?

This lets a beginner see instructions and lets others say "no".

TIE A STRING AROUND THE USERS FINGER

Use a "prompt" to remind users what choices they have.

Example: <Y/N> where the choice is Y for "yes" or N for "no".

Beginners need long prompts. Others like short prompts.

DON'T GIVE THE USER A HEADACHE

If you are writing your program using the text window, remember **scrolling** gives headaches!

Text windows can scroll - if you start writing things at the end of the window, the new line push the old lines up. It is like the scrolls the Romans used for writing. They unwound at the bottom and wound up at the top.

Avoid scrolling. Use the **CursorLeft** and **CursorTop** properties to write exactly where you want. Erase by writing a string of blanks to the same spot.

Use delays, if needed, to keep writing in the window while a user reads it.

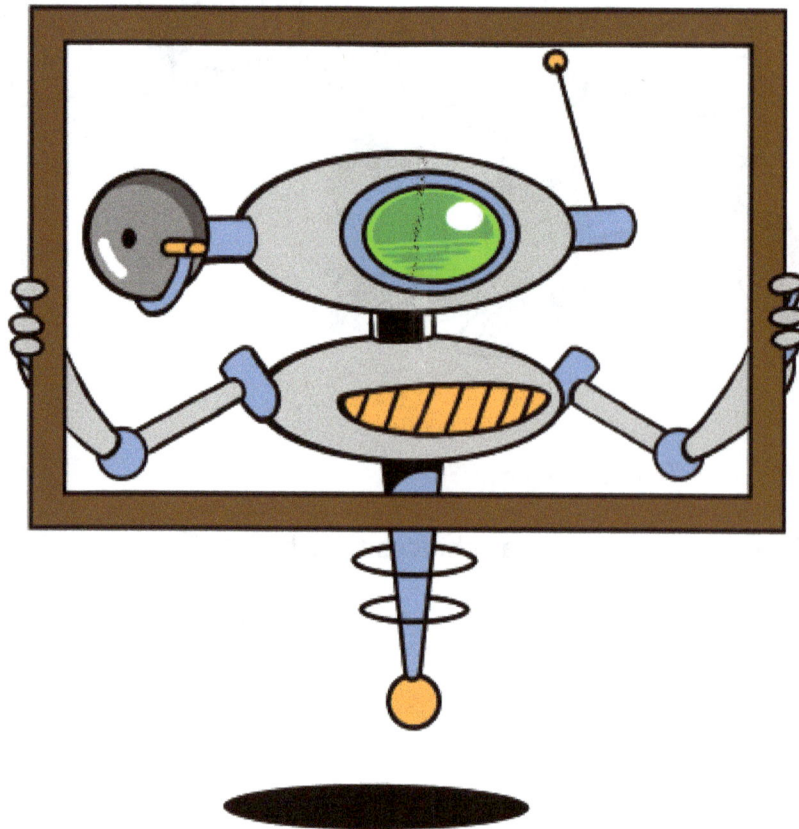

SET TRAPS FOR ERRORS

Remember the question asking the user if they wanted instructions:

Do you want instructions <Y/N>?

There are only two possible answers (Y or N). What happens if the user enters something else? You might get undesired results. Check for such possibilities using an "error trap."

Traps make your program "bomb proof" so that users will be unable to goof up!

DEBUGGING

In addition to not letting users make mistakes, you want to make sure your program doesn't make mistakes. Little mistakes in your programs are called "bugs." Before you let someone use your program, you want to make sure it's bug free.

Test your program thoroughly. If you have **If** statements, make sure you test to make sure they work correctly when the condition is "true" and when it's "false". Make input errors on purpose to make sure your program still works.

LONG PROGRAMS

In the final lessons, we will take you through the building of two long game programs. The first is a **Hangman** game written for the text window. The second is a simple video game (**Pizza Zapper**) written for the graphics window. These programs will illustrate many of the steps in writing user-friendly programs.

Assignment 25:

1. Make a program to write a very large number, 50 digits. Pick the digits at random. Put a comma between each set of three digits.

2. Write a secret cipher program. The user chooses a password and it is used to make a cipher alphabet like this:

   If the password is DRAGONETTE, remove the repeated letters to get DRAGONET. Put it at the front of the alphabet and the rest of the letters after it in normal order.

   Cipher alphabet – DRAGONETBCFHIJKLMPQSUVWXYZ
   Normal alphabet – ABCDEFGHIJKLMNOPQRSTUVWXYZ

   The user chooses to code or decode from a menu.

INSTRUCTOR NOTES 26   HANGMAN GAME - PART 1

This lesson begins to demonstrate top down organization of a task using a **Hangman** game as an example.

One of the hardest habits to form in some students (and even some professionals) is to impose structure on the program. Structuring has gone by many names such as "structured programming" and "top down programming," and uses various techniques to discipline the programmer.

Here we outline the program right in the Small Basic editor. The task is "chunked" into sections by using subroutines. This leads to clarity in the articulation of the program parts and allows testing and debugging of each part separately from the others.

After the outline is done, each subroutine is expanded with comments about what needs to be done. Then the programming begins.

Of course, there is always some backing and filling to be done as the program is written. The number of subroutines may change and the tasks performed in each will also change, usually expanding.

There are those who advocate performing all planning of the program on paper before starting to code. This may work for some programmers, but children especially are unlikely to adopt to this style of work. Besides, if one uses word processors for interactively writing text on a computer, it would seem equally appropriate to plan computer programs in a similar fashion.

QUESTIONS:

1. Why is it good to outline the program in the code editor?

2. If you have trouble deciding which steps go in a game program, how can you, a friend, or a piece of paper help?

3. When do you test each subroutine you have written?

LESSON 26   HANGMAN GAME - PART 1

In these next two lessons, we are going to write a long, detailed program. Why two lessons? Because it is a long program and you'll need a break. And it shows you that you can build a program in stages, stopping along the way.

We are going to write a **Hangman** game. This, by the way, is the first computer game your author ever programmed on a computer. **Hangman** is a word guessing game where you draw another part of the person each time you guess a letter that is not in a secret word. Don't worry – no one really gets "hanged" – it's a non-violent game.

First, we make an outline following the steps of the game.

PROGRAM OUTLINE

The brief outline is:

```
'Hangman Game
'Main program
New:
' New game
'Get the word to guess
Guess:
'Make a guess at a letter
'Test if letter is right-add to the drawing if wrong
'Test if game is over - will determine variable GameOver
'If not over, get another guess
If (GameOver = "false") Then
  Goto Guess
EndIf
If (GameOver = "true") Then
  Goto New
EndIf
```

Now, we fill in more details, with subroutine names (type in this code):

```
'Hangman Game
'Main program
New:
' New game
NewGame()
'Get the word to guess
GetWord()
Guess:
'Make a guess at a letter
GetGuess()
'Test if letter is right-add to the drawing if wrong
TestGuess()
'Test if game is over - will determine variable GameOver
TestGameOver()
'If not over, get another guess
If (GameOver = "false") Then
  Goto Guess
EndIf
If (GameOver = "true") Then
  Goto New
EndIf

'subroutines
Sub NewGame
  'play a new game
EndSub

Sub GetWord
  'enter a word to guess - draw game screen
EndSub

Sub GetGuess
  'get users guess at letter
EndSub

Sub TestGuess
  'see if guess is in word - if not, draw body part
EndSub

Sub TestGameOver
  'if there are seven wrong guesses or the word is complete
  'the game is over
EndSub
```

NEWGAME SUBROUTINE

Now, we just "march down" the list of subroutines filling in the needed code. Type this code for the **NewGame** subroutine:

```
Sub NewGame
    'play a new game
    'clear window
    GameOver = "false"
    TextWindow.BackgroundColor = "White"
    TextWindow.ForegroundColor = "Black"
    TextWindow.Title = "Hangman"
    TextWindow.Clear()
EndSub
```

This initializes the **GameOver** variable and sets up the text window where the game will be played.

Even though we've just begun, you can **Run** the program to test what we have so far. You will get an empty text window with the **Hangman** title bar:

BUILDING AND TESTING PROGRAM IN CHUNKS

When writing long programs like the **Hangman** game, always build your program in little chunks and run and test along the way. This eliminates your errors as you go. Working with subroutines makes this an easy thing to do.

You should also to remember to **Save** your program often. A good habit is to **Save** it everytime you're about to try some new code.

GETWORD SUBROUTINE

One player enters a word, while the other looks away from the computer. Use this code in the **GetWord** subroutine to do this task (we will only use upper case letters for the word):

```
Sub GetWord
  'enter a word to guess - draw game screen
  TextWindow.ForegroundColor = "Black"
  TextWindow.WriteLine("One player enters a word, the other guesses
it.")
  TextWindow.WriteLine("The guessing player should look away from the
computer.")
  TextWindow.WriteLine("")
  TextWindow.WriteLine("Enter a word to be guessed (it will be
converted to all capital letters): ")
  'Word is word to be guessed,
  'NumberLetters is length of word
  Word = Text.ConvertToUpperCase(TextWindow.Read())
  NumberLetters = Text.GetLength(Word)
EndSub
```

Run the program and you can now enter a word (I used alphabet):

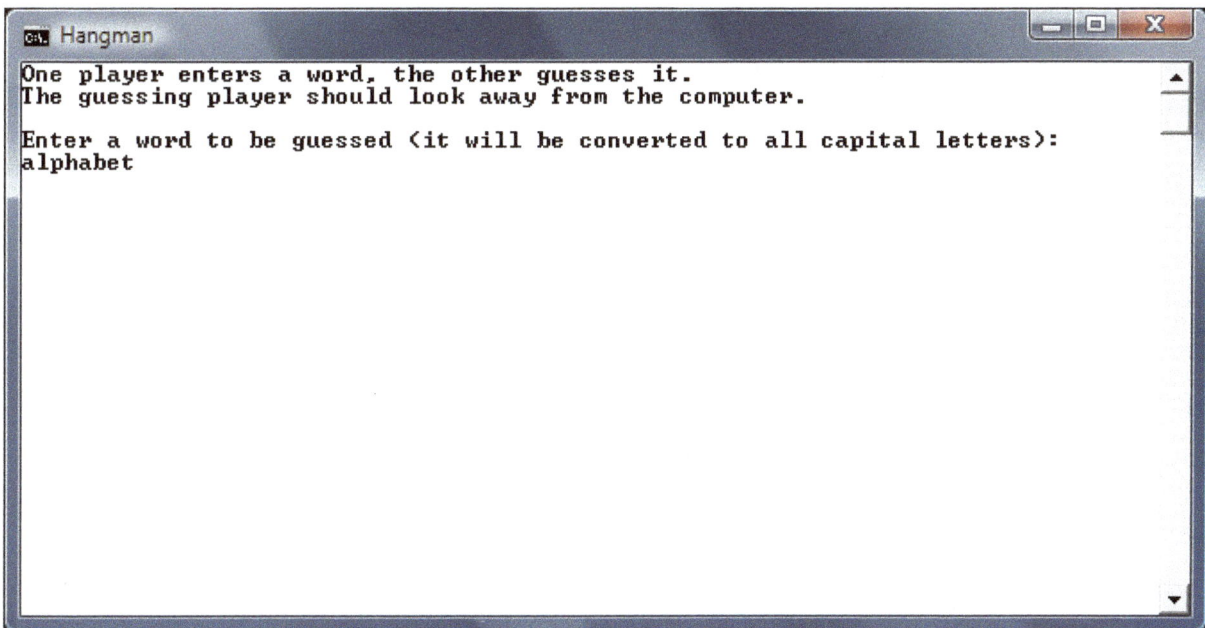

```
Hangman
One player enters a word, the other guesses it.
The guessing player should look away from the computer.

Enter a word to be guessed (it will be converted to all capital letters):
alphabet
```

We need to do more once a word is entered. We need to clear the window so the player doing the guessing doesn't know what the word is.

We also want to show the user how many letters are in the word to be guessed and we want to display the letters that can still be guessed. We need to initialize the number of wrong guesses. Add this code at the end of the **GetWord** subroutine:

```
'Guess is players guess, Remaining are letters remaining to be guessed
'Wrong is number of wrong guesses made
Guess = ""
For I =1 To NumberLetters
  Guess = Guess + "."
EndFor
Wrong = 0
Remaining = "ABCDEFGHIJKLMNOPQRSTUVWXYZ"
'draw screen
TextWindow.Clear()
TextWindow.CursorLeft = 30
TextWindow.CursorTop = 6
TextWindow.WriteLine("Word to Guess:")
TextWindow.WriteLine("")
TextWindow.CursorLeft = 30
TextWindow.Write(Guess)
TextWindow.CursorLeft = 30
TextWindow.CursorTop = 12
TextWindow.WriteLine("Letters Remaining:")
TextWindow.WriteLine("")
TextWindow.CursorLeft = 30
TextWindow.Write(Remaining)
```

Run the program again. Enter 'alphabet' as the word and you see:

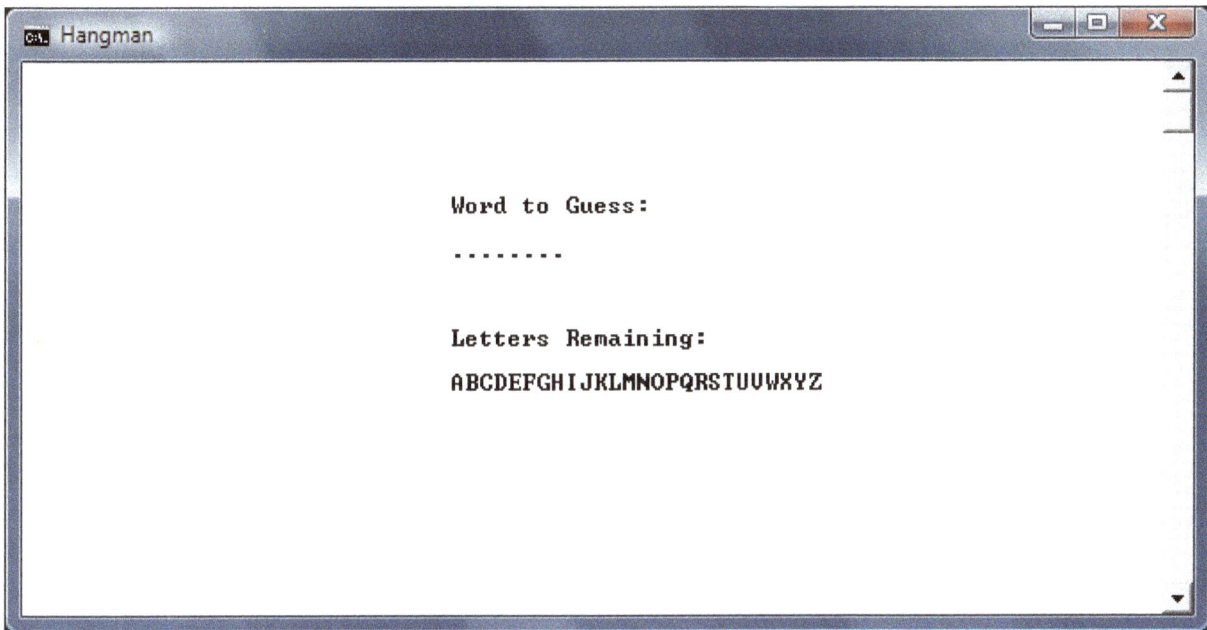

The window has been cleared. Using the **CursorLeft** and **CursorTop** properties, we have written two variables **Guess** (the user's guess using dots to represent letters still to be guessed – all dots in the beginning) and **Remaining** (the letters you can still guess – the entire alphabet to start).

Notice the meaningful variable names we've used. The **GetWord** subroutine is complete.

GETGUESS SUBROUTINE

The player needs to input his or her guesses at letters in the word. Put this code in the **GetGuess** subroutine (notice we make sure whatever is entered is converted to upper case):

```
Sub GetGuess
  'get users guess at letter
  TextWindow.ForegroundColor = "Black"
  TextWindow.CursorLeft = 30
  TextWindow.CursorTop = 2
  TextWindow.Write("Guess a letter:        ")
  TextWindow.CursorLeft = 46
  Letter = Text.ConvertToUpperCase(TextWindow.Read())
EndSub
```

Run the program and enter some guesses. Notice how your old guess is erased before a new guess is entered:

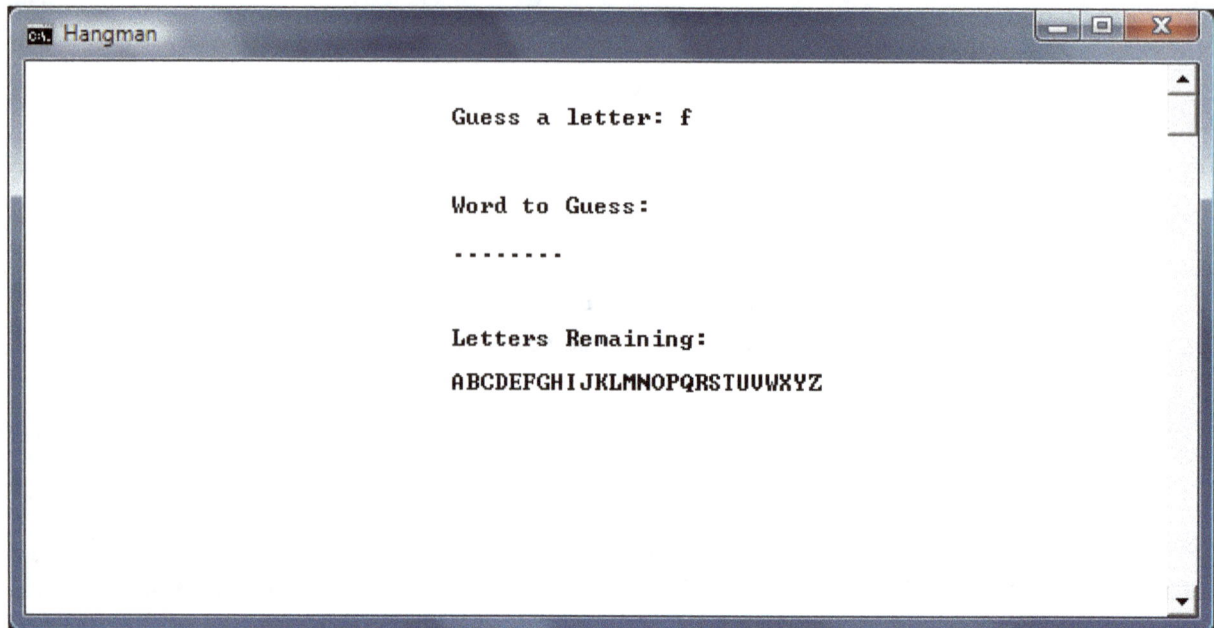

```
┌─────────────────────────────────────────────────────────────────────┐
│ C:\ Hangman                                          [_] [□] [X]      │
├─────────────────────────────────────────────────────────────────────┤
│                                                              ▲        │
│                                                                       │
│                    Guess a letter: f                                  │
│                                                                       │
│                                                                       │
│                    Word to Guess:                                     │
│                                                                       │
│                    . . . . . . . .                                    │
│                                                                       │
│                                                                       │
│                    Letters Remaining:                                 │
│                                                                       │
│                    ABCDEFGHIJKLMNOPQRSTUVWXYZ                          │
│                                                                       │
│                                                                       │
│                                                              ▼        │
└─────────────────────────────────────────────────────────────────────┘
```

The next step is to test the guess to see if it's in the 'secret' word. But we also want to remove any guess made from the **Letters Remaining** string. Add this code to the end of the **GetGuess** subroutine:

```
'remove guess from remaining letters
S = ""
For I = 1 to Text.GetLength(Remaining)
  T = Text.GetSubText(Remaining, I, 1)
  If (T = Letter) Then
    S = S + " "
  EndIf
  If (T <> Letter) Then
    S = S + T
  EndIf
EndFor
Remaining = S
TextWindow.CursorTop = 14
TextWindow.CursorLeft = 30
TextWindow.Write(Remaining)
```

This new code goes through the **Remaining** string, finds the letter (**Letter**) that was guessed, removes it from the string and replaces it with a space. It then rewrites the string to window.

Run the program again. Enter several guesses to make sure the letters are properly removed from the **Remaining** string. Here's what I got after guessing a, e, i, o, and u:

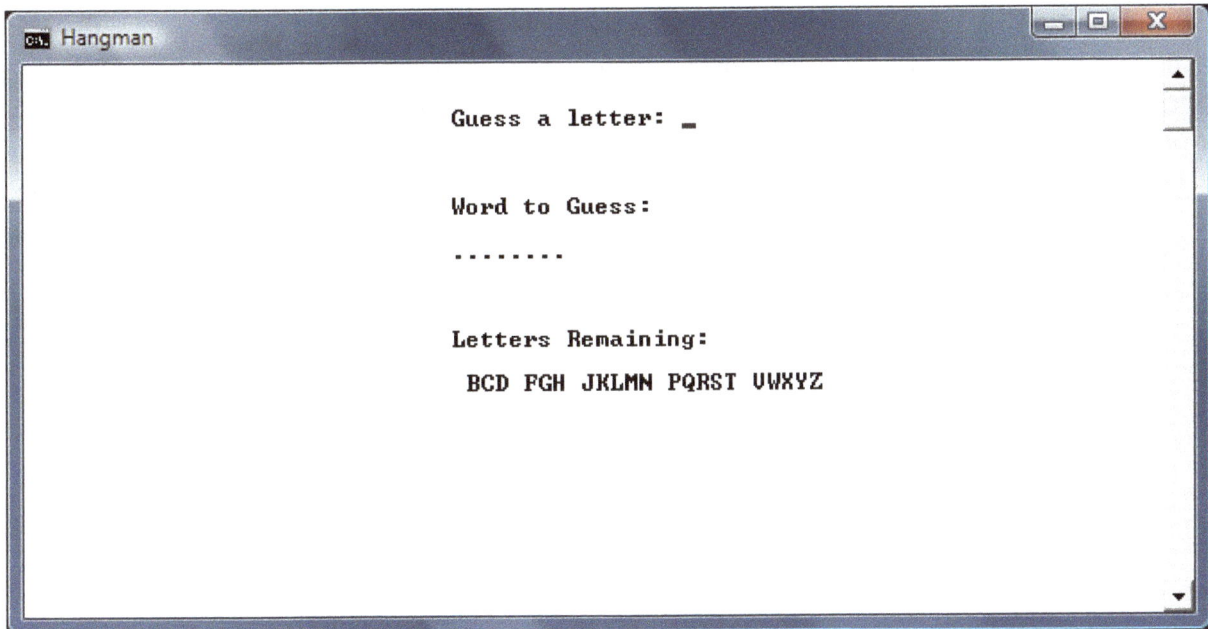

```
Hangman                                            _ □ X

                    Guess a letter: _


                    Word to Guess:

                    . . . . . . . .


                    Letters Remaining:
                     BCD FGH JKLMN PQRST UWXYZ
```

The **GetGuess** subroutine is now complete. Time for a break – you deserve it!

Make sure you **Save** your program.

Assignment 26:

1. Go back over the code you've done so far and make sure you understand how it works.

2. Do you see how building in chunks (or stages) really makes your job as a programmer much easier?

This lesson continues the top down programming of the **Hangman** game.

It illustrates that, by building in "chunks", you can write some code, test some code and stop without having to write the entire program. Make sure to stress saving the work along the way.

1. How can graph paper help plan a program displayed in the text window?

2. Can you think of other ways to draw the 'hanged' figure? Is there something else you could draw using seven different parts?

When we last worked on the **Hangman** game, we just finished the **GetGuess** subroutine. Now, it's time to check the guess. Once checked, we see if the game is over – either the word is complete or we've used all of our guesses.

Open your saved program.

TESTGUESS SUBROUTINE

The **GetGuess** subroutine has the variable **Letter** which has the users guess. In the **TestGuess** subroutine, we see if the guessed letter is in the 'secret' word. If so, we put the letter in it proper place (it could appear more than once). If it is not in the word, we increment the **Wrong** variable and draw a part of the hangman body.

Type this code in the **TestGuess** subroutine:

```
Sub TestGuess
  'see if guess is in word - if not, draw body part
  S = ""
  InWord = "false"
  For I = 1 to NumberLetters
    'check only letters we still need
    If (Text.GetSubText(Guess, I, 1) = ".") Then
      T = Text.GetSubText(Word, I, 1)
      If (T = Letter) Then
        InWord = "true"
        S = S + T
      EndIf
      If (T <> Letter) Then
        S = S + "."
      EndIf
    EndIf
    If (Text.GetSubText(Guess, I, 1) <> ".") Then
      S = S + Text.GetSubText(Guess, I, 1)
    EndIf
  EndFor
  Guess = S
  TextWindow.ForegroundColor = "Black"
  TextWindow.CursorLeft = 30
  TextWindow.CursorTop = 8
  TextWindow.Write(Guess)
  If (InWord = "false") Then
    Wrong = Wrong + 1
```

```
    'draw body part
  EndIf
EndSub
```

The first part of this code is very similar to the code used in **GetGuess** to remove the guessed letter from **Remaining**. The difference here is we look at each 'unguessed' letter in **Word** and see if it matches **Letter**. If it does, we put **Letter** in its proper place in the current value of **Guess**.

If the guess is in the word, the variable **InWord** is "true". If not, **InWord** is "false" – in this case, we increment **Wrong** by 1 and draw the body part (just represented by a comment at this point).

Run the program. Enter a word (I used alphabet again). Try guesses and make sure they appear in the proper place. Here is what I see after guessing a, b, c ,d, e and f:

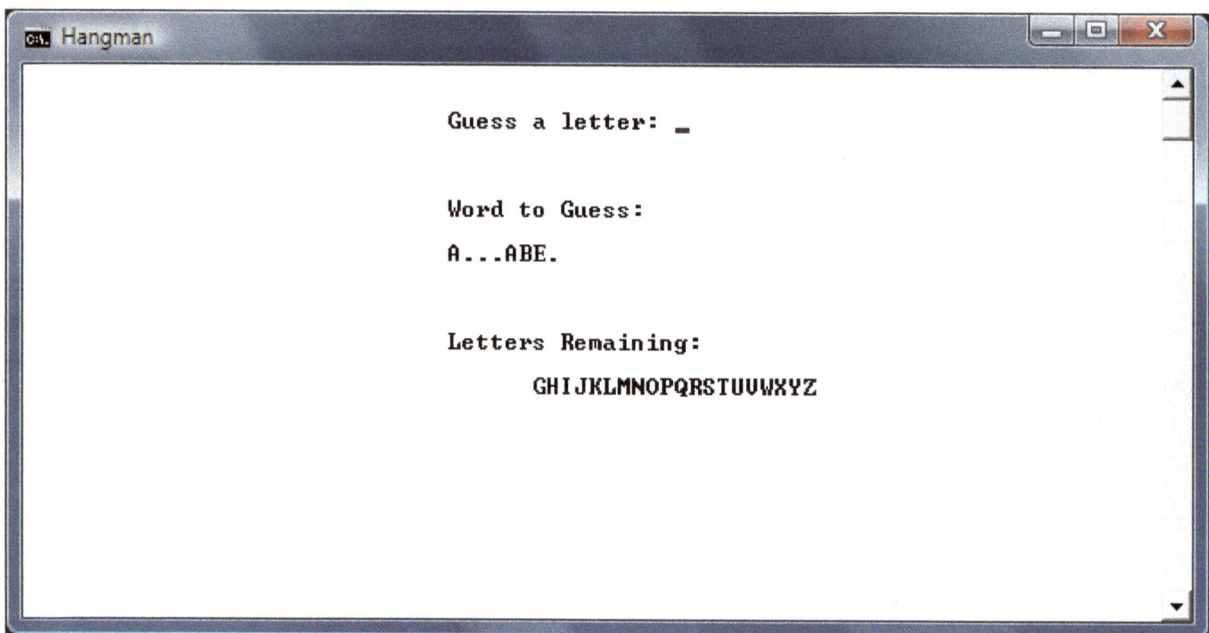

DRAWING BODY PARTS

With each wrong guess, a body part for the 'hanged' guy is drawn. We allow seven wrong guesses before the game ends. I chose these body parts for each wrong guess:

Guess 1 – draw head
Guess 2 – draw body
Guess 3 – draw left arm
Guess 4 – draw right arm
Guess 5 – draw left leg
Guess 6 – draw right leg
Guess 7 – draw face

Since we are using the text window, each part will be drawn with characters on the keyboard – the hanged guy will be a little stick figure.

Here is a section of graph paper where I sketched out my stick figure. The columns are used to establish the **CursorLeft** property and the rows are used to set the **CursorTop** property when "drawing":

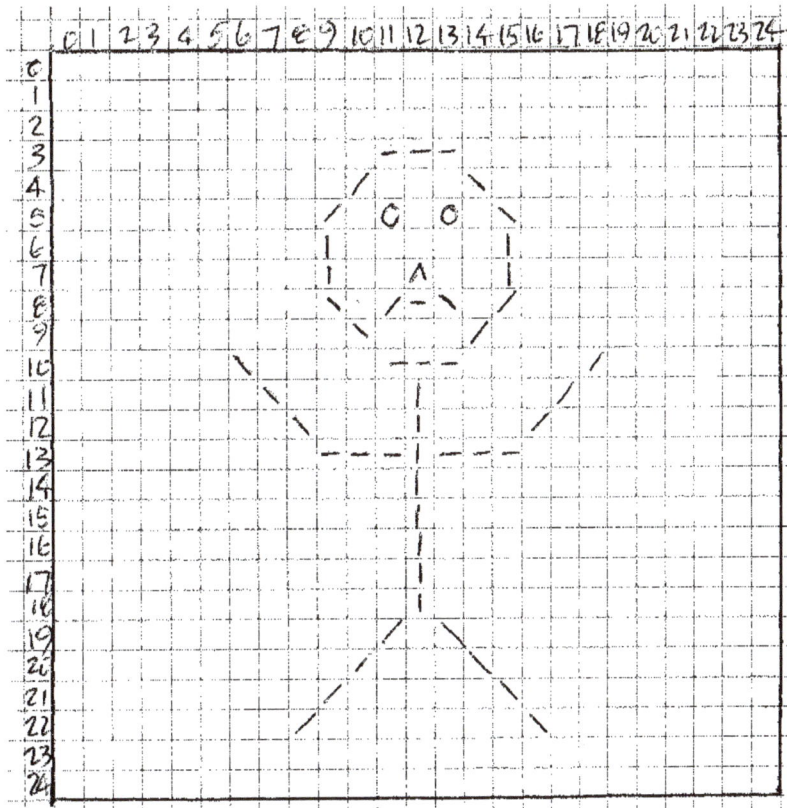

Add this code after the *'draw body part* comment. Yes, it's a lot of code, but notice many lines are similar. You might want to try your 'copy and paste' skills here:

```smallbasic
If (Wrong = 1) Then
  'head
  TextWindow.ForegroundColor = "Blue"
  TextWindow.CursorLeft = 11
  TextWindow.CursorTop = 3
  TextWindow.WriteLine("---")
  TextWindow.CursorLeft = 10
  TextWindow.WriteLine("/   \")
  TextWindow.CursorLeft = 9
  TextWindow.WriteLine("/     \")
  TextWindow.CursorLeft = 9
  TextWindow.WriteLine("|      |")
  TextWindow.CursorLeft = 9
  TextWindow.WriteLine("|      |")
  TextWindow.CursorLeft = 9
  TextWindow.WriteLine("\      /")
  TextWindow.CursorLeft = 10
  TextWindow.WriteLine("\   /")
  TextWindow.CursorLeft = 11
  TextWindow.WriteLine("---")
EndIf
If (Wrong = 2) Then
  'body
  TextWindow.ForegroundColor = "Blue"
  TextWindow.CursorTop = 11
  For I = 1 To 8
    TextWindow.CursorLeft = 12
    TextWindow.WriteLine("|")
  EndFor
EndIf
If (Wrong = 3) Then
  'left arm
  TextWindow.ForegroundColor = "Blue"
  TextWindow.CursorTop = 10
  TextWindow.CursorLeft = 6
  TextWindow.WriteLine("\")
  TextWindow.CursorLeft = 7
  TextWindow.WriteLine("\")
  TextWindow.CursorLeft = 8
  TextWindow.WriteLine("\")
  TextWindow.CursorLeft = 9
  TextWindow.WriteLine("---")
EndIf
```

```smallbasic
If (Wrong = 4) Then
  'right arm
  TextWindow.ForegroundColor = "Blue"
  TextWindow.CursorTop = 10
  TextWindow.CursorLeft = 18
  TextWindow.WriteLine("/")
  TextWindow.CursorLeft = 17
  TextWindow.WriteLine("/")
  TextWindow.CursorLeft = 16
  TextWindow.WriteLine("/")
  TextWindow.CursorLeft = 13
  TextWindow.WriteLine("---")
EndIf
If (Wrong = 5) Then
  'left leg
  TextWindow.ForegroundColor = "Blue"
  TextWindow.CursorTop = 19
  TextWindow.CursorLeft = 11
  TextWindow.WriteLine("/")
  TextWindow.CursorLeft = 10
  TextWindow.WriteLine("/")
  TextWindow.CursorLeft = 9
  TextWindow.WriteLine("/")
  TextWindow.CursorLeft = 8
  TextWindow.WriteLine("/")
EndIf
If (Wrong = 6) Then
  'right leg
  TextWindow.ForegroundColor = "Blue"
  TextWindow.CursorTop = 19
  TextWindow.CursorLeft = 13
  TextWindow.WriteLine("\")
  TextWindow.CursorLeft = 14
  TextWindow.WriteLine("\")
  TextWindow.CursorLeft = 15
  TextWindow.WriteLine("\")
  TextWindow.CursorLeft = 16
  TextWindow.WriteLine("\")
EndIf
If (Wrong = 7) Then
  'face
  TextWindow.ForegroundColor = "Black"
  TextWindow.CursorLeft = 11
  TextWindow.CursorTop = 5
  TextWindow.WriteLine("O O")
  TextWindow.CursorLeft = 12
```

```
    TextWindow.CursorTop = 7
    TextWindow.WriteLine("^")
    TextWindow.CursorLeft = 11
    TextWindow.CursorTop = 8
    TextWindow.WriteLine("/-\")
EndIf
```

This code just takes what's on the graph paper and converts it to code.

Run the program again, with the same inputs just tried (make the word alphabet and guess a, b, c, d, e, and f). Three body parts (head, body, left arm) will be drawn:

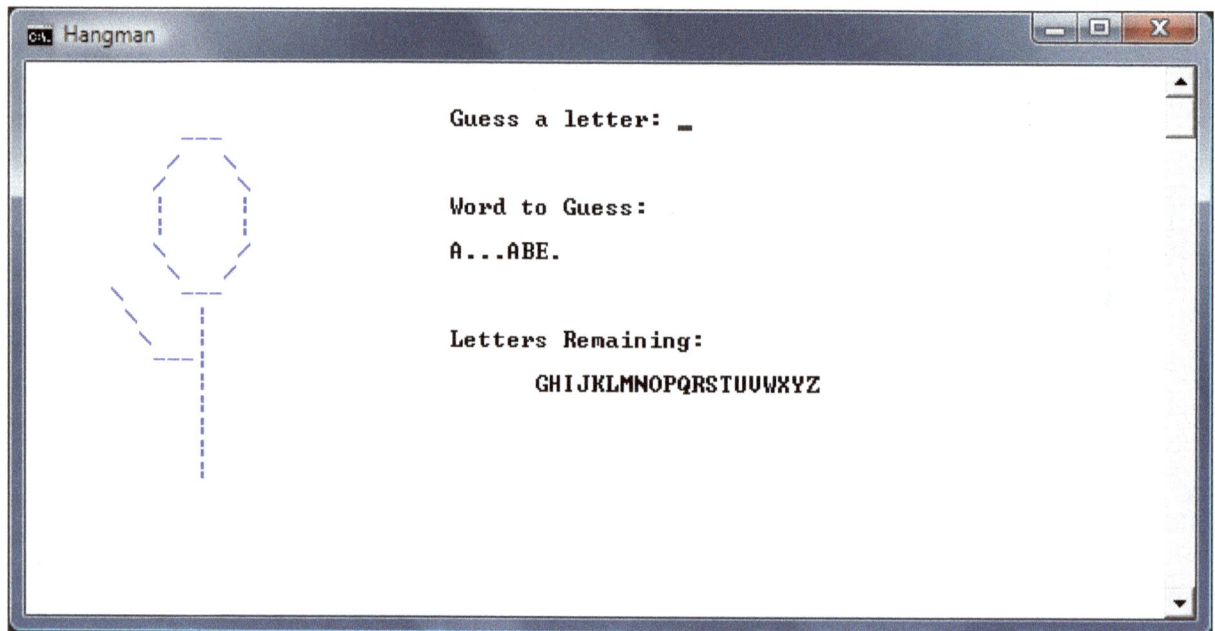

The **TestGuess** subroutine is complete. One subroutine to go!

TESTGAMEOVER SUBROUTINE

A last step is to see if the game is over. It is over if one of two things happen:

> You run out of guesses (Wrong = 7)
> You guess all the letters in the word (Guess = Word).

Use this code in the **TestGameOver** subroutine:

```
Sub TestGameOver
  'if there are seven wrong guesses or the word is complete
  'the game is over
  If (Wrong = 7 Or Guess = Word) Then
    GameOver = "true"
    TextWindow.ForegroundColor = "Black"
    TextWindow.CursorLeft = 30
    TextWindow.CursorTop = 18
    TextWindow.Write("Game Over - Press Enter To Continue")
    TextWindow.Read()
  EndIf
EndSub
```

Save your program. **Run** the program. Try the word alphabet again. First, type in letters that give you the correct word. Here's my try:

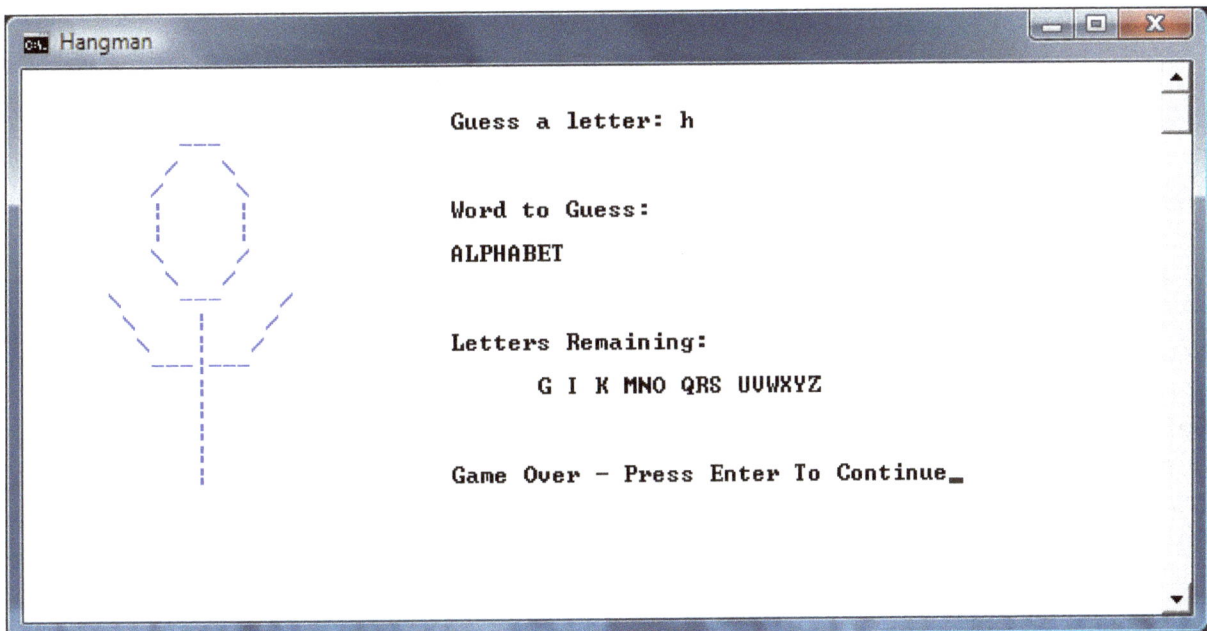

Run again, but don't guess the correct letters. This makes sure the game stops when we run out of guesses. Always try all program possibilities. Here's the 'hanged' figure:

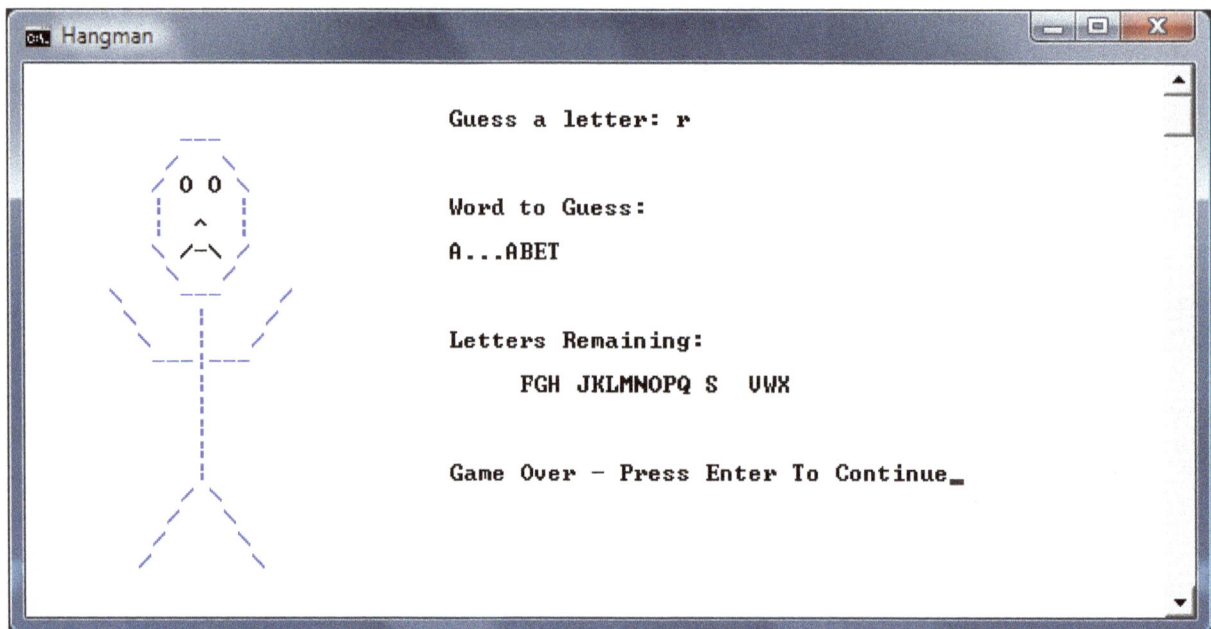

The **TestGameOver** subroutine works and the game is complete. Congratulations!! Have fun playing it with your friends.

COMPLETE CODE LISTING

For reference purposes, here is the complete **Hangman** game code listing.

```
'Hangman Game
'Main program
New:
' New game
NewGame()
'Get the word to guess
GetWord()
Guess:
'Make a guess at a letter
GetGuess()
'Test if letter is right-add to the drawing if wrong
TestGuess()
'Test if game is over - will determine variable GameOver
TestGameOver()
'If not over, get another guess
If (GameOver = "false") Then
```

```
      Goto Guess
EndIf
If (GameOver = "true") Then
   Goto New
EndIf

'subroutines
Sub NewGame
   'play a new game
   'clear window
   GameOver = "false"
   TextWindow.BackgroundColor = "White"
   TextWindow.ForegroundColor = "Black"
   TextWindow.Title = "Hangman"
   TextWindow.Clear()
EndSub

Sub GetWord
   'enter a word to guess - draw game screen
      TextWindow.ForegroundColor = "Black"
   TextWindow.WriteLine("One player enters a word, the other guesses
it.")
   TextWindow.WriteLine("The guessing player should look away from the
computer.")
   TextWindow.WriteLine("")
   TextWindow.WriteLine("Enter a word to be guessed (it will be
converted to all capital letters): ")
   'Word is word to be guessed,
   'NumberLetters is length of word
   Word = Text.ConvertToUpperCase(TextWindow.Read())
   NumberLetters = Text.GetLength(Word)
   'Guess is players guess, Remaining are letters remaining to be
guessed
   'Wrong is number of wrong guesses made
   Guess = ""
   For I =1 To NumberLetters
     Guess = Guess + "."
   EndFor
   Wrong = 0
   Remaining = "ABCDEFGHIJKLMNOPQRSTUVWXYZ"
   'draw screen
   TextWindow.Clear()
   TextWindow.CursorLeft = 30
   TextWindow.CursorTop = 6
   TextWindow.WriteLine("Word to Guess:")
   TextWindow.WriteLine("")
```

```
    TextWindow.CursorLeft = 30
    TextWindow.Write(Guess)
    TextWindow.CursorLeft = 30
    TextWindow.CursorTop = 12
    TextWindow.WriteLine("Letters Remaining:")
    TextWindow.WriteLine("")
    TextWindow.CursorLeft = 30
    TextWindow.Write(Remaining)
EndSub

Sub GetGuess
    'get users guess at letter
    TextWindow.ForegroundColor = "Black"
    TextWindow.CursorLeft = 30
    TextWindow.CursorTop = 2
    TextWindow.Write("Guess a letter:        ")
    TextWindow.CursorLeft = 46
    Letter = Text.ConvertToUpperCase(TextWindow.Read())
    'remove guess from remaining letters
    S = ""
    For I = 1 to Text.GetLength(Remaining)
      T = Text.GetSubText(Remaining, I, 1)
      If (T = Letter) Then
        S = S + " "
      EndIf
      If (T <> Letter) Then
        S = S + T
      EndIf
    EndFor
    Remaining = S
    TextWindow.CursorTop = 14
    TextWindow.CursorLeft = 30
    TextWindow.Write(Remaining)
EndSub

Sub TestGuess
    'see if guess is in word - if not, draw body part
    S = ""
    InWord = "false"
    For I = 1 to NumberLetters
      'check only letters we still need
      If (Text.GetSubText(Guess, I, 1) = ".") Then
        T = Text.GetSubText(Word, I, 1)
        If (T = Letter) Then
          InWord = "true"
          S = S + T
```

261

```
          EndIf
        If (T <> Letter) Then
          S = S + "."
        EndIf
      EndIf
    If (Text.GetSubText(Guess, I, 1) <> ".") Then
      S = S + Text.GetSubText(Guess, I, 1)
    EndIf
  EndFor
Guess = S
TextWindow.ForegroundColor = "Black"
TextWindow.CursorLeft = 30
TextWindow.CursorTop = 8
TextWindow.Write(Guess)
If (InWord = "false") Then
  Wrong = Wrong + 1
  'draw body part
  If (Wrong = 1) Then
    'head
    TextWindow.ForegroundColor = "Blue"
    TextWindow.CursorLeft = 11
    TextWindow.CursorTop = 3
    TextWindow.WriteLine("---")
    TextWindow.CursorLeft = 10
    TextWindow.WriteLine("/   \")
    TextWindow.CursorLeft = 9
    TextWindow.WriteLine("/     \")
    TextWindow.CursorLeft = 9
    TextWindow.WriteLine("|      |")
    TextWindow.CursorLeft = 9
    TextWindow.WriteLine("|     |")
    TextWindow.CursorLeft = 9
    TextWindow.WriteLine("\     /")
    TextWindow.CursorLeft = 10
    TextWindow.WriteLine("\   /")
    TextWindow.CursorLeft = 11
    TextWindow.WriteLine("---")
  EndIf
  If (Wrong = 2) Then
    'body
    TextWindow.ForegroundColor = "Blue"
    TextWindow.CursorTop = 11
    For I = 1 To 8
      TextWindow.CursorLeft = 12
      TextWindow.WriteLine("|")
    EndFor
```

```
    EndIf
    If (Wrong = 3) Then
      'left arm
      TextWindow.ForegroundColor = "Blue"
      TextWindow.CursorTop = 10
      TextWindow.CursorLeft = 6
      TextWindow.WriteLine("\")
      TextWindow.CursorLeft = 7
      TextWindow.WriteLine("\")
      TextWindow.CursorLeft = 8
      TextWindow.WriteLine("\")
      TextWindow.CursorLeft = 9
      TextWindow.WriteLine("---")
    EndIf
    If (Wrong = 4) Then
      'right arm
      TextWindow.ForegroundColor = "Blue"
      TextWindow.CursorTop = 10
      TextWindow.CursorLeft = 18
      TextWindow.WriteLine("/")
      TextWindow.CursorLeft = 17
      TextWindow.WriteLine("/")
      TextWindow.CursorLeft = 16
      TextWindow.WriteLine("/")
      TextWindow.CursorLeft = 13
      TextWindow.WriteLine("---")
    EndIf
    If (Wrong = 5) Then
      'left leg
      TextWindow.ForegroundColor = "Blue"
      TextWindow.CursorTop = 19
      TextWindow.CursorLeft = 11
      TextWindow.WriteLine("/")
      TextWindow.CursorLeft = 10
      TextWindow.WriteLine("/")
      TextWindow.CursorLeft = 9
      TextWindow.WriteLine("/")
      TextWindow.CursorLeft = 8
      TextWindow.WriteLine("/")
    EndIf
    If (Wrong = 6) Then
      'right leg
      TextWindow.ForegroundColor = "Blue"
      TextWindow.CursorTop = 19
      TextWindow.CursorLeft = 13
      TextWindow.WriteLine("\")
```

```
        TextWindow.CursorLeft = 14
        TextWindow.WriteLine("\")
        TextWindow.CursorLeft = 15
        TextWindow.WriteLine("\")
        TextWindow.CursorLeft = 16
        TextWindow.WriteLine("\")
      EndIf
      If (Wrong = 7) Then
        'face
        TextWindow.ForegroundColor = "Black"
        TextWindow.CursorLeft = 11
        TextWindow.CursorTop = 5
        TextWindow.WriteLine("O O")
        TextWindow.CursorLeft = 12
        TextWindow.CursorTop = 7
        TextWindow.WriteLine("^")
        TextWindow.CursorLeft = 11
        TextWindow.CursorTop = 8
        TextWindow.WriteLine("/-\")
      EndIf
    EndIf
  EndSub

  Sub TestGameOver
    'if there are seven wrong guesses or the word is complete
    'the game is over
    If (Wrong = 7 Or Guess = Word) Then
      GameOver = "true"
      TextWindow.ForegroundColor = "Black"
      TextWindow.CursorLeft = 30
      TextWindow.CursorTop = 18
      TextWindow.Write("Game Over - Press Enter To Continue")
      TextWindow.Read()
    EndIf
  EndSub
```

264

The **Hangman** game is pretty cool as it is, but there are some improvements that could be made to make it a better program. Try any or all of these:

1. When the user enters a letter, there is nothing from keep them from typing in more than one letter. There is nothing to keep them from guessing a letter more than once. Correct this with some 'error trapping'.

2. Similarly, the user can type in characters that are not letters. Can you correct this?

3. When the game ends, ask the user this question:

    Want to play again <Y/N>?

    Make sure the user enters a Y (yes) or N (no), then do as the user requests.

INSTRUCTOR NOTES 28   PIZZA ZAPPER GAME – PART 1

In this lesson, we begin the writing of a fairly elaborate little video game. It's a classic shoot-em-up where a zapper is used to shoot falling pizzas. Yeah, I know, a bit weird, but fun!

We use all of the same top down development rules followed for the **Hangman** game. The program is first outlined. All tasks but a few initializations are moved to subroutines. This is because we are using the **KeyDown** event. Most of the program logic moves to its associated subroutine (**KeyDownSub**).

There are several steps game design we discuss in this and the next two lessons. In this lesson, we address rules and "player" movement. A fun part of making up a game is that you can make up the rules. You adjust the rules as you design the game to make it fun to play.

In this lesson, we use the same code used a few lessons ago to move a submarine from left to right (demonstrating the **KeyDown** event). Here the left and right arrow keys move the pizza zapper.

Another key, the **Space** bar, is used to fire the zapper. In this lesson, we draw the zapper, but do nothing with it. In the next lesson, we will get the pizzas falling and see if the zapper "collides" with the pizza. Collision detection is an important part of game design.

QUESTIONS:

1. Why do longer variable names help your job as a programmer?

2. Why do you think the pizza zapper was not completely erased by the original line of code?

3. Instead of having a variable for the zapper width (**ZapperW**) and height (**ZapperH**), would it be a good idea to just use numbers like 50 and 25? Why or why not?

266

LESSON 28   PIZZA ZAPPER GAME – PART 1

Are you ready to try another game? This one's even longer than the **Hangman** game, so we'll spread it over three lessons.

Like the **Hangman** game, we will build this new program in steps. Unlike the **Hangman** game, this game will be made using the graphics, not the text, window.

One of the more popular games to play is one where you 'zap' things coming at you. In this game, cheese pizzas are falling from the sky! Nobody knows why, but you must 'zap' them before they hit the ground. We call the game **Pizza Zapper**.

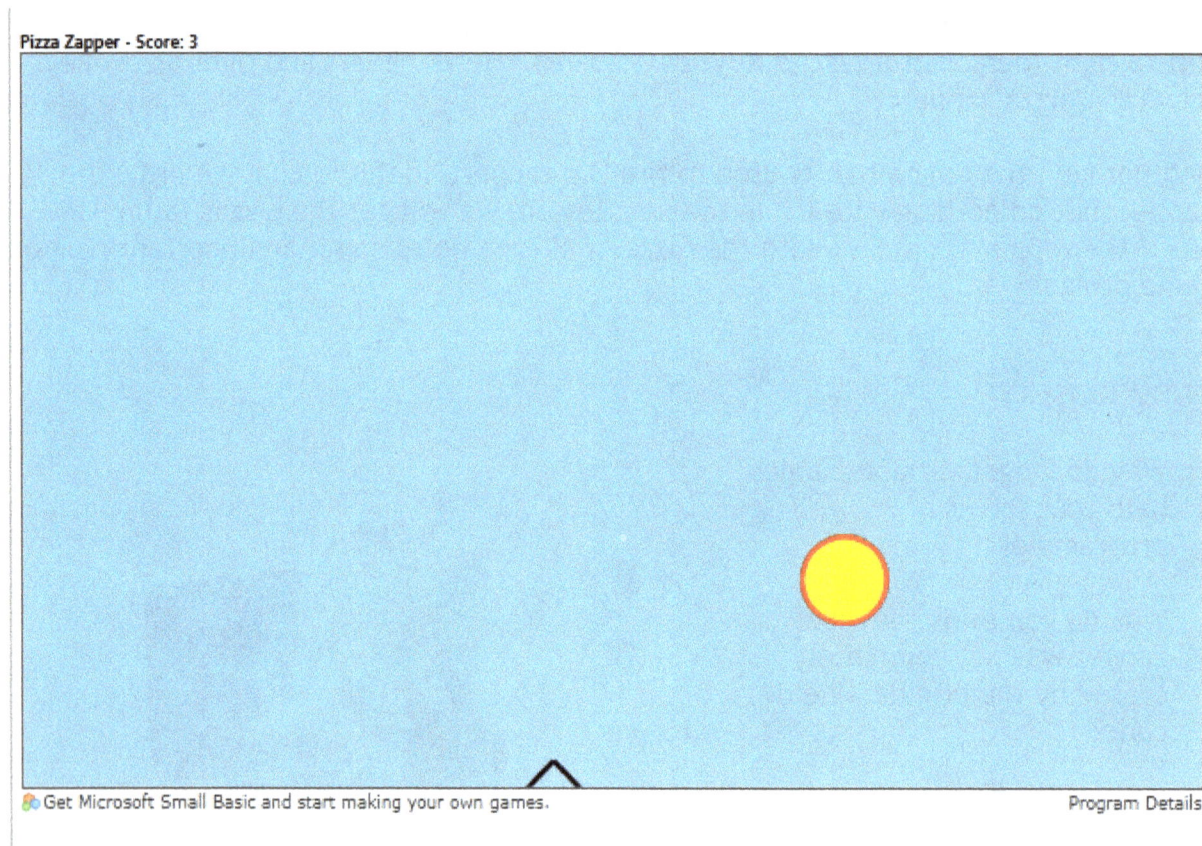

PIZZA ZAPPER RULES

In the **Hangman** game, there were some well-accepted rules for play. When you make up your own games, you can make up your own rules. That's a fun part of programming games. You're in charge!

Here are the rules for **Pizza Zapper**:

1. Pizzas fall randomly from the sky.
2. Use the left and right arrow keys on the keyboard to move your zapper under a pizza.
3. Use the **Space** bar to zap your pizza.
4. You get one point for each zapped pizza.
5. Once you miss zapping three pizzas, the game ends.

PROGRAM OUTLINE

Here's our first shot at a program outline (with empty subroutines):

```
'Pizza Zapper
'Set up graphics window
'initializations
NewGame()

Sub NewGame
  'reinitialize everything for a new game
EndSub

Sub MoveZapper
  'move the zapper
EndSub

Sub FireZapper
  'fire the zapper
EndSub

Sub NewPizza
  ' start a new pizza falling
EndSub

Sub DrawPizza
  'draw a pizza
EndSub

Sub ErasePizza
  'erase a pizza
EndSub

Sub MovePizza
  'move a pizza
EndSub
```

Type in the above code.

PROGRAM INITIALIZATIONS

Let's draw the game screen – you get to choose how big you want it. We also know we are going to use the keyboard for input, so we need a subroutine to handle the **KeyDown** Event. Put this code before the call to the **NewGame** subroutine:

```
GraphicsWindow.Show()
GraphicsWindow.Width = 1000
GraphicsWindow.Height = 600
GraphicsWindow.BackgroundColor = "SkyBlue"
GraphicsWindow.KeyDown = KeyDownSub
```

And add this empty subroutine:

```
Sub KeyDownSub
   'handle key presses
EndSub
```

Save the program now and after each set of changes. **Run** the program to make sure the game screen appears.

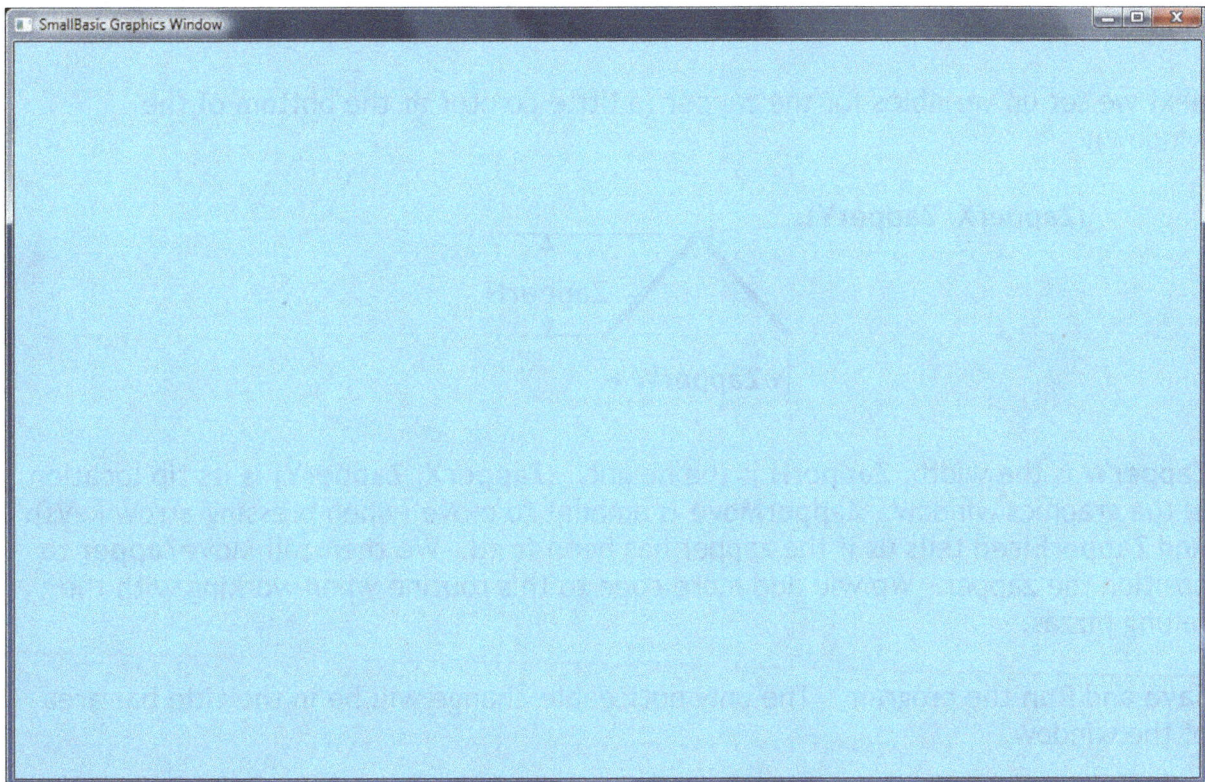

The window is 1000 pixels wide by 600 pixels high.

NEWGAME SUBROUTINE

Type this code for the **NewGame** subroutine:

```
Sub NewGame
    'reinitialize everything for a new game
    GraphicsWindow.Clear()
    GraphicsWindow.Title = "Pizza Zapper - Score: 0"
    Score = 0
    Missed = 0
    ZapperW = 50
    ZapperH = 25
    ZapperX = 500
    ZapperY = 575
    ZapperMove = 0
    ZapperFired = "false"
    MoveZapper()
EndSub
```

We use the **Title** property of the window to keep track of the score (**Score**) – this keeps the window clear for the game. **Missed** keeps track of how many pizzas are missed.

Next we set up variables for the zapper (a little pointer at the bottom of the window):

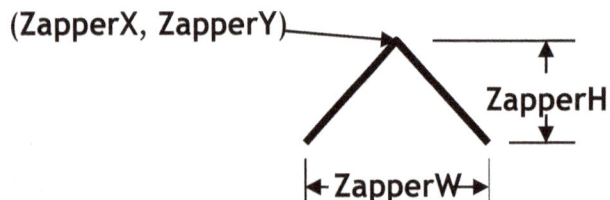

ZapperW is the width, **ZapperH** is the height. (**ZapperX, ZapperY**) is its tip location in the graphics window. **ZapperMove** is amount to move (when pressing arrow keys). And **ZapperFired** tells us if the zapper has been fired. We then call **MoveZapper** to position the zapper. We will add more code to this routine when working with the falling pizzas.

Save and **Run** the program. The only noticeable change will be in the title bar area of the window.

MOVEZAPPER SUBROUTINE

The **MoveZapper** subroutine uses the variables just defined to position the zapper along the bottom of the window. Type in this code:

```
Sub MoveZapper
  'move the zapper
  'erase first
  GraphicsWindow.BrushColor = GraphicsWindow.BackgroundColor
  GraphicsWindow.FillRectangle(ZapperX - ZapperW / 2, ZapperY,
ZapperW, ZapperH)
  'move by ZapperMove
  ZapperX = ZapperX + ZapperMove
  If (ZapperX < 0) Then
    ZapperX = 0
  EndIf
  If (ZapperX > GraphicsWindow.Width) Then
    ZapperX = GraphicsWindow.Width
  EndIf
  ' draw zapper
  GraphicsWindow.PenWidth = 5
  GraphicsWindow.PenColor = "Black"
  GraphicsWindow.DrawLine(ZapperX, ZapperY, ZapperX - ZapperW / 2,
ZapperY + ZapperH)
  GraphicsWindow.DrawLine(ZapperX, ZapperY, ZapperX + ZapperW / 2,
ZapperY + ZapperH)
EndSub
```

The zapper is erased from its previous location. Then it is drawn at its updated location (new value of **ZapperX**) with two thick lines (width is 5). Notice how we make sure the zapper stays in the window.

Run the program. The zapper should appear in the middle of the window near the bottom:

You can't move the zapper yet (**ZapperMove** = 0). We take care of that next.

KEYDOWNSUB SUBROUTINE

The left and right cursor arrow keys are used to move the zapper. Pressing of these keys is detected by the graphics window **KeyDown** event which "points" to the **KeyDownSub** subroutine. Use this code:

```
Sub KeyDownSub
  'handle key presses
  K = GraphicsWindow.LastKey
  ZapperMove = 0
  If (K = "Left") Then
    ZapperMove = -10
  EndIf
  If (K = "Right") Then
    ZapperMove = 10
  EndIf
  MoveZapper()
EndSub
```

Save and **Run** the program. The zapper will move. Try it:

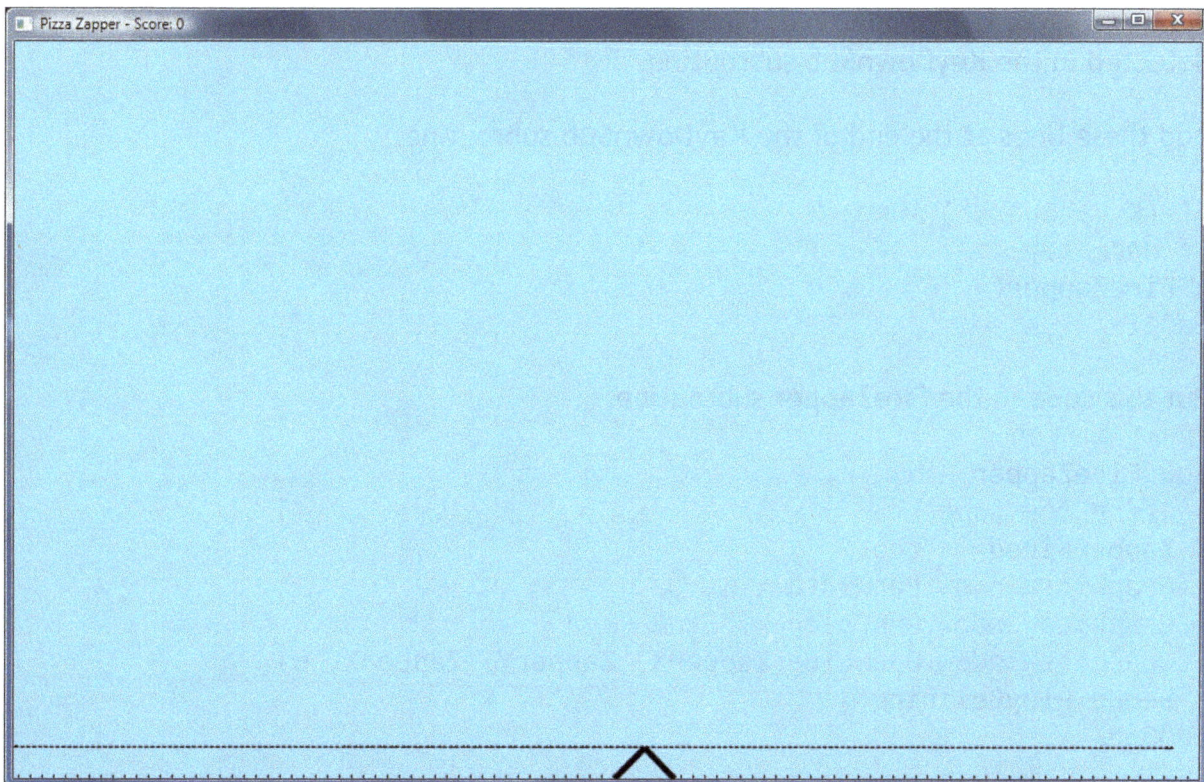

Make sure the zapper does not leave the window. Notice the zapper is not completely erased as it moves. This is a common problem. We just need to expand the 'erasing' area a bit.

The line of code that currently erases the zapper is in the **MoveZapper** subroutine:

```
GraphicsWindow.FillRectangle(ZapperX - ZapperW / 2, ZapperY, ZapperW, ZapperH)
```

Expand the area (5 pixels in all directions) by changing the line to:

```
GraphicsWindow.FillRectangle(ZapperX - ZapperW / 2 - 5, ZapperY - 5, ZapperW + 10, ZapperH + 10)
```

Save and **Run** the program again. The zapper should be erased completely with each move.

FIREZAPPER SUBROUTINE

Another keyboard operation is to fire the zapper whenever the **Space** bar is pressed. The drawing of the zapping ray is in the subroutine **FireZapper**. The key press is detected in the **KeyDownSub** subroutine.

Add these lines at the end of the **KeyDownSub** subroutine:

```
If (K = "Space") Then
  'draw ray
  FireZapper()
EndIf
```

Put this code in the **FireZapper** subroutine:

```
Sub FireZapper
  'fire the zapper
  ZapperFired = "true"
  GraphicsWindow.PenWidth = 3
  GraphicsWindow.PenColor = "Blue"
  GraphicsWindow.DrawLine(ZapperX, ZapperY, ZapperX, 0)
  Sound.PlayBellRing()
EndSub
```

275

When the zapper is fired, a blue line is drawn to the top of the window and a bell sound is heard:

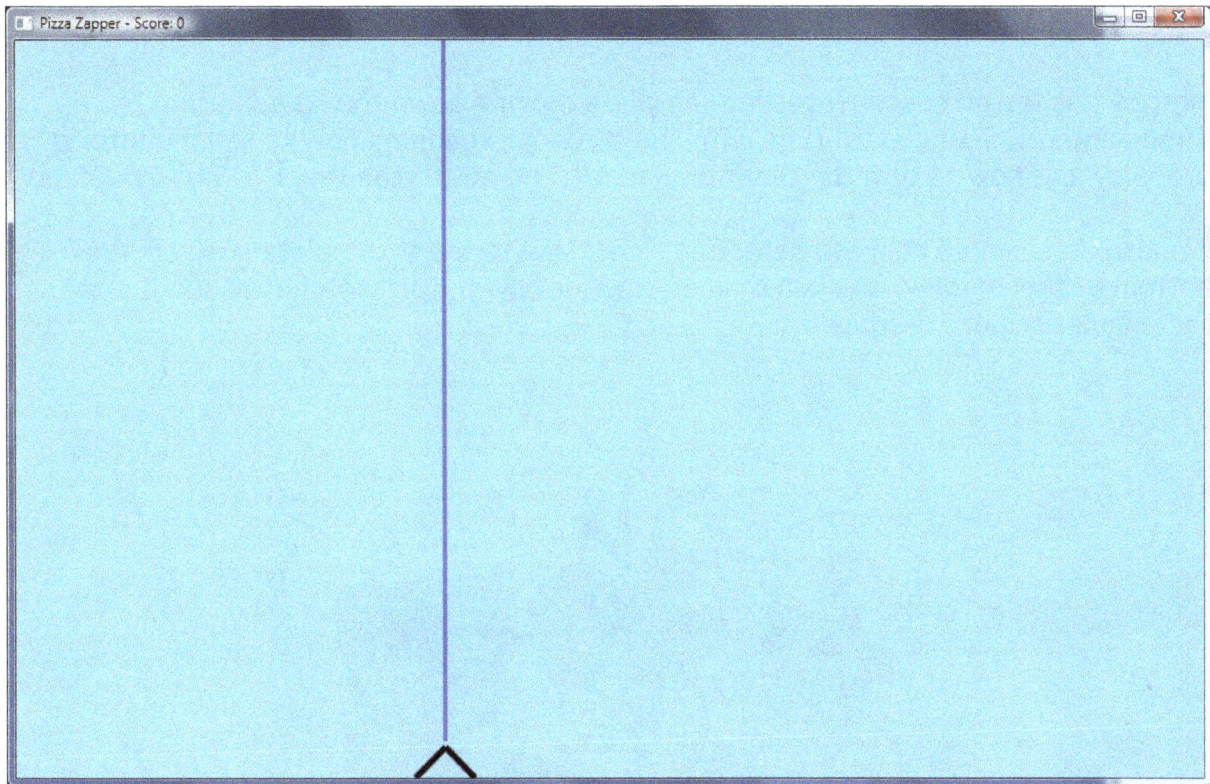

We are done with the beginning stages of the **Pizza Zapper** game. We have the initial screen built and we can move and fire the zapper.

Time for a break ... how about ordering in some pizza for dinner? Make sure to **Save** your work!

Assignment 28:

1. Try making the zapper using a colored triangle. Modify the movement code.

2. Change any colors you want to. It's your game!

We continue building the **Pizza Zapper** game.

Most of this lesson concerns getting the pizza moving down the screen using the **Timer** object. Spend extra time with the student explaining how to set the **Interval** property and how to turn the timer on and off. Be aware the timer is 'on' by default.

We also do a simple collision detection - checking to see if the pizza goes off the bottom of the window. Explain to your student how to use sketches to see if two rectangular regions overlap.

QUESTIONS:

1. How would you make a non-circular pizza? How would the 'falling off the window' logic change?

2. Explain how the **Timer** works.

3. What **Timer Interval** would you use if you want something to happen 5 times per second? What if you want something to happen every two seconds?

LESSON 29   PIZZA ZAPPER GAME – PART 2

Welcome Back! We have started the **Pizza Zapper** game, but there is still lots to be done. In the last lesson, we got the window all set up and wrote code to move the zapper and fire the zapper. In this lesson, we get the pizzas moving.

Open your saved program.

PIZZA INITIALIZATION

Here is what our pizza will look like (a cheese pizza with tomato sauce):

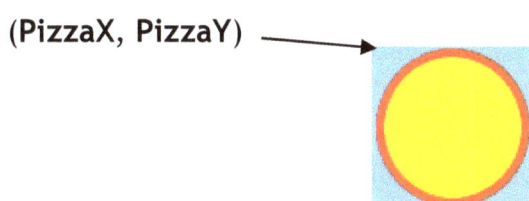

(PizzaX, PizzaY) ⟶

It is a circle (diameter **PizzaD**). It is located at (**PizzaX**, **PizzaY**). It will travel down the window at a speed of **PizzaSpeed**. Add the indicated new lines at the end of the **NewGame** subroutine to establish some initial values:

```
PizzaD = 75
PizzaSpeed = 10
NewPizza()
```

Initial values for **PizzaX** and **PizzaY** are set in the **NewPizza** subroutine.

You might be asking – where did these numbers come from? I made them up. As a game designer, you can use any numbers you want. You usually play the game as you build it to come up with numbers that make sense. In this case, you don't want a speed so slow, the game is easy and boring. And, you don't want a speed that's so fast, you can't possibly zap the pizza.

PIZZA SUBROUTINES

There are several subroutines associated with placing and moving the pizza. Let's get those done.

The most basic routine is one to draw a pizza at (**PizzaX**, **PizzaY**). This is done in the **DrawPizza** subroutine:

```
Sub DrawPizza
  'draw a pizza
  'yellow pizza red crust
  GraphicsWindow.BrushColor = "Yellow"
  GraphicsWindow.FillEllipse(PizzaX, PizzaY, PizzaD, PizzaD)
  GraphicsWindow.PenWidth = 4
  GraphicsWindow.PenColor = "Red"
  GraphicsWindow.DrawEllipse(PizzaX, PizzaY, PizzaD, PizzaD)
EndSub
```

The pizza is a "square" ellipse with both width and height set to **PizzaD**.

We are going to want to move pizzas, so we need a corresponding **ErasePizza** subroutine:

```
Sub ErasePizza
  'erase a pizza
  GraphicsWindow.BrushColor = GraphicsWindow.BackgroundColor
  GraphicsWindow.FillEllipse(PizzaX - 5, PizzaY - 5, PizzaD + 10, PizzaD + 10)
EndSub
```

We have 'expanded' the erase area to make sure we get complete erasure.

With these two subroutines, we can write a **MovePizza** routine (it erases, adjusts **PizzaY**, then redraws):

```
Sub MovePizza
  'move a pizza
  'erase first
  ErasePizza()
  'move
  PizzaY = PizzaY + PizzaSpeed
  DrawPizza()
EndSub
```

Lastly, every time we need to display a new pizza, it is randomly placed at the top of the game window. Type this code in the **NewPizza** subroutine:

```
Sub NewPizza
  ' start a new pizza falling
  PizzaX = Math.GetRandomNumber(GraphicsWindow.Width - PizzaD)
  PizzaY = 0
  DrawPizza()
EndSub
```

Save the program. **Run** the program and you'll see your first pizza (it will most likely be in a different position than this one since it is placed randomly):

MOVING PIZZA

It's time to get the pizza moving. We want it to drop down the screen all by itself. We don't want anyone to have to press a key or anything. We can do this, but it's needs a little explanation.

Remember when we talked about waiting for key presses using the **KeyDown** event. We saw that Small Basic can "secretly" wait for this event, then execute the code in its subroutine. There's another "secret" event we can make happen.

Small Basic has something called a **Timer**. The **Timer** has a very interesting feature. It can generate events (called **Tick** events) without any input from the user. The **Timer** works in the background, generating events at time intervals you specify. If we update the pizza position every time one of these events occurs, we get the sense of motion, or animation.

It's really pretty easy. There are just a couple of steps:

1. Assign the timer's **Tick** event to a subroutine that contains code to be executed with each event.
2. Decide how often you want to generate **Tick** events; this is the timer's **Interval** property. The **Interval** is measured in milliseconds. There are 1000 milliseconds in one second.

To start a timer and begin event processing, use:

Timer.Resume()

To stop the timer and stop event processing, use:

Timer.Pause()

To review, here's what happens. When a timer is running, every **Interval** milliseconds, Small Basic will generate an event and execute the corresponding **Tick** event subroutine. No user interaction is needed.

The **Interval** property is important. This property is set to the number of milliseconds between timer events. A millisecond is 1/1000th of a second, or there are 1,000 milliseconds in a second. If you want to generate N events per second, set the **Interval** to 1000 / N. For example, if you want a timer event to occur 4 times per second, use an **Interval** of 250. Now, let's use this to move the pizza.

Add this code in the 'main program' (before the `NewGame()` line) to set up the **Timer:**

```
Timer.Interval = 50
Timer.Tick = TickSub
Timer.Pause()
```

We use an **Interval** of 50 (causing 20 events per second). When a **Tick** event occurs, it processes the code in the **TickSub** subroutine. Lastly, we make sure the **Timer** is stopped when we begin.

Add this line at the end of the **NewGame** subroutine to start the timer:

```
Timer.Resume()
```

This, by the way, completes the initialization code and the **NewGame** subroutine.

Lastly, add the **TickSub** subroutine:

```
Sub TickSub
  'move pizza
  MovePizza()
EndSub
```

After all this work, we have simply said "every 50 milliseconds move the pizza down the screen."

Save the program. **Run** the program and the pizza will fall:

Uh-oh, the pizza just keeps falling out the bottom of the window!

GETTING A NEW PIZZA

If a pizza falls off the bottom of the window before being zapped, we call that a **miss**. The rules we set up said we could have three misses before the game ends. Let's finish this lesson by setting up that logic.

We will define a miss just a little differently. We will say the pizza is missed if it reaches the zapper top without being zapped. Look at this picture showing the vertical locations of the pizza and the zapper:

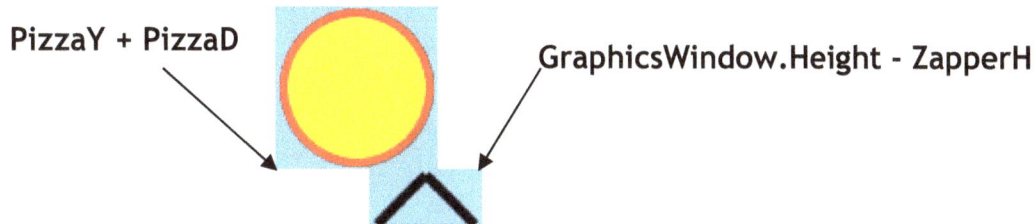

So, a miss occurs when:

PizzaY + PizzaD > GraphicsWindow.Height - ZapperH

We check for misses in the **TickSub** subroutine after we move the pizza:

```
Sub TickSub
  'move pizza
  MovePizza()
  'check for miss
  If (PizzaY + PizzaD > GraphicsWindow.Height - ZapperH) Then
    ErasePizza()
    Missed = Missed + 1
    If (Missed = 3) Then
      GraphicsWindow.Title = "Pizza Zapper - Game Over - Final Score:
" + Score
      Timer.Pause()
    EndIf
    If (Missed <> 3) Then
      NewPizza()
    EndIf
  EndIf
EndSub
```

If there is a miss, we erase the pizza then increment **Missed**. If there are three misses, we stop the timer and display a game over message in the title bar area. If there are not three misses, we display a new pizza and the game continues.

Save the program. **Run** the program. Watch three pizzas fall out the bottom of the window and you will see the game over message:

Time for another break. In the final lesson, we will finish the game. We will see if pizzas are zapped (changing the score), look at ways to make the game more difficult as it proceeds and will add a prompt to let the user play again.

Assignment 29:

1. For practice with the **Timer**, see if you can write a program that makes a bell sound every second.

We complete the **Pizza Zapper** game.

We discuss collision logic to see if the zapper hits a pizza. Again, a sketch helps.

With a zap, the score is incremented and displayed. We talk about making the game more difficult as scores increase. We change pizza size and pizza speed. Your students might have other ideas to change. Maybe slow down the zapper. Make the zapper random in its firing ability. Here is where the student can use their imagination.

Lastly, we illustrate the use of a prompt to continue game play. Make sure the student understands the **KeyDownSub** subroutine is used for both zapper movement and zapper fire, as well as detecting Y or N answers for the prompt.

In any game, there's always room for improvement. The student's assignment has some suggestions. See if your students can come up with ideas of their own.

QUESTIONS:

1. When the program starts, can you give the user the option to see game insructions? Tell them what keys do what and what the game rules are.

2. Notice you can move the zapper and fire the zapper even when the game is stopped. Can you think of how to keep this from happening?

3. Similarly, you can press Y or N at anytime to start a new game or stop the game. How can you keep this from happening?

These questions are also part of the assignment. Encourage your student to make these changes. They make the game more "user-friendly."

LESSON 30   PIZZA ZAPPER GAME - PART 3

Let's finish the **Pizza Zapper** game. Here's what's left to do:

> Zap pizzas
> Keep score
> Make game harder as it goes on
> Provide 'Play Again?' Prompt

DID THE PIZZA GET ZAPPED?

After a player fires the zapper, we need to see if it zapped a pizza. In "game design talk," we want to know if the zapper "**collides**" with the pizza.

A picture helps. Here are the horizontal edges of a pizza:

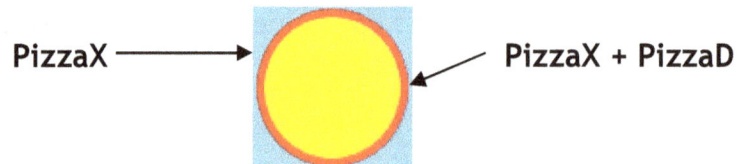

If the horizontal position of the zapper (**ZapperX**) lies between these edges, we have a collision and the pizza is zapped. When a pizza is zapped, the score variable (**Score**) is increased by one.

Where do we check for collisions? In the same place we check if the pizzas fall off the window – in the **TickSub** subroutine. Add these lines at the beginning of the subroutine:

```
'zapper fired?  if so, check for zap
If (ZapperFired = "true") Then
  ZapperFired = "false"
  'check for  zapper hit
  If (ZapperX > PizzaX And ZapperX < PizzaX + PizzaD) Then
    ' a hit
    Score = Score + 1
    GraphicsWindow.Title = "Pizza Zapper - Score: " + Score
    ErasePizza()
    NewPizza()
  EndIf
  'erase ray
  GraphicsWindow.BrushColor = GraphicsWindow.BackgroundColor
  GraphicsWindow.FillRectangle(ZapperX - 5, 0, 10,
GraphicsWindow.Height - ZapperH)
EndIf
```

This code is only checked if the zapper has been fired (**ZapperFired** is "true"). If there is a collision, the score is incremented and displayed. The zapped pizza is erased and a new pizza is started. Lastly, the zapper is erased (with an expanded erasure area).

Run the program. Move the zapper under a pizza and fire away! Remember you press **Space** to fire. You can now play a game to completion – until you have three misses.

Here's a game I played zapping 16 pizzas:

289

LET'S MAKE IT HARDER

After playing a while, you get good at the game and zapping pizzas is kind of easy. In most games, as you continue to play, the game becomes more difficult. Let's add that feature to the **Pizza Zapper**.

Here's another chance to make up your own rules. You are the game designer, so you can pick how you want to make the game harder. Here's what I chose: every time the score reaches a multiple of 10, make the pizza smaller and make the pizza faster.

Again, this code goes in the **TickSub** subroutine. Find these lines in the **TickSub** subroutine:

```
' a hit
Score = Score + 1
```

Add this code after these lines:

```
'make harder?
If (Math.Remainder(Score, 10) = 0) Then
  PizzaD = PizzaD - 5
  PizzaSpeed = PizzaSpeed + 1
EndIf
```

The **Remainder** function tells you the remainder when you divide **Score** by **10**. When it is zero, **Score** is a multiple of 10.

Save and **Run** the program again. Once the score reaches 10, notice you have smaller faster pizzas:

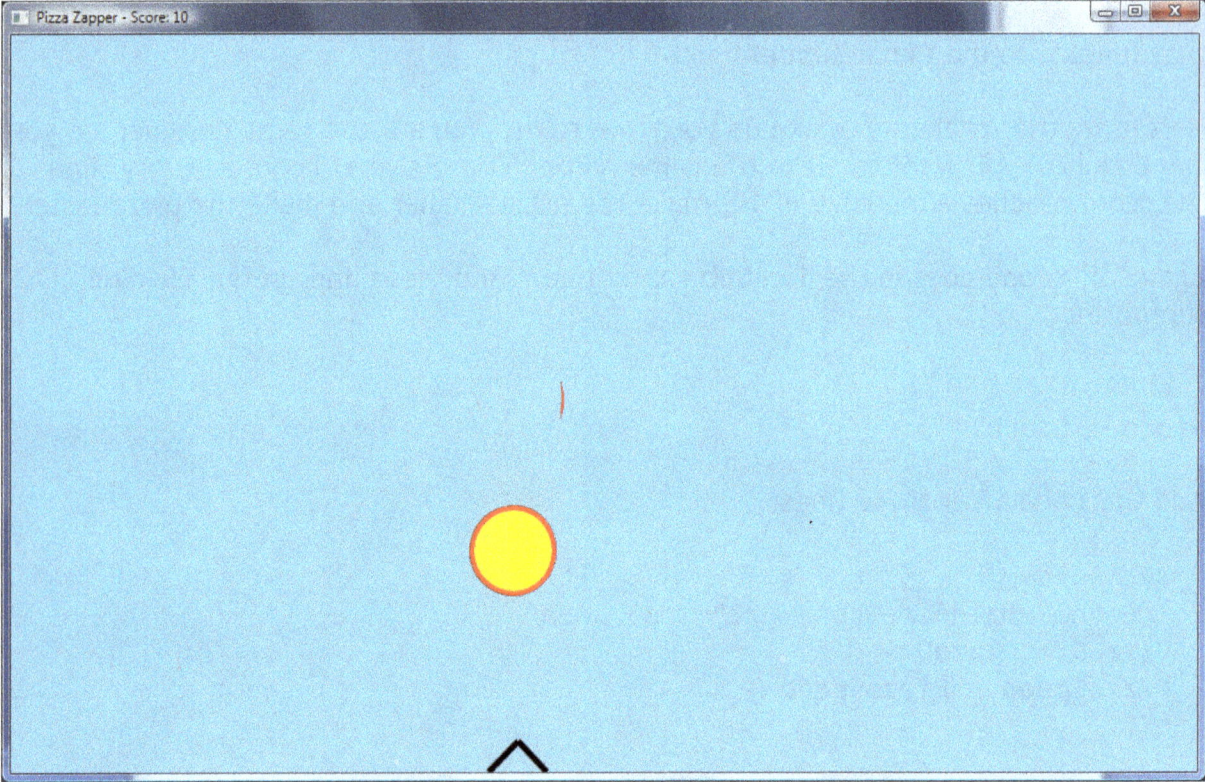

WANT TO PLAY AGAIN?

When the game stops, your only option is to stop the program. Let's give the player an option to play again.

Add this code in the **TickSub** subroutine after the lines displaying the game over message and stopping the **Timer**:

```
GraphicsWindow.BrushColor = "Black"
GraphicsWindow.FontSize = 24
GraphicsWindow.DrawText(100, 100, "Want to play again (Y or N)?")
```

Run the program. Let the game end and you see this message:

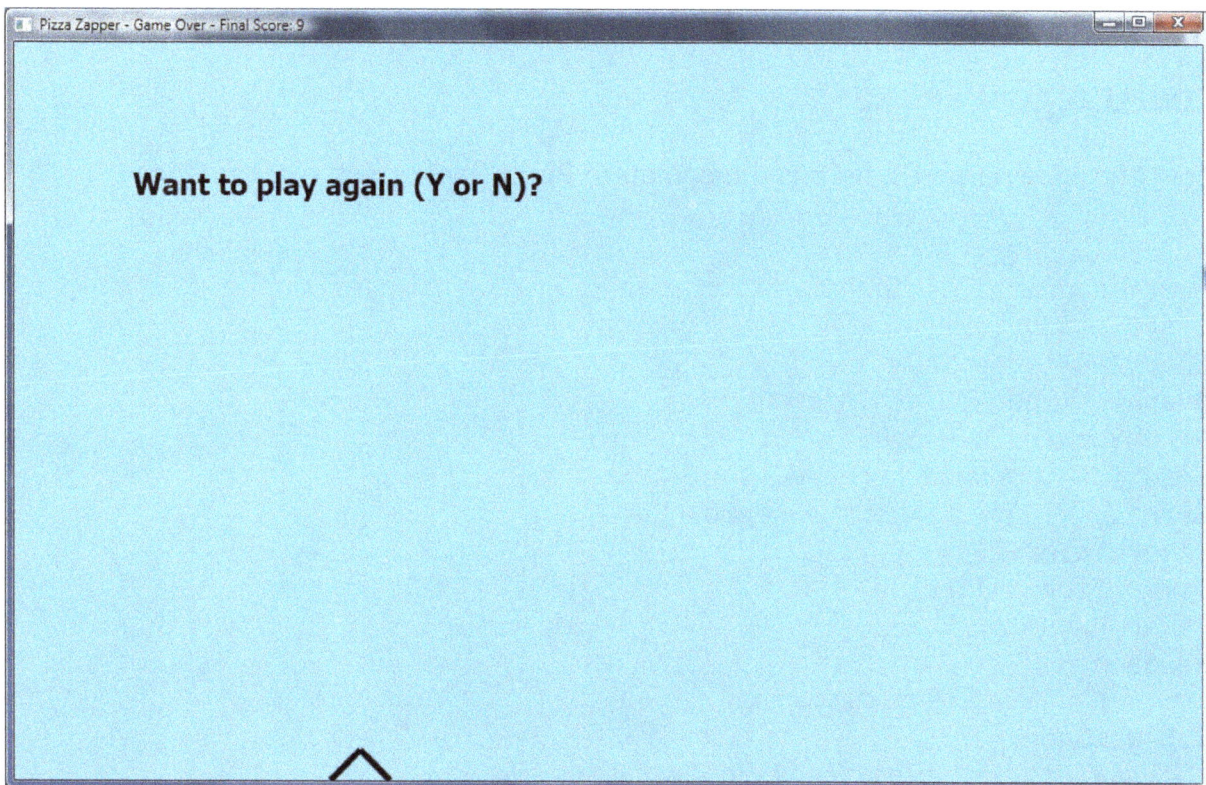

We need to recognize the user input (Y or N). **Stop** the program by clicking the X in the upper right corner.

Add these lines at the end of the **KeyDownSub** subroutine to enable recognizing when the user presses Y (for yes) or N (for no):

```
If (K = "Y") Then
  NewGame()
EndIf
If (K = "N") then
  Program.End()
EndIf
```

Save the program. **Run** it again. Test the 'Play Again' feature.

At long last, the **Pizza Zapper** game is complete. Can you think of ways to make it even better? Try them. We give you some suggestions in this lesson's assignments.

COMPLETE CODE LISTING

For reference purposes, here is the complete **Pizza Zapper** game code listing.

```
'Pizza Zapper
'Set up graphics window
'initializations
GraphicsWindow.Show()
GraphicsWindow.Width = 1000
GraphicsWindow.Height = 600
GraphicsWindow.BackgroundColor = "SkyBlue"
GraphicsWindow.KeyDown = KeyDownSub
Timer.Interval = 50
Timer.Tick = TickSub
Timer.Pause()
NewGame()

Sub NewGame
  'reinitialize everything for a new game
  GraphicsWindow.Clear()
  GraphicsWindow.Title = "Pizza Zapper - Score: 0"
  Score = 0
  Missed = 0
  ZapperW = 50
  ZapperH = 25
  ZapperX = 500
  ZapperY = 575
  ZapperMove = 0
  ZapperFired = "false"
  MoveZapper()
```

```
  PizzaD = 75
  PizzaSpeed = 10
  NewPizza()
  Timer.Resume()
EndSub

Sub MoveZapper
  'move the zapper
  'erase first
  GraphicsWindow.BrushColor = GraphicsWindow.BackgroundColor
  GraphicsWindow.FillRectangle(ZapperX - ZapperW / 2 - 5, ZapperY - 5,
ZapperW + 10, ZapperH + 10)
  'move by ZapperMove
  ZapperX = ZapperX + ZapperMove
  If (ZapperX < 0) Then
    ZapperX = 0
  EndIf
  If (ZapperX > GraphicsWindow.Width) Then
    ZapperX = GraphicsWindow.Width
  EndIf
  ' draw zapper
  GraphicsWindow.PenWidth = 5
  GraphicsWindow.PenColor = "Black"
  GraphicsWindow.DrawLine(ZapperX, ZapperY, ZapperX - ZapperW / 2,
ZapperY + ZapperH)
  GraphicsWindow.DrawLine(ZapperX, ZapperY, ZapperX + ZapperW / 2,
ZapperY + ZapperH)
EndSub

Sub FireZapper
  'fire the zapper
  ZapperFired = "true"
  GraphicsWindow.PenWidth = 3
  GraphicsWindow.PenColor = "Blue"
  GraphicsWindow.DrawLine(ZapperX, ZapperY, ZapperX, 0)
  Sound.PlayBellRing()
EndSub

Sub NewPizza
  ' start a new pizza falling
  PizzaX = Math.GetRandomNumber(GraphicsWindow.Width - PizzaD)
  PizzaY = 0
  DrawPizza()
EndSub

Sub DrawPizza
```

```
    'draw a pizza
    'yellow pizza red crust
    GraphicsWindow.BrushColor = "Yellow"
    GraphicsWindow.FillEllipse(PizzaX, PizzaY, PizzaD, PizzaD)
    GraphicsWindow.PenWidth = 4
    GraphicsWindow.PenColor = "Red"
    GraphicsWindow.DrawEllipse(PizzaX, PizzaY, PizzaD, PizzaD)
EndSub

Sub ErasePizza
    'erase a pizza
    GraphicsWindow.BrushColor = GraphicsWindow.BackgroundColor
    GraphicsWindow.FillEllipse(PizzaX - 5, PizzaY - 5, PizzaD + 10,
PizzaD + 10)
EndSub

Sub MovePizza
    'move a pizza
    'erase first
    ErasePizza()
    'move
    PizzaY = PizzaY + PizzaSpeed
    DrawPizza()
EndSub

Sub KeyDownSub
    'handle key presses
    K = GraphicsWindow.LastKey
    ZapperMove = 0
    If (K = "Left") Then
      ZapperMove = -10
    EndIf
    If (K = "Right") Then
      ZapperMove = 10
    EndIf
    MoveZapper()
    If (K = "Space") Then
      'draw ray
      FireZapper()
    EndIf
    If (K = "Y") Then
      NewGame()
    EndIf
    If (K = "N") then
      Program.End()
    EndIf
```

```
EndSub

Sub TickSub
  'zapper fired?  if so, check for zap
  If (ZapperFired = "true") Then
    ZapperFired = "false"
    'check for  zapper hit
    If (ZapperX > PizzaX And ZapperX < PizzaX + PizzaD) Then
      ' a hit
      Score = Score + 1
      'make harder?
      If (Math.Remainder(Score, 10) = 0) Then
        PizzaD = PizzaD - 5
        PizzaSpeed = PizzaSpeed + 1
      EndIf
      GraphicsWindow.Title = "Pizza Zapper - Score: " + Score
      ErasePizza()
      NewPizza()
    EndIf
    'erase ray
    GraphicsWindow.BrushColor = GraphicsWindow.BackgroundColor
    GraphicsWindow.FillRectangle(ZapperX - 5, 0, 10,
GraphicsWindow.Height - ZapperH)
  EndIf
  'move pizza
  MovePizza()
  'check for miss
  If (PizzaY + PizzaD > GraphicsWindow.Height - ZapperH) Then
    ErasePizza()
    Missed = Missed + 1
    If (Missed = 3) Then
      GraphicsWindow.Title = "Pizza Zapper - Game Over - Final Score:
" + Score
      Timer.Pause()
      GraphicsWindow.BrushColor = "Black"
      GraphicsWindow.FontSize = 24
      GraphicsWindow.DrawText(100, 100, "Want to play again (Y or
N)?")
    EndIf
    If (Missed <> 3) Then
      NewPizza()
    EndIf
  EndIf
EndSub
```

1. When the program starts, give the user the option to see game insructions. Tell them what keys do what and what the game rules are.

2. Notice you can move the zapper and fire the zapper even when the game is stopped. Can you think of how to keep this from happening?

3. Similarly, you can press Y or N at anytime to start a new game or stop the game. How can you keep this from happening?

4. Many video games give you rewards as scores increase. Change this game so you get an extra miss for achieving a certain score level.

5. Many video games give you limited shots in a shooting game. Change this game so you can only take so many zaps. Allow extra zaps as you achieve different levels.

6. Many video games keep track of highest scores. Change this game so you know what the highest score yet is.

In this last lesson, we illustrate a really neat feature of Small Basic – the ability to share a program by "publishing" it to the Internet.

By clicking the **Publish** button, the contents of the current code editor are written to a special Microsoft website that archives Small Basic programs. With the provided link, anyone can access and run the published program.

The **Publish** feature doesn't work well with text windows – the text window does not appear in full size. So, this feature is best used with graphics windows programs.

Another cool feature is the ability to embed a Small Basic program in any website. This is something you might like to teach if student (or your school) has a website where such embedding makes sense. When you **Publish** a program, the code needed to do this embedding is given to you in a box marked **Embed this in your website**.

QUESTIONS:

1. What does the Publish button do?

2. How can you share a published program with a friend?

3. What does the Import button do?

LESSON 31   SHARING YOUR PROGRAMS

I bet you'd like to show your friends the **Pizza Zapper** game you just programmed and let them play it.

Here's one way to do that:

> Give them a copy of your code
> Have them install Small Basic on their computer
> Teach them how to open and run a program
> Have them open your **Pizza Zapper** program and run it

I think you'll agree this might be asking a lot of your friends!

Let's look at an easier way to share your work – letting users access and run your programs over the Internet! Take a look at the Small Basic toolbar. There are two buttons there we haven't talked about yet. Between the buttons to **Open** and **Save** programs and the ones for editing are buttons marked **Publish** and **Import**:

Publish allows you to store your programs on the Internet for others to use.

Clicking **Import** will take you to a Microsoft website where you can import and open a program stored on the Internet by you or other programmers.

Make sure your computer is connected to the Internet. **Open** the **Pizza Zapper** program. Click **Publish.** You will see a message something like this where your program is assigned an **ID** number (**WQV496**):

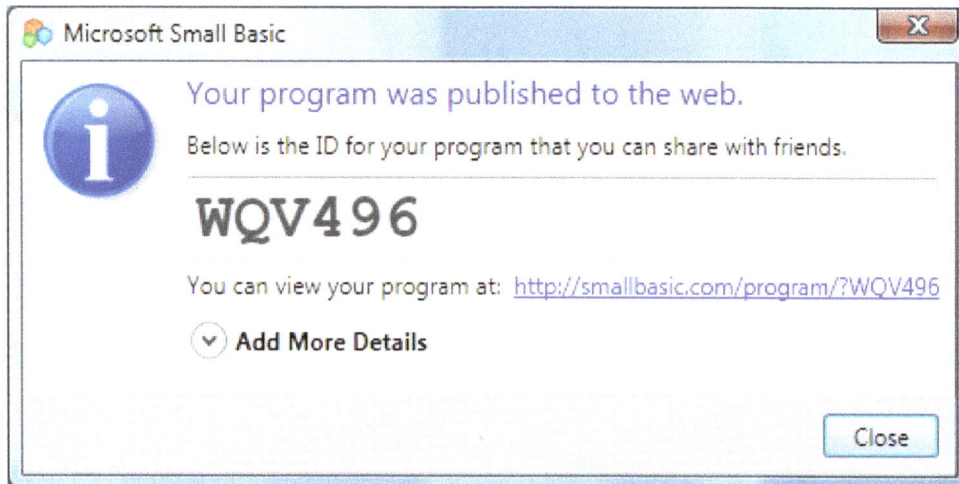

Also listed in this window is this very interesting piece of information:

You can view your program at:

http://smallbasic.com/program/?WQV496

If you click this link (or give the link to others and let them click it), "magic" occurs.

When I click the link, I am taken to this website hosted by Microsoft:

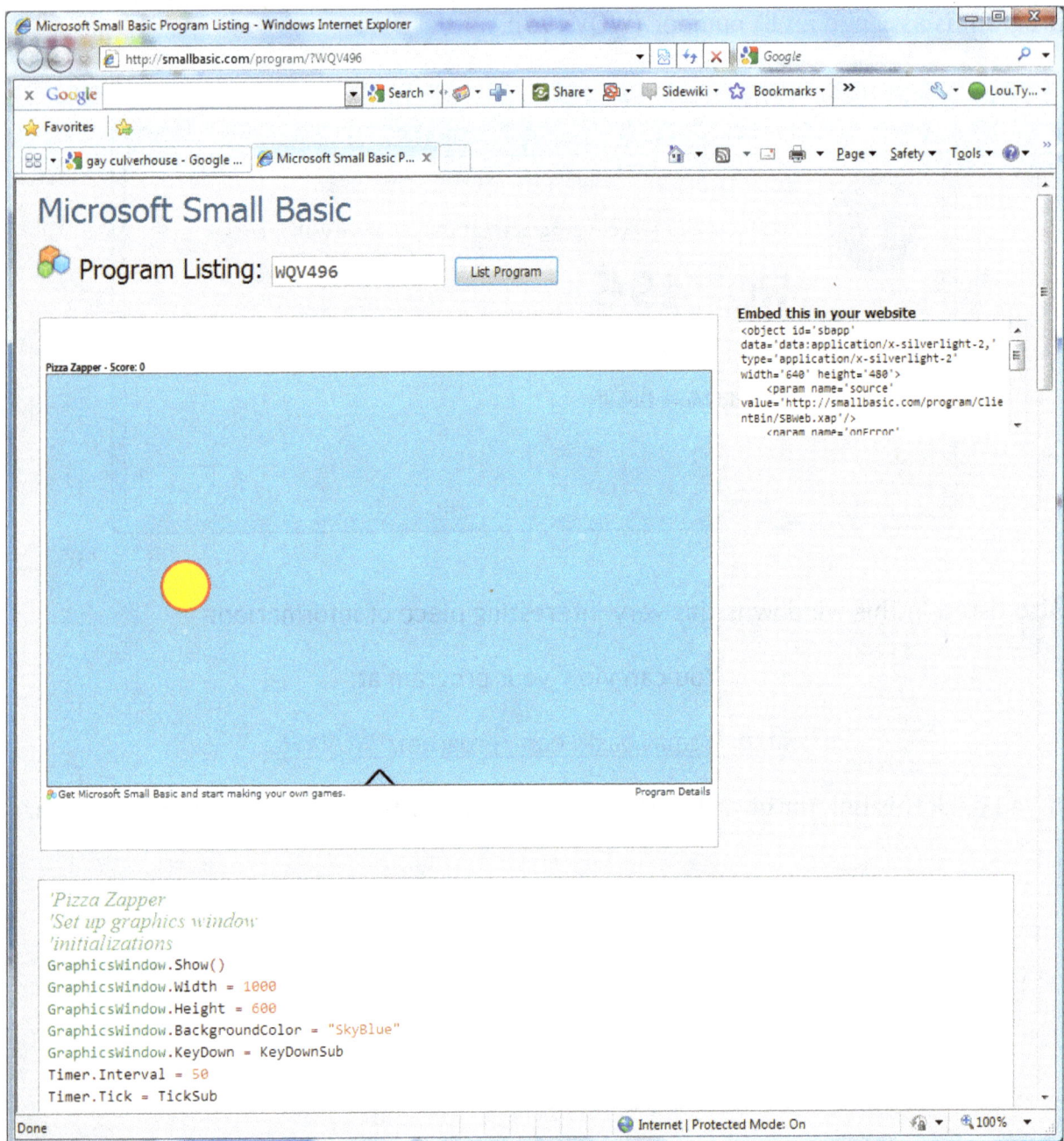

The running **Pizza Zapper** program is shown, along with a code listing.

You (and others) can play the game on-line!

Program Details

I think you'll agree this pretty neat.

To share your programs with other users, **Publish** them, then give them the program link given to you. If they click the link, they can run the program. Well, almost.

To use this feature, a user's computer must have a Microsoft product called **Silverlight** installed on their computer. It can be downloaded and installed from this website:

http://www.silverlight.net/

If a user attempts to access your Small Basic program via a provided link and they do not have the required Silverlight product, they will be taken through the installation steps.

Before leaving, let's return to the **Import** button in Small Basic. Click it again and enter the program ID for your program (I used **WQV496**):

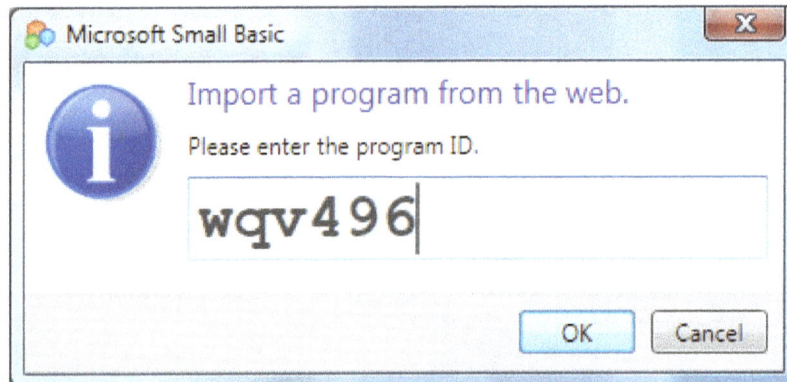

Click **OK**. The imported code will appear in your editor:

So, you have access to any code published to the Microsoft Small Basic library. I'm guessing this library will be growing very quickly.

1. Write a really cool program. Publish it to the Internet.

2. Have your other Small Basic programming friends write a program and share it with you.

APPENDIX I   SMALL BASIC COLORS

Color	Name	RGB Value
	AliceBlue	#F0F8FF
	AntiqueWhite	#FAEBD7
	Aqua	#00FFFF
	Aquamarine	#7FFFD4
	Azure	#F0FFFF
	Beige	#F5F5DC
	Bisque	#FFE4C4
	Black	#000000
	BlanchedAlmond	#FFEBCD
	Blue	#0000FF
	BlueViolet	#8A2BE2
	Brown	#A52A2A
	BurlyWood	#DEB887
	CadetBlue	#5F9EA0

	Chartreuse	#7FFF00
	Chocolate	#D2691E
	Coral	#FF7F50
	CornflowerBlue	#6495ED
	Cornsilk	#FFF8DC
	Crimson	#DC143C
	Cyan	#00FFFF
	DarkBlue	#00008B
	DarkCyan	#008B8B
	DarkGoldenrod	#B8860B
	DarkGray / DarkGrey[+]	#A9A9A9
	DarkGreen	#006400
	DarkKhaki	#BDB76B
	DarkMagenta	#8B008B
	DarkOliveGreen	#556B2F
	DarkOrange	#FF8C00

	DarkOrchid	#9932CC
	DarkRed	#8B0000
	DarkSalmon	#E9967A
	DarkSeaGreen	#8FBC8F
	DarkSlateBlue	#483D8B
	DarkSlateGray / DarkSlateGrey[†]	#2F4F4F
	DarkTurquoise	#00CED1
	DarkViolet	#9400D3
	DeepPink	#FF1493
	DeepSkyBlue	#00BFFF
	DimGray / DimGrey[†]	#696969
	DodgerBlue	#1E90FF
	FireBrick	#B22222
	FloralWhite	#FFFAF0
	ForestGreen	#228B22
	Fuchsia	#FF00FF

	Gainsboro	#DCDCDC
	GhostWhite	#F8F8FF
	Gold	#FFD700
	Goldenrod	#DAA520
	Gray / Grey[+]	#808080
	Green	#008000
	GreenYellow	#ADFF2F
	Honeydew	#F0FFF0
	HotPink	#FF69B4
	IndianRed	#CD5C5C
	Indigo	#4B0082
	Ivory	#FFFFF0
	Khaki	#F0E68C
	Lavender	#E6E6FA
	LavenderBlush	#FFF0F5
	LawnGreen	#7CFC00

	LemonChiffon	#FFFACD
	LightBlue	#ADD8E6
	LightCoral	#F08080
	LightCyan	#E0FFFF
	LightGoldenrodYellow	#FAFAD2
	LightGreen	#90EE90
	LightGray[†] / LightGrey	#D3D3D3
	LightPink	#FFB6C1
	LightSalmon	#FFA07A
	LightSeaGreen	#20B2AA
	LightSkyBlue	#87CEFA
	LightSlateGray / LightSlateGrey[†]	#778899
	LightSteelBlue	#B0C4DE
	LightYellow	#FFFFE0
	Lime	#00FF00
	LimeGreen	#32CD32

	Color	Hex
	Linen	#FAF0E6
	Magenta	#FF00FF
	Maroon	#800000
	MediumAquamarine	#66CDAA
	MediumBlue	#0000CD
	MediumOrchid	#BA55D3
	MediumPurple	#9370DB
	MediumSeaGreen	#3CB371
	MediumSlateBlue	#7B68EE
	MediumSpringGreen	#00FA9A
	MediumTurquoise	#48D1CC
	MediumVioletRed	#C71585
	MidnightBlue	#191970
	MintCream	#F5FFFA
	MistyRose	#FFE4E1
	Moccasin	#FFE4B5

	NavajoWhite	#FFDEAD
	Navy	#000080
	OldLace	#FDF5E6
	Olive	#808000
	OliveDrab	#6B8E23
	Orange	#FFA500
	OrangeRed	#FF4500
	Orchid	#DA70D6
	PaleGoldenrod	#EEE8AA
	PaleGreen	#98FB98
	PaleTurquoise	#AFEEEE
	PaleVioletRed	#DB7093
	PapayaWhip	#FFEFD5
	PeachPuff	#FFDAB9
	Peru	#CD853F
	Pink	#FFC0CB

	Plum	#DDA0DD
	PowderBlue	#B0E0E6
	Purple	#800080
	Red	#FF0000
	RosyBrown	#BC8F8F
	RoyalBlue	#4169E1
	SaddleBrown	#8B4513
	Salmon	#FA8072
	SandyBrown	#F4A460
	SeaGreen	#2E8B57
	Seashell	#FFF5EE
	Sienna	#A0522D
	Silver	#C0C0C0
	SkyBlue	#87CEEB
	SlateBlue	#6A5ACD
	SlateGray / SlateGrey[†]	#708090

	Color	Hex
	Snow	#FFFAFA
	SpringGreen	#00FF7F
	SteelBlue	#4682B4
	Tan	#D2B48C
	Teal	#008080
	Thistle	#D8BFD8
	Tomato	#FF6347
	Turquoise	#40E0D0
	Violet	#EE82EE
	Wheat	#F5DEB3
	White	#FFFFFF
	WhiteSmoke	#F5F5F5
	Yellow	#FFFF00
	YellowGreen	#9ACD32

APPENDIX II   ANSWERS TO ASSIGNMENTS

Many of these solutions are based on solutions in the original text.

Assignment 1:

2. Write a program that uses one comment and two **WriteLine** statements. **Run** your new program.

```
'Assignment 1 - Question 2
TextWindow.WriteLine("I am enjoying my study")
TextWindow.WriteLine("of Small Basic.")
```

Assignment 2:

4. Write a program that prints your first, middle and last names. Make the letters black on a yellow screen.

```
'Assignment 2 - Question 1
TextWindow.BackgroundColor = "Yellow"
TextWindow.ForegroundColor = "Black"
TextWindow.Clear()
TextWindow.WriteLine("Minda")
TextWindow.WriteLine("Anne")
TextWindow.WriteLine("Carlson")
TextWindow.WriteLine("")
```

5. Now, add a "bell ring" before it prints each name.

```
'Assignment 2 - Question 2
TextWindow.BackgroundColor = "Yellow"
TextWindow.ForegroundColor = "Black"
TextWindow.Clear()
Sound.PlayBellRingAndWait()
TextWindow.WriteLine("Minda")
Sound.PlayBellRingAndWait()
TextWindow.WriteLine("Anne")
Sound.PlayBellRingAndWait()
TextWindow.WriteLine("Carlson")
TextWindow.WriteLine("")
```

6. Write a program that draws three flying birds in the text window.

```
'Assignment 2 - Question 3
TextWindow.BackgroundColor = "Blue"
TextWindow.ForegroundColor = "White"
TextWindow.Clear()
TextWindow.WriteLine(" /-O-\ ")
TextWindow.WriteLine("/     \")
TextWindow.WriteLine("")
TextWindow.WriteLine(" /-O-\ ")
TextWindow.WriteLine("/     \")
TextWindow.WriteLine("")
TextWindow.WriteLine(" /-O-\ ")
TextWindow.WriteLine("/     \")
TextWindow.WriteLine("")
```

Assignment 4:

3. Write a program that makes a valentine. Use red letters on a white background.
    Try to draw a heart using characters.

```
'Assignment 4 - Question 3
TextWindow.BackgroundColor = "White"
TextWindow.ForegroundColor = "Red"
TextWindow.Clear()
TextWindow.WriteLine(" XXX   XXX")
TextWindow.WriteLine("X   X X   X")
TextWindow.WriteLine("X     X    X")
TextWindow.WriteLine("X          X")
TextWindow.WriteLine(" X        X")
TextWindow.WriteLine("  X      X")
TextWindow.WriteLine("   X    X")
TextWindow.WriteLine("    X X")
TextWindow.WriteLine("     X")
TextWindow.WriteLine("")
```

3. Write a program that asks for a person's name and then says something silly to the person, by name.

```
'Assignment 5 - Question 1
TextWindow.WriteLine("What is your name?")
N = TextWindow.Read()
TextWindow.WriteLine("")
TextWindow.WriteLine(N)
TextWindow.WriteLine("I'm a computer and you're not!")
TextWindow.WriteLine("")
```

4. Write a program that asks you to **Read** your favorite color and put it into a box called C. Now the program asks your favorite animal and puts this into box C too. Have the program write C. What will be written? **Run** the program and see if you are right.

```
'Assignment 5 - Question 2
TextWindow.WriteLine("What is your favorite color?")
C = TextWindow.Read()
TextWindow.WriteLine("I put that in box C")
TextWindow.WriteLine("")
TextWindow.WriteLine("What is your favorite animal?")
C = TextWindow.Read()
TextWindow.WriteLine("I put that in box C too")
TextWindow.WriteLine("")
TextWindow.WriteLine("Now here is what is in box C:")
TextWindow.WriteLine(C)
TextWindow.WriteLine("")
```

Assignment 6:

3. Write a program that asks for the name of a musical group and one of their tunes. Then, write the group name and the tune name, with the word "plays" in between.

```
'Assignment 6 - Question 1
TextWindow.Write("What is your favorite music group? ")
G = TextWindow.Read()
TextWindow.Write("What is one of their songs? ")
S = TextWindow.Read()
TextWindow.Write(G)
TextWindow.Write(" plays ")
TextWindow.WriteLine(S)
TextWindow.WriteLine("")
```

4. Write a program that asks for a famous person's name and the year they were born? Write out the input information.

```
'Assignment 6 - Question 2
TextWindow.Write("Name someone famous ... ")
N = TextWindow.Read()
TextWindow.Write("What year were they born? ")
Y = TextWindow.ReadNumber()
TextWindow.Write(N)
TextWindow.Write(" was born in ")
TextWindow.WriteLine(Y)
TextWindow.WriteLine("")
```

Assignment 7:

2. Write a program that reads two strings, glues them together and writes them in the text window.

```
'Assignment 7 - Question 2
TextWindow.Write("How is the weather? ")
X = TextWindow.Read()
TextWindow.Write("And how do you feel? ")
Y = TextWindow.Read()
TextWindow.Write("You mean: " + X + " and " + Y)
TextWindow.WriteLine("")
```

7. Just for practice in understanding the **Goto** statement and line labels, draw the road map for this spaghetti program:

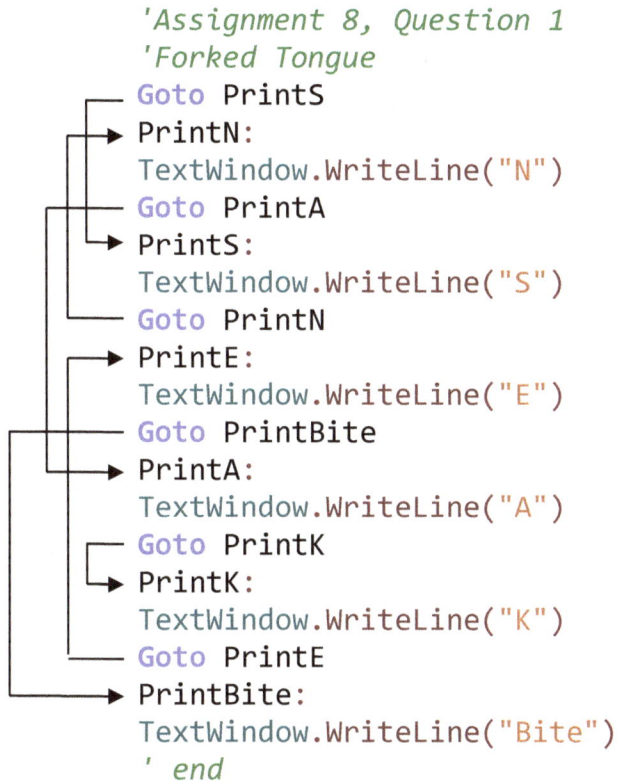

```
'Assignment 8, Question 1
'Forked Tongue
Goto PrintS
PrintN:
TextWindow.WriteLine("N")
Goto PrintA
PrintS:
TextWindow.WriteLine("S")
Goto PrintN
PrintE:
TextWindow.WriteLine("E")
Goto PrintBite
PrintA:
TextWindow.WriteLine("A")
Goto PrintK
PrintK:
TextWindow.WriteLine("K")
Goto PrintE
PrintBite:
TextWindow.WriteLine("Bite")
' end
```

8. Rewrite the snake program above, leaving out the **Goto** statements, making the program "clean and lean."

```
'Assignment 8, Question 2
' Forked Tongue
TextWindow.WriteLine("S")
TextWindow.WriteLine("N")
TextWindow.WriteLine("A")
TextWindow.WriteLine("K")
TextWindow.WriteLine("E")
TextWindow.WriteLine("Bite")
' end
```

9. Write a program that writes "Teen Power" over and over.

```
'Assignment 8, Question 3
PrintAgain:
TextWindow.WriteLine("Teen Power")
Goto PrintAgain
```

10. Write another program that prints your name on one line, then a friend's name on the next, over and over. Sound a ringing bell as each name is written. Stop the program.

```
'Assignment 8, Question 4
PrintAgain:
TextWindow.WriteLine("Minda")
Sound.PlayBellRingAndWait()
TextWindow.WriteLine("Nell")
Sound.PlayBellRingAndWait()
Goto PrintAgain
```

11. Write a program that uses **WriteLine**, **Read**, assignment statements and **Goto**. It also should glue strings together.

```
'Assignment 8, Question 5
GetAgain:
TextWindow.WriteLine("Name a state ... ")
S = TextWindow.Read()
TextWindow.WriteLine("What is its capital city?")
C = TextWindow.Read()
M = "The capital of " + S + " is " + C
TextWindow.WriteLine(M)
Goto GetAgain
```

2. Start a **New** program. Write code that asks if you are a "BOY" or a "GIRL". If the answer is "BOY", the program prints "SNIPS AND SNAILS". If the answer is "GIRL", write "SUGAR AND SPICE".

```
'Assignment 9A, Question 1
TextWindow.Write("Are you a BOY or a GIRL? ")
A = TextWindow.Read()
If (A = "BOY") Then
  TextWindow.WriteLine("SNIPS AND SNAILS")
EndIf
If (A = "GIRL") Then
  TextWindow.WriteLine("SUGAR AND SPICE")
EndIf
```

Assignment 9B:

3. Write a "pizza" program. Ask what topping is wanted. You can choose mushrooms, pepperoni, anchovies, green peppers, etc. You can also ask what size.

```
'Assignment 9B, Question 1
' Original by Chris Clark, Jr (14 years old in 1983)
TextWindow.WriteLine("Hallo, Ay am Mario, your pizza man")
TextWindow.WriteLine("Just tell me ze gory details and I'll do the
rest")
TextWindow.WriteLine("")
TextWindow.Write("What size (s, m, l)? ")
S = TextWindow.Read()
If (S = "s") Then
  TextWindow.WriteLine("On a diet?  Ho-Ho!")
EndIf
If (S = "m") Then
  TextWindow.WriteLine("Good choice - not too big, but filling!")
EndIf
If (S = "l") Then
  TextWindow.WriteLine("You must have a big bunch at home!")
EndIf
TextWindow.WriteLine("")
TextWindow.WriteLine("Now, pick your toppings (STOP to stop)")
GetTopping:
T = TextWindow.Read()
If (T <> "STOP") Then
  Goto GetTopping
EndIf
```

4. Write a color guessing game. One player inputs a color in string C and the other keeps inputting guesses into string G. Use two **If** statements to tell the user if their guess is right or wrong.

```
'Assignment 9B, Question 2
TextWindow.WriteLine("Player 2, turn your back")
TextWindow.WriteLine("")
TextWindow.Write("Player 1, enter a color ")
C = TextWindow.Read()
TextWindow.WriteLine("")
TextWindow.WriteLine("Player 2, turn around and guess until right ...
")
GetGuess:
G = TextWindow.Read()
If (G <> C) Then
  Goto GetGuess
EndIf
TextWindow.WriteLine("That's it!")
```

Assignment 10:

3. Write a program that asks for your age and the current year. Then subtract and write out the year of your birth. Be sure to use **Write** or **WriteLine** statements to tell what is wanted and what the final number means.

```
'Assignment 10, Question 1
TextWindow.Write("How old are you? ")
A = TextWindow.ReadNumber()
TextWindow.Write("And what year is it now? ")
Y = TextWindow.ReadNumber()
B = Y - A
TextWindow.Write("Has your birthday come yet this year (Y or N)? ")
A = TextWindow.Read()
If (A = "N") Then
  B = B - 1
EndIf
TextWindow.WriteLine("")
TextWindow.WriteLine("So, you were born in " + B)
```

4. Write a program that asks for two numbers and then writes out their product (multiplies them). Be sure to use lots of output statements to tell the user what is happening.

```
'Assignment 10, Question 2
TextWindow.Write("Give me a number ")
N = TextWindow.ReadNumber()
TextWindow.Write("Give me another number ")
M = TextWindow.ReadNumber()
P = N * M
TextWindow.Write("Here is their product: ")
TextWindow.WriteLine(P)
```

Assignment 11:

4. Write a "slow poke" program that prints out a three word message with a couple of seconds between each word. Have the computer ring a bell before each word.

```
'Assignment 11, Question 1
TextWindow.WriteLine("I'm")
Program.Delay(2000)
TextWindow.WriteLine("so")
Program.Delay(2000)
TextWindow.WriteLine("tired!!!")
Program.Delay(2000)
Sound.PlayBellRing()
```

5. Write a program that rolls two dice. Show the number on each die and the sum. Maybe add a delay between displaying the two values.

```
'Assignment 11, Question 2
Roll:
A = Math.GetRandomNumber(6)
TextWindow.WriteLine("Die 1: " + A)
B = Math.GetRandomNumber(6)
TextWindow.WriteLine("Die 2: " + B)
S = A + B
TextWindow.WriteLine("Sum:    " + S)
TextWindow.Write("Again? (Y or N) ")
R = TextWindow.Read()
If (R = "Y") Then
  Goto Roll
EndIf
```

6. Write a "coin flipping" game, you against the computer. If you get heads and computer gets tails, you win. If computer gets heads and you get tails, the computer wins. If you both get the same, it's a tie. Use the computer to flip a coin, choose 1 or 2 using **GetRandomNumber**: 1 is heads, 2 is tails. Let the computer figure out who wins and keep score.

```smallbasic
'Assignment 11, Question 3
'P your points, Q computer points, R tie points
P = 0
Q = 0
R = 0
PlayAgain:
TextWindow.WriteLine("")
TextWindow.WriteLine("Flipping coins against the computer ...")
TextWindow.WriteLine("Your wins: " + P)
TextWindow.WriteLine("Computer wins: " + Q)
TextWindow.WriteLine("Ties: " + R)
TextWindow.Write("Press Enter to Flip")
X = TextWindow.Read()
TextWindow.WriteLine("")
'your flip
V = Math.GetRandomNumber(2)
F = "Heads"
If (V = 2) Then
  F = "Tails"
EndIf
Y = F
TextWindow.WriteLine("You flipped a " + Y)
'computer flip
V = Math.GetRandomNumber(2)
F = "Heads"
If (V = 2) Then
  F = "Tails"
EndIf
C = F
TextWindow.WriteLine("Computer flipped a " + C)
'tie?
If (Y <> C) Then
  Goto NoTie
EndIf
'tie
TextWindow.WriteLine("It's a Tie!")
R = R + 1
Goto PlayAgain
NoTie:
'computer win?
```

```
If (C = "Heads") Then
  Goto ComputerWin
EndIf
'if got here, you win
TextWindow.WriteLine("You Win!")
P = P + 1
Goto PlayAgain
ComputerWin:
TextWindow.WriteLine("Computer Wins!")
Q = Q + 1
Goto PlayAgain
```

Assignment 12:

2. Write a program that says something about each number from one to ten. The player enters a number and the computer prints something about each number: "three strikes, you're out" or "seven is lucky" etc.

```
'Assignment 12, Question 2
TryAgain:
TextWindow.WriteLine("")
TextWindow.Write("Give me a number between 0 and 10 ... ")
N = TextWindow.Read()
TextWindow.WriteLine("")
If (N = 0) Then
  TextWindow.WriteLine("I got plenty of nothing!")
EndIf
If (N = 1) Then
  TextWindow.WriteLine("We're number one!")
EndIf
If (N = 2) Then
  TextWindow.WriteLine("Tea for two!")
EndIf
If (N = 3) Then
  TextWindow.WriteLine("Three to get ready!")
EndIf
If (N = 4) Then
  TextWindow.WriteLine("Four seasons - winter, spring, summer, fall!")
EndIf
If (N = 5) Then
  TextWindow.WriteLine("Take five!")
EndIf
If (N = 6) Then
  TextWindow.WriteLine("Six legged creatures!")
EndIf
```

```
If (N = 7) Then
  TextWindow.WriteLine("Seven swans a swimming!")
EndIf
If (N = 8) Then
  TextWindow.WriteLine("Eight days a week!")
EndIf
If (N = 9) Then
  TextWindow.WriteLine("Number nine, number nine!")
EndIf
If (N = 10) Then
  TextWindow.WriteLine("Ten little Indians!")
EndIf
If (N > 10) Then
  Goto EndProgram
EndIf
Program.Delay(1000)
Goto TryAgain
EndProgram:
TextWindow.WriteLine("That's all folks!")
```

3. Add to the **Guessing Game** program so that it prints "You're Hot" whenever the guesser is close to the right number.

```
'Assignment 12, Question 3
' Guessing Game
N = Math.GetRandomNumber(100)
TextWindow.WriteLine("I have a number between 1 and 100")
GetGuess:
TextWindow.Write("Make a guess ")
G = TextWindow.ReadNumber()
If (G < N) Then
  TextWindow.WriteLine("Too small")
EndIf
If (G > N) Then
  TextWindow.WriteLine("Too big")
EndIf
If (G - N > 0) Then
  If (G - N < 5) Then
    TextWindow.WriteLine("But, you're hot!")
  EndIf
EndIf
If (G - N < 0) Then
  If (G - N > -5) Then
    TextWindow.WriteLine("But, you're hot!")
  EndIf
EndIf
If (G = N) Then
  Goto GotIt
EndIf
Goto GetGuess
GotIt:
'game is over
TextWindow.WriteLine("")
TextWindow.WriteLine("That's it!")
```

4. Write a game for guessing a card that the computer has selected. Have the computer select the suit (club, diamond, heart, or spade) and the value (1 through 13). First, you guess the suit, then the program goes on to ask the value.

```
'Assignment 12, Question 4
' Card Guessing Game
S = Math.GetRandomNumber(4)
TextWindow.WriteLine("I pulled a card from the deck ... guess the
suit")
GetSuit:
TextWindow.WriteLine("")
TextWindow.WriteLine("1-Hearts")
TextWindow.WriteLine("2-Diamonds")
TextWindow.WriteLine("3-Hearts")
TextWindow.WriteLine("4-Hearts")
A = TextWindow.ReadNumber()
If (A <> S) Then
  Goto GetSuit
EndIf
TextWindow.WriteLine("")
TextWindow.WriteLine("That's the suit!")
TextWindow.WriteLine("")
C = Math.GetRandomNumber(13)
TextWindow.WriteLine("Now, guess the card ... ")
GetCard:
TextWindow.WriteLine("")
TextWindow.WriteLine("1-Ace")
TextWindow.WriteLine("2-Two")
TextWindow.WriteLine("3-Three")
TextWindow.WriteLine("4-Four")
TextWindow.WriteLine("5-Five")
TextWindow.WriteLine("6-Six")
TextWindow.WriteLine("7-Seven")
TextWindow.WriteLine("8-Eight")
TextWindow.WriteLine("9-Nine")
TextWindow.WriteLine("10-Ten")
TextWindow.WriteLine("11-Jack")
TextWindow.WriteLine("12-Queen")
TextWindow.WriteLine("13-King")
A = TextWindow.ReadNumber()
If (A <> C) Then
  Goto GetCard
EndIf
'game is over
TextWindow.WriteLine("")
TextWindow.WriteLine("That's it!")
```

Assignment 13A:

2. Have the computer count by fives from 0 to 100.

```
'Assignment 13A, Question 1
' Counting by fices
For I = 0 To 100 Step 5
  TextWindow.WriteLine(I)
EndFor
TextWindow.WriteLine("Done counting")
```

Assignment 13B:

4. Write a program that writes your name 15 times.

```
'Assignment 13B, Question 1
N = "Santa Claus"
For I = 1 To 15
  TextWindow.WriteLine(N)
EndFor
```

5. Now, make it write your name on one line, your friend's name on the next and keep switching until each name is written five times.

```
'Assignment 13B, Question 2
N = "Santa Claus"
B = "Buddy the Elf"
For I = 1 To 5
  TextWindow.WriteLine(N)
  TextWindow.WriteLine(B)
EndFor
```

6. Write a program that writes out addition facts using the digits from zero to nine.

```
'Assignment 13B, Question 3
''addition facts
For M = 0 To 9
  For N = 0 To 9
    TextWindow.WriteLine(M + " + " + N + " = " + (M + N))
  EndFor
EndFor
```

4. Use the **GetRandomNumber** method to write your name at random places in the text window. Make it write your name many times.

```
'Assignment 15, Question 1
For I = 1 To 100
  C = Math.GetRandomNumber(80)
  R = Math.GetRandomNumber(25)
  TextWindow.CursorLeft = C - 1
  TextWindow.CursorTop = R - 1
  TextWindow.Write("Lou")
  Program.Delay(200)
EndFor
```

5. Use **CursorTop** and **CursorLeft** to write your name in a large "X" shape in the text window.

```
'Assignment 15, Question 2
TextWindow.CursorLeft = 1
TextWindow.CursorTop = 1
TextWindow.WriteLine("R   N")
TextWindow.CursorLeft = 2
TextWindow.WriteLine("O I")
TextWindow.CursorLeft = 3
TextWindow.WriteLine("B")
TextWindow.CursorLeft = 2
TextWindow.WriteLine("O I")
TextWindow.CursorLeft = 1
TextWindow.WriteLine("R   N")
```

6. Write a program that makes a bird flap its wings and fly across the text window.

```
'Assignment 15, Question 3
For I = 3 To 80 Step 2
  'wings straight
  TextWindow.CursorTop = 8
  For J = 1 To 5
    TextWindow.CursorLeft = I - 1
    TextWindow.WriteLine("X")
  EndFor
  Program.Delay(200)
  'erase
  TextWindow.CursorTop = 8
  For J = 1 To 5
    TextWindow.CursorLeft = I - 1
    TextWindow.WriteLine(" ")
  EndFor
  'wings back
  TextWindow.CursorTop = 8
  TextWindow.CursorLeft = I - 3
  TextWindow.WriteLine("X")
  TextWindow.CursorLeft = I - 2
  TextWindow.WriteLine("X")
  TextWindow.CursorLeft = I - 1
  TextWindow.WriteLine("X")
  TextWindow.CursorLeft = I - 2
  TextWindow.WriteLine("X")
  TextWindow.CursorLeft = I - 3
  TextWindow.WriteLine("X")
  Program.Delay(200)
  'erase again
  TextWindow.CursorTop = 8
  For J = 1 To 5
    TextWindow.CursorLeft = I - 3
    TextWindow.WriteLine("   ")
  EndFor
EndFor
```

3. Use the **DrawLine** method to draw a rectangle. Use a pen width of 10 and a pen color of Blue.

```
'Assignment 16, Question 1
GraphicsWindow.Show()
GraphicsWindow.PenWidth = 10
GraphicsWindow.PenColor = "Blue"
GraphicsWindow.DrawLine(50, 50, 500, 50)
GraphicsWindow.DrawLine(500, 50, 500, 350)
GraphicsWindow.DrawLine(500, 350, 50, 350)
GraphicsWindow.DrawLine(50, 350, 50, 50)
```

4. Use the **DrawLine** method to draw your school's initials. Make each letter a different color. Save your program.

```
'Assignment 16, Question 2
GraphicsWindow.Show()
GraphicsWindow.PenWidth = 5
GraphicsWindow.PenColor = "Red"
GraphicsWindow.DrawLine(150, 50, 150, 350)
GraphicsWindow.DrawLine(150, 350, 50, 350)
GraphicsWindow.PenColor = "Green"
GraphicsWindow.DrawLine(250, 50, 250, 350)
GraphicsWindow.DrawLine(250, 50, 350, 50)
GraphicsWindow.DrawLine(250, 200, 325, 200)
GraphicsWindow.PenColor = "Blue"
GraphicsWindow.DrawLine(400, 50, 400, 350)
GraphicsWindow.DrawLine(400, 200, 500, 50)
GraphicsWindow.DrawLine(400, 200, 500, 350)
```

Assignment 17:

4. Draw a snowman using **DrawEllipse** for the body and head and **DrawLine** for his arms. How can you draw his face?

```
'Assignment 17, Question 1
GraphicsWindow.Show()
GraphicsWindow.PenColor = "Black"
'head and body
GraphicsWindow.DrawEllipse(150, 100, 100, 100)
GraphicsWindow.DrawEllipse(100, 200, 200, 200)
'arms
GraphicsWindow.PenWidth = 5
GraphicsWindow.DrawLine(130, 230, 50, 125)
GraphicsWindow.DrawLine(270, 230, 350, 125)
'face
GraphicsWindow.PenWidth = 2
GraphicsWindow.DrawEllipse(175, 125, 10, 10)
GraphicsWindow.DrawEllipse(215, 125, 10, 10)
GraphicsWindow.DrawEllipse(195, 150, 10, 10)
GraphicsWindow.DrawLine(175, 175, 225, 175)
```

5. Draw a flag for a country you are doing a report for.

```
'Assignment 17, Question 2
'french flag
GraphicsWindow.Show()
GraphicsWindow.BrushColor = "Blue"
GraphicsWindow.FillRectangle(50, 50, 150, 300)
GraphicsWindow.BrushColor = "Red"
GraphicsWindow.FillRectangle(350, 50, 150, 300)
GraphicsWindow.PenWidth = 3
GraphicsWindow.PenColor = "Black"
GraphicsWindow.DrawRectangle(50, 50, 450, 300)
```

6. Write a program to draw "Sinbad's Magic Carpet." Have many colors in the rug.

```
'Assignment 17, Question 3
GraphicsWindow.Show()
For I = 50 To 300 Step 50
  For J = 50 To 500 Step 50
    GraphicsWindow.BrushColor = GraphicsWindow.GetRandomColor()
    GraphicsWindow.FillRectangle(J, I, 50, 50)
  EndFor
EndFor
```

Assignment 18:

3. Write you name close to the center of the graphics window. Use colors and large font size.

```
'Assignment 18, Question 1
GraphicsWindow.Show()
GraphicsWindow.FontSize = 64
GraphicsWindow.BrushColor = "Red"
GraphicsWindow.DrawText(50, 100, "Computer Guy")
```

4. Write a program that randomly displays the digits from 1 to 9 in the graphics window.

```
'Assignment 18, Question 2
GraphicsWindow.Show()
GraphicsWindow.FontSize = 24
For I = 1 To 100
  For J = 1 To 9
    GraphicsWindow.BrushColor = GraphicsWindow.GetRandomColor()
    X = Math.GetRandomNumber(GraphicsWindow.Width)
    Y = Math.GetRandomNumber(GraphicsWindow.Height)
    GraphicsWindow.DrawText(X, Y, J)
  EndFor
EndFor
```

Assignment 19:

4. Draw a green rectangle using the turtle.

```
'Assignment 19, Question 1
Turtle.Show()
GraphicsWindow.PenColor = "Green"
Turtle.PenUp()
Turtle.Move(150)
Turtle.TurnLeft()
Turtle.PenDown()
Turtle.Move(250)
Turtle.TurnLeft()
Turtle.Move(300)
Turtle.TurnLeft()
Turtle.Move(500)
Turtle.TurnLeft()
Turtle.Move(300)
Turtle.TurnLeft()
Turtle.Move(250)
```

5. Draw a Tic-Tac-Toe grid using the turtle.

```
'Assignment 19, Question 2
Turtle.Show()
GraphicsWindow.PenColor = "Black"
GraphicsWindow.PenWidth = 5
Turtle.Speed = 9
'get to starting point
Turtle.PenUp()
Turtle.Move(150)
Turtle.TurnLeft()
Turtle.Move(50)
Turtle.TurnLeft()
'first vertical
Turtle.PenDown()
Turtle.Move(300)
'move to next
Turtle.PenUp()
Turtle.TurnLeft()
Turtle.Move(100)
Turtle.TurnLeft()
'second vertical
Turtle.PenDown()
Turtle.Move(300)
'move to next
```

```
Turtle.PenUp()
Turtle.TurnLeft()
Turtle.Move(200)
Turtle.TurnLeft()
Turtle.Move(100)
Turtle.TurnLeft()
'first horizontal
Turtle.PenDown()
Turtle.Move(300)
'move to last
Turtle.PenUp()
Turtle.TurnRight()
Turtle.Move(100)
Turtle.TurnRight()
'second horizontal
Turtle.PenDown()
Turtle.Move(300)
```

Assignment 20:

4. Change the string in "Row, Row, Row Your Boat" program so that it plays very fast, very slow, an octave higher, an octave lower, staccato, legato.

```
'Assignment 21, Question 1
'fast
Sound.PlayMusic("T255 O3 C4 C4 C6 D16 E4 E6 D16 E6 F16 G2 O4 C12 C12
C12 O3 G12 G12 G12 E12 E12 E12 C12 C12 C12 G8 F8 E8 D8 C2")
'slow
Sound.PlayMusic("T32 O3 C4 C4 C6 D16 E4 E6 D16 E6 F16 G2 O4 C12 C12
C12 O3 G12 G12 G12 E12 E12 E12 C12 C12 C12 G8 F8 E8 D8 C2")
'octave higher
Sound.PlayMusic("T100 O4 C4 C4 C6 D16 E4 E6 D16 E6 F16 G2 O4 C12 C12
C12 O3 G12 G12 G12 E12 E12 E12 C12 C12 C12 G8 F8 E8 D8 C2")
'octave lower
Sound.PlayMusic("T100 O2 C4 C4 C6 D16 E4 E6 D16 E6 F16 G2 O4 C12 C12
C12 O3 G12 G12 G12 E12 E12 E12 C12 C12 C12 G8 F8 E8 D8 C2")
'staccato
Sound.PlayMusic("MS T100 O3 C4 C4 C6 D16 E4 E6 D16 E6 F16 G2 O4 C12
C12 C12 O3 G12 G12 G12 E12 E12 E12 C12 C12 C12 G8 F8 E8 D8 C2")
'legato
Sound.PlayMusic("ML T100 O3 C4 C4 C6 D16 E4 E6 D16 E6 F16 G2 O4 C12
C12 C12 O3 G12 G12 G12 E12 E12 E12 C12 C12 C12 G8 F8 E8 D8 C2")
```

5. Play some other tune with **PlayMusic**.

```
'Assignment 21, Question 2
Sound.PlayMusic("T100 O3 C4 C4 G4 G4 A4 A4 G1 F4 F4 E4 E4 D4 D4 C1")
```

6. Crossing friends. While music plays, make your name move down the screen while a friend's name move along the screen. Use the MB symbol in the string. The names cross in the middle.

```
'Assignment 21, Question 3
TextWindow.Show()
Sound.PlayMusic("MB T100 O3 C4 C4 C6 D16 E4 E6 D16 E6 F16 G2 O4 C12
C12 C12 O3 G12 G12 G12 E12 E12 E12 C12 C12 C12 G8 F8 E8 D8 C2")
For I = 1 To 20
  TextWindow.CursorTop = I
  TextWindow.CursorLeft = 20
  TextWindow.Write("Player 1")
  TextWindow.CursorTop = 10
  TextWindow.CursorLeft = I + 5
  TextWindow.Write("Player 2")
  Program.Delay(100)
EndFor
```

Assignment 21:

3. Go back to the coin flip game in Assignment 11. Clean up the main program by using subroutines. Use a subroutine to flip the coin, one to check the results and one to display the score.

```
'Assignment 21, Question 1
'P your points, Q computer points, R tie points
P = 0
Q = 0
R = 0
PlayAgain:
DisplayScore()
TextWindow.Write("Press Enter to Flip")
X = TextWindow.Read()
TextWindow.WriteLine("")
'your flip
FlipCoin()
Y = F
TextWindow.WriteLine("You flipped a " + Y)
'computer flip
FlipCoin()
```

```
C = F
TextWindow.WriteLine("Computer flipped a " + C)
CheckResults()
Goto PlayAgain

Sub DisplayScore
  TextWindow.WriteLine("")
  TextWindow.WriteLine("Flipping coins against the computer ...")
  TextWindow.WriteLine("Your wins: " + P)
  TextWindow.WriteLine("Computer wins: " + Q)
  TextWindow.WriteLine("Ties: " + R)
EndSub

Sub FlipCoin
  V = Math.GetRandomNumber(2)
  F = "Heads"
  If (V = 2) Then
    F = "Tails"
  EndIf
EndSub

Sub CheckResults
  'tie?
  If (Y <> C) Then
    Goto NoTie
  EndIf
  'tie
  TextWindow.WriteLine("It's a Tie!")
  R = R + 1
  Goto LeaveSub
  NoTie:
  'computer win?
  If (C = "Heads") Then
    Goto ComputerWin
  EndIf
  'if got here, you win
  TextWindow.WriteLine("You Win!")
  P = P + 1
  Goto LeaveSub
  ComputerWin:
  TextWindow.WriteLine("Computer Wins!")
  Q = Q + 1
  LeaveSub:
EndSub
```

4. Change the moving submarine program. Make the graphics window taller. Then, make the submarine move from the lower right corner to the upper left corner. This makes it look like the sub is surfacing.

```
'Assignment 21, Question 2
'Moving submarine
GraphicsWindow.Show()
GraphicsWindow.Width = 600
GraphicsWindow.Height = 700
GraphicsWindow.BackgroundColor = "Black"
GraphicsWindow.BrushColor = "SkyBlue"
GraphicsWindow.FillRectangle(0, 0, 600, 55)
X = 425
Y = 650
D = -25
E = -35
For I = 1 To 17
  MoveSubmarine()
EndFor

Sub MoveSubmarine
  'erase
  GraphicsWindow.BrushColor = GraphicsWindow.BackgroundColor
  GraphicsWindow.FillRectangle(X, Y, 175, 50)
  'move by D, E
  X = X + D
  Y = Y + E
  ' draw body
  GraphicsWindow.BrushColor = "Red"
  GraphicsWindow.FillEllipse(X, Y, 150, 50)
  'draw fin
  GraphicsWindow.BrushColor = "Silver"
  GraphicsWindow.FillTriangle(X + 150, Y + 25, X + 170, Y, X + 170, Y
+ 50)
  Program.Delay(200)
EndSub
```

Assignment 22:

4. Write a program where the user can change the graphics window color by pressing a key. Use R for red, G for green, B for blue, etc.

```
'Assignment 22, Question 1
'change colors
'R-red
'B-blue
'G-green
'Y-yellow
'W-white
'P-purple
GraphicsWindow.Show()
GraphicsWindow.Width = 300
GraphicsWindow.Height = 200
GraphicsWindow.KeyDown = KeyDownSub

Sub KeyDownSub
  K = GraphicsWindow.LastKey
  If (K = "R") Then
    GraphicsWindow.BackgroundColor = "Red"
  EndIf
  If (K = "B") Then
    GraphicsWindow.BackgroundColor = "Blue"
  EndIf
  If (K = "G") Then
    GraphicsWindow.BackgroundColor = "Green"
  EndIf
  If (K = "Y") Then
    GraphicsWindow.BackgroundColor = "Yellow"
  EndIf
  If (K = "W") Then
    GraphicsWindow.BackgroundColor = "White"
  EndIf
  If (K = "P") Then
    GraphicsWindow.BackgroundColor = "Purple"
  EndIf
EndSub
```

5. Write a program where the user enters a password. Have the program form the password from the entered keys, but display asterisks (*) in the graphics window.

```
'Assignment 22, Question 2
GraphicsWindow.Show()
GraphicsWindow.Width = 500
GraphicsWindow.Height = 250
P = ""
D = ""
GraphicsWindow.FontSize = 24
GraphicsWindow.BrushColor = "Blue"
GraphicsWindow.DrawText(30, 30, "Type a password, then press Enter")
GraphicsWindow.KeyDown = KeyDownSub

Sub KeyDownSub
  K = GraphicsWindow.LastKey
  If (K <> "Return") Then
    P = P + K
    D = D + "*"
    GraphicsWindow.BrushColor = "Black"
    GraphicsWindow.DrawText(30, 80, D)
  EndIf
  If (K = "Return") Then
    GraphicsWindow.BrushColor = "Blue"
    GraphicsWindow.DrawText(30, 130, "Entered: " + P)
  EndIf
EndSub
```

6. For the moving submarine program, write code that keeps the submarine from moving out of the window. Can you make the fin change sides when the direction changes?

```
'Assignment 22, Question 3
'Moving submarine with keys
GraphicsWindow.Show()
GraphicsWindow.Width = 600
GraphicsWindow.Height = 100
GraphicsWindow.BackgroundColor = "Black"
X = 275
Y = 25
D = 0
MoveSubmarine()
GraphicsWindow.KeyDown = KeyDownSub

Sub KeyDownSub
  K = GraphicsWindow.LastKey
```

```
  D = 0
  If (K = "Left") Then
    D = -10
  EndIf
  If (K = "Right") Then
    D = 10
  EndIf
  MoveSubmarine()
EndSub

Sub MoveSubmarine
  'erase
  GraphicsWindow.BrushColor = GraphicsWindow.BackgroundColor
  GraphicsWindow.FillRectangle(X - 20, Y, 195, 50)
  'move by D
  X = X + D
  ' draw body
  GraphicsWindow.BrushColor = "Red"
  GraphicsWindow.FillEllipse(X, Y, 150, 50)
  'draw fin
  GraphicsWindow.BrushColor = "Silver"
  If (D >= 0) Then
    'fin on left
    GraphicsWindow.FillTriangle(X, Y + 25, X - 20, Y, X - 20, Y + 50)
  EndIf
  If (D < 0) Then
    'fin on right
    GraphicsWindow.FillTriangle(X + 150, Y + 25, X + 170, Y, X + 170,
Y + 50)
  EndIf
EndSub
```

Assignment 23:

4. Write a secret cipher making program. You give it a sentence and it finds out how long the sentence is, then switches the first letter with the second, third with the fourth, etc. Example:

THIS IS A DRAGON

Becomes

HTSII S ARDGANO

```
'Assignment 23, Question 1
GetSentence:
TextWindow.WriteLine("")
TextWindow.WriteLine("Enter a sentence for coding:")
S = TextWindow.Read()
L = Text.GetLength(S)
S = S + " "
W = ""
For I = 1 to L step 2
  P = Text.GetSubText(S, I, 2)
  Q = Text.GetSubText(P, 2, 1) + Text.GetSubText(P, 1, 1)
  W = W + Q
EndFor
TextWindow.WriteLine("")
TextWindow.WriteLine("Here is the code sentence:")
TextWindow.WriteLine(W)
Goto GetSentence
```

5. Write a question answering program? You give it a question starting with a verb and it reverses verb and noun to answer the question. Example:

ARE YOU A TURKEY?
YOU ARE A TURKEY.

```
'Assignment 23, Question 2
GetQuestion:
TextWindow.WriteLine("")
TextWindow.WriteLine("Enter a question:")
Q = TextWindow.Read()
L = Text.GetLength(Q)
'take off question mark
Q = Text.GetSubText(Q, 1, L - 1)
'find end of first word
For I = 1 To L
  C = Text.GetSubText(Q, I, 1)
  If (C = " ") Then
    Goto Got1
  EndIf
EndFor
Got1:
S = I
'find end of second word
For I = S + 1 To L
  C = Text.GetSubText(Q, I, 1)
  If (C = " ") Then
    Goto Got2
  EndIf
EndFor
Got2:
T = I
'turn words around
X = Text.GetSubText(Q, S + 1, T - S)
Y = Text.GetSubText(Q, 1, S)
TextWindow.WriteLine(X + Y + Text.GetSubText(Q, T + 1, L - T))
Goto GetQuestion
```

6. Write a pig latin program. It asks for a word. Then it takes all the letters up to the first vowel and puts them on the back of the word, followed by AY. If the word starts with a vowel, it only adds AY. Examples:

BOX becomes OXBAY
APPLE becomes APPLEAY

```
'Assignment 23, Question 3
GetWord:
TextWindow.WriteLine("")
TextWindow.WriteLine("Pig Latin")
TextWindow.WriteLine("Enter a word (all capital letters):")
W = TextWindow.Read()
L = Text.GetLength(W)
'find first vowel
For I = 1 To L
  V = Text.GetSubText(W, I, 1)
  If (V = "A") Then
    Goto GotVowel
  EndIf
  If (V = "E") Then
    Goto GotVowel
  EndIf
  If (V = "I") Then
    Goto GotVowel
  EndIf
  If (V = "O") Then
    Goto GotVowel
  EndIf
  If (V = "U") Then
    Goto GotVowel
  EndIf
EndFor
GotVowel:
If (I = 1) Then
  Goto VowelFirst
EndIf
L = Text.GetSubText(W, I, L - I + 1)
L = L + Text.GetSubText(W, 1, I - 1)
L = L + "AY"
Goto WriteWord
VowelFirst:
L = W + "AY"
WriteWord:
TextWindow.WriteLine(L)
Goto GetWord
```

Assignment 25:

3. Make a program to write a very large number, 50 digits. Pick the digits at random. Put a comma between each set of three digits.

```
'Assignment 25, Question 1
'generate NumberLength random digits with comma separators
'put a letter in Number to start to trick it into thinking it's a string
'remove letter when done
Number = "A"
NumberLength = 50
'first digit can't be zero
Digit = Math.GetRandomNumber(9)
Number = Number + Digit
'get remaining digits
For I = 1 To NumberLength - 1
  Digit = Math.GetRandomNumber(10) - 1
  Number = Number + Digit
EndFor
'strip off A at beginning
Number = Text.GetSubText(Number, 2, NumberLength)
'put commas every three characters starting at right
NumberWithCommas = ""
NumberOfChunks = 0
For I = NumberLength To 1 Step -3
  'only add chunks of three
  If (I >= 3) Then
    NumberWithCommas = "," + Text.GetSubText(Number, I - 2, 3) +
NumberWithCommas
    NumberOfChunks = NumberOfChunks + 1
  EndIf
EndFor
'do we have entire number - if so strip off comma
If (NumberOfChunks * 3 = NumberLength) Then
  NumberWithCommas = Text.GetSubText(NumberWithCommas, 2,
Text.GetLength(NumberWithCommas) - 1)
EndIf
'otherwise add rest of digits
If (NumberOfChunks * 3 <> NumberLength) Then
  NumberWithCommas = Text.GetSubText(Number, 1, NumberLength -
NumberOfChunks * 3) + NumberWithCommas
EndIf
TextWindow.WriteLine("Big Number: " + NumberWithCommas)
```

2. Write a secret cipher program. The user chooses a password and it is used to make a cipher alphabet like this:

> If the password is DRAGONETTE, remove the repeated letters to get DRAGONET. Put it at the front of the alphabet and the rest of the letters after it in normal order.

> Cipher alphabet -   DRAGONETBCFHIJKLMPQSUVWXYZ
> Normal alphabet -   ABCDEFGHIJKLMNOPQRSTUVWXYZ

The user chooses to code or decode from a menu.

```
'Assignment 25, Question 2
GetPassword()
FormAlphabet()
GetMessage:
TextWindow.WriteLine("")
TextWindow.Write("Code or Decode (C or D)? ")
A = TextWindow.Read()
If (A = "C") Then
  Code()
EndIf
If (A = "D") Then
  Decode()
EndIf
Goto GetMessage

Sub GetPassword
  TextWindow.WriteLine("")
  TextWindow.WriteLine("Cipher Program - Best to Use Capital Letters")
  TextWindow.WriteLine("")
  TextWindow.Write("Enter password: ")
  Password = text.ConvertToUpperCase(TextWindow.Read())
  'removed repeated letters
  T = Text.GetSubText(Password, 1, 1)
  For I = 2 To Text.GetLength(Password)
    Letter1 = Text.GetSubText(Password, I, 1)
    For J = 1 To Text.GetLength(T)
      Letter2 = Text.GetSubText(T, J, 1)
      If (Letter1 = Letter2) Then
        Goto NextLetter
      EndIf
    EndFor
    T = T + Letter1
    NextLetter:
  EndFor
```

```
    Password = T
    TextWindow.WriteLine("Shortened password: " + Password)
EndSub

Sub FormAlphabet
  'remove password letters from alphabet
  Alphabet = "ABCDEFGHIJKLMNOPQRSTUVWXYZ"
  Cipher = ""
  For I = 1 To 26
    For J = 1 To Text.GetLength(Password)
      If (Text.GetSubText(Alphabet, I, 1) = Text.GetSubText(Password,
J, 1)) Then
        Goto NoAdd
      EndIf
    EndFor
    Cipher = Cipher + Text.GetSubText(Alphabet, I, 1)
    NoAdd:
  EndFor
  'tack password to front of cipher
  Cipher = Password + Cipher
  TextWindow.WriteLine("Normal alphabet: " + Alphabet)
  TextWindow.WriteLine("Cipher alphabet: " + Cipher)
EndSub

Sub Code
  TextWindow.WriteLine("")
  TextWindow.WriteLine("Input message to code:")
  Message = text.ConvertToUpperCase(TextWindow.Read())
  CodedMessage = ""
  'go through every character if in alphabet, replace with ciphered
value
  ''otherwise just replace with same character
  For I = 1 To Text.GetLength(Message)
    T = Text.GetSubText(Message, I, 1)
    For J = 1 To 26
      If (T = Text.GetSubText(Alphabet, J, 1)) Then
        Goto InAlphabet
      EndIf
    EndFor
    'not in alphabet
    CodedMessage = CodedMessage + T
    Goto NextOne
    InAlphabet:
    CodedMessage = CodedMessage + Text.GetSubText(Cipher, J, 1)
    NextOne:
  EndFor
```

```
    TextWindow.WriteLine("Coded Message:")
    TextWindow.WriteLine(CodedMessage)
EndSub

Sub Decode
    TextWindow.WriteLine("")
    TextWindow.WriteLine("Input message to decode:")
    Message = text.ConvertToUpperCase(TextWindow.Read())
    DecodedMessage = ""
    'go through every character if in cipher, replace with deciphered
value
    ''otherwise just replace with same character
    For I = 1 To Text.GetLength(Message)
      T = Text.GetSubText(Message, I, 1)
      For J = 1 To 26
        If (T = Text.GetSubText(Cipher, J, 1)) Then
          Goto InCipher
        EndIf
      EndFor
      'not in cipher
      DecodedMessage = DecodedMessage + T
      Goto NextOneAgain
      InCipher:
      DecodedMessage = DecodedMessage + Text.GetSubText(Alphabet, J, 1)
      NextOneAgain:
    EndFor
    TextWindow.WriteLine("Decoded Message:")
    TextWindow.WriteLine(DecodedMessage)
EndSub
```

2. For practice with the **Timer**, see if you can write a program that makes a bell sound every second.

```
'Assignment 29, Question 1
Timer.Interval = 1000
Timer.Tick = TickSub

Sub TickSub
  Sound.PlayBellRing()
EndSub
```

We publish several Self-Study or Instructor-Led Computer Programming Tutorials for Microsoft® Small Basic:

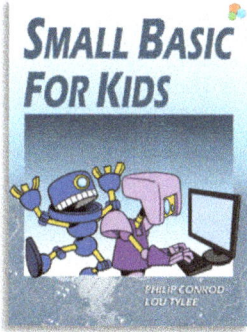

Small Basic For Kids is an illustrated introduction to computer programming that provides an interactive, self-paced tutorial to the new Small Basic programming environment. The book consists of 30 short lessons that explain how to create and run a Small Basic program. Elementary students learn about program design and many elements of the Small Basic language. Numerous examples are used to demonstrate every step in the building process. The tutorial also includes two complete games (Hangman and Pizza Zapper) for students to build and try. Designed for kids ages 8 and up.

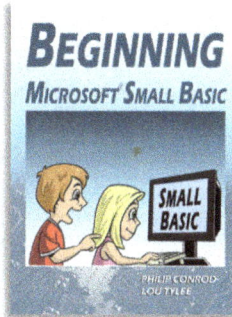

The Beginning Microsoft Small Basic Programming Tutorial is a self-study first semester "beginner" programming tutorial consisting of 11 chapters explaining (in simple, easy-to-follow terms) how to write Microsoft Small Basic programs. Numerous examples are used to demonstrate every step in the building process. The last chapter of this tutorial shows you how four different Small Basic games could port to Visual Basic, Visual C# and Java. This beginning level self-paced tutorial can be used at home or at school. The tutorial is simple enough for kids ages 10 and above yet engaging enough for beginning adults.

Programming Games with Microsoft Small Basic is a self-paced second semester "intermediate" level programming tutorial consisting of 10 chapters explaining (in simple, easy-to-follow terms) how to write video games in Microsoft Small Basic. The games built are non-violent, family-friendly, and teach logical thinking skills. Students will learn how to program the following Small Basic video games: Safecracker, Tic Tac Toe, Match Game, Pizza Delivery, Moon Landing, and Leap Frog. This intermediate level self-paced tutorial can be used at home or school. The tutorial is simple enough for kids yet engaging enough for beginning adults.

Programming Home Projects with Microsoft Small Basic is a self-paced programming tutorial explains (in simple, easy-to-follow terms) how to build Small Basic Windows applications. Students learn about program design, Small Basic objects, many elements of the Small Basic language, and how to debug and distribute finished programs. Sequential file input and output is also introduced.. The projects built include a Dual-Mode Stopwatch, Flash Card Math Quiz, Multiple Choice Exam, Blackjack Card Game, Weight Monitor, Home Inventory Manager and a Snowball Toss Game.

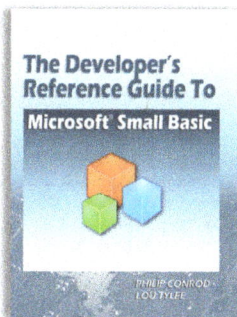

The Developer's Reference Guide to Microsoft Small Basic
While developing all the different Microsoft Small Basic tutorials we found it necessary to write The Developer's Reference Guide to Microsoft Small Basic. The Developer's Reference Guide to Microsoft Small Basic is over 500 pages long and includes over 100 Small Basic programming examples for you to learn from and include in your own Microsoft Small Basic programs. It is a detailed reference guide for new developers.

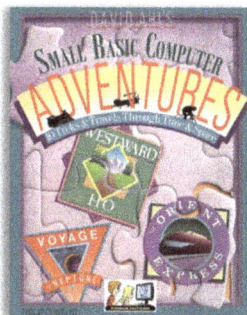

David Ahl's Small Basic Computer Adventures is a Microsoft Small Basic re-make of the classic *Basic Computer Games* programming *book* originally written by David H. Ahl. This new book includes the following classic adventure simulations; Marco Polo, Westward Ho!, The Longest Automobile Race, The Orient Express, Amelia Earhart: Around the World Flight, Tour de France, Subway Scavenger, Hong Kong Hustle, and Voyage to Neptune. Learn how to program these classic computer simulations in Microsoft Small Basic. This "intermediate" level self-paced tutorial can be used at home or school.

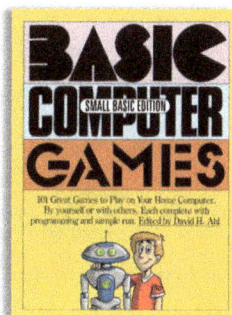

Basic Computer Games - Small Basic Edition is a re-make of the classic BASIC COMPUTER GAMES book originally edited by David H. Ahl. It contains 100 of the original text based BASIC games that inspired a whole generation of programmers. Now these classic BASIC games have been re-written in Microsoft Small Basic for a new generation to enjoy! The new Small Basic games look and act like the original text based games. The book includes all the original spaghetti code GOTO commands and it will make you appreciate the structured programming techniques found in our other tutorials.

We also publish several Self-Study or Instructor-Led Computer Programming Tutorials for Microsoft® Visual Basic® Express and Visual C#® Express:

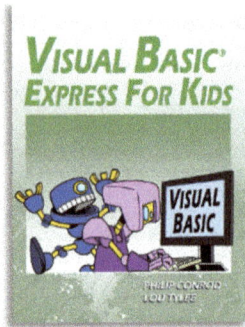

Visual Basic® Express For Kids is a beginning programming tutorial consisting of 10 chapters explaining (in simple, easy-to-follow terms) how to build a Visual Basic Express Windows application. Students learn about project design, the Visual Basic Express toolbox, and many elements of the BASIC language. The tutorial also includes several detailed computer projects for students to build and try. These projects include a number guessing game, a card game, an allowance calculator, a drawing program, a state capitals game, Tic-Tac-Toe and even a simple video game. Designed for kids ages 12 and up.

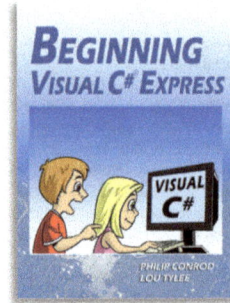

Beginning Visual Basic® Express is a semester long self-paced "beginner" programming tutorial consisting of 10 chapters explaining (in simple, easy-to-follow terms) how to build a Visual Basic Express Windows application. The tutorial includes several detailed computer projects for students to build and try. These projects include a number guessing game, card game, allowance calculator, drawing program, state capitals game, and a couple of video games like Pong. We also include several college prep bonus projects including a loan calculator, portfolio manager, and checkbook balancer. Designed for students age 15 and up.

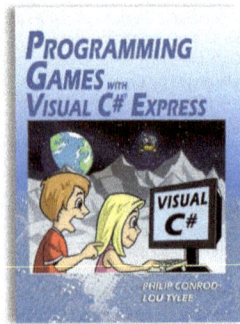

Programming Games with Visual Basic® Express is a semester long "intermediate" programming tutorial consisting of 10 chapters explaining (in simple, easy-to-follow terms) how to build Visual Basic Video Games. The games built are non-violent, family-friendly, and teach logical thinking skills. Students will learn how to program the following Visual Basic video games: Safecracker, Tic Tac Toe, Match Game, Pizza Delivery, Moon Landing, and Leap Frog. This intermediate level self-paced tutorial can be used at home or school. The tutorial is simple enough for kids yet engaging enough for beginning adults.

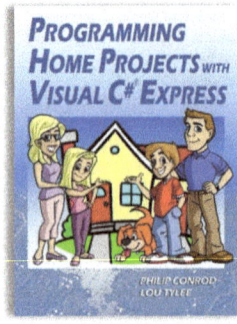

Programming Home Projects with Visual Basic® Express is a semester long self-paced programming tutorial explains (in simple, easy-to-follow terms) how to build a Visual Basic Express Windows project. Students learn about project design, the Visual Basic Express toolbox, many elements of the Visual Basic language, and how to debug and distribute finished projects. The projects built include a Dual-Mode Stopwatch, Flash Card Math Quiz, Multiple Choice Exam, Blackjack Card Game, Weight Monitor, Home Inventory Manager and a Snowball Toss Game.

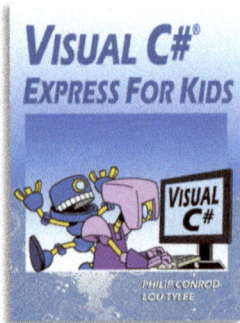

Visual C#® Express For Kids is a beginning programming tutorial consisting of 10 chapters explaining (in simple, easy-to-follow terms) how to build a Visual C# Express Windows application. Students learn about project design, the Visual C# Express toolbox, and many elements of the C# language. Numerous examples are used to demonstrate every step in the building process. The projects include a number guessing game, a card game, an allowance calculator, a drawing program, a state capitals game, Tic-Tac-Toe and even a simple video game. Designed for kids ages 12 and up.

Beginning Visual C#® Express is a semester long "beginning" programming tutorial consisting of 10 chapters explaining (in simple, easy-to-follow terms) how to build a C# Express Windows application. The tutorial includes several detailed computer projects for students to build and try. These projects include a number guessing game, card game, allowance calculator, drawing program, state capitals game, and a couple of video games like Pong. We also include several college prep bonus projects including a loan calculator, portfolio manager, and checkbook balancer. Designed for students age 15 and up.

Programming Games with Visual C#® Express is a semester long "intermediate" programming tutorial consisting of 10 chapters explaining (in simple, easy-to-follow terms) how to build a Visual C# Video Games. The games built are non-violent, family-friendly, and teach logical thinking skills. Students will learn how to program the following Visual C# video games: Safecracker, Tic Tac Toe, Match Game, Pizza Delivery, Moon Landing, and Leap Frog. This intermediate level self-paced tutorial can be used at home or school. The tutorial is simple enough for kids yet engaging enough for beginning adults.

Programming Home Projects with Visual C#® Express is a semester long self-paced programming tutorial explains (in simple, easy-to-follow terms) how to build a Visual C# Express Windows project. Students learn about project design, the Visual C# Express toolbox, many elements of the Visual C# language, and how to debug and distribute finished projects. The projects built include a Dual-Mode Stopwatch, Flash Card Math Quiz, Multiple Choice Exam, Blackjack Card Game, Weight Monitor, Home Inventory Manager and a Snowball Toss Game.

We also publish several Self-Study or Instructor-Led Computer Programming Tutorials for Oracle® Java® :

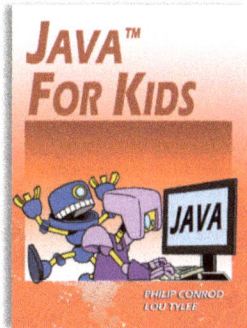

Java™ For Kids is a beginning programming tutorial consisting of 10 chapters explaining (in simple, easy-to-follow terms) how to build a Java application. Students learn about project design, object-oriented programming, console applications, graphics applications and many elements of the Java language. Numerous examples are used to demonstrate every step in the building process. The projects include a number guessing game, a card game, an allowance calculator, a state capitals game, Tic-Tac-Toe, a simple drawing program, and even a basic video game. Designed for kids ages 12 and up.

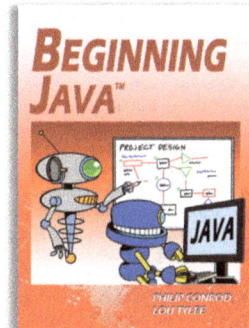

Beginning Java™ is a semester long "beginning" programming tutorial consisting of 10 chapters explaining (in simple, easy-to-follow terms) how to build a Java application. The tutorial includes several detailed computer projects for students to build and try. These projects include a number guessing game, card game, allowance calculator, drawing program, state capitals game, and a couple of video games like Pong. We also include several college prep bonus projects including a loan calculator, portfolio manager, and checkbook balancer. Designed for students age 15 and up.

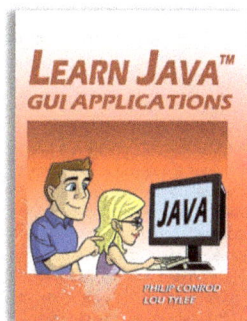

Learn Java™ GUI Applications is a 9 lesson Tutorial covering object-oriented programming concepts, using a integrated development environment to create and test Java projects, building and distributing GUI applications, understanding and using the Swing control library, exception handling, sequential file access, graphics, multimedia, advanced topics such as printing, and help system authoring. Our **Beginning Java** tutorial is a pre-requisite for this tutorial.

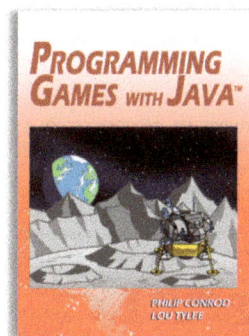

Programming Games with Java™ is a semester long "intermediate" programming tutorial consisting of 10 chapters explaining (in simple, easy-to-follow terms) how to build a Visual C# Video Games. The games built are non-violent, family-friendly and teach logical thinking skills. Students will learn how to program the following Visual C# video games: Safecracker, Tic Tac Toe, Match Game, Pizza Delivery, Moon Landing, and Leap Frog. This intermediate level self-paced tutorial can be used at home or school. The tutorial is simple enough for kids yet engaging enough for beginning adults. Our **Beginning Java** and **Learn Java GUI Applications** tutorials are required pre-requisites for this tutorial.

Programming Home Projects with Java™ is a Java GUI Swing tutorial covering object-oriented programming concepts. It explains (in simple, easy-to-follow terms) how to build Java GUI project to use around the home. Students learn about project design, the Java Swing controls, many elements of the Java language, and how to distribute finished projects. The projects built include a Dual-Mode Stopwatch, Flash Card Math Quiz, Multiple Choice Exam, Blackjack Card Game, Weight Monitor, Home Inventory Manager and a Snowball Toss Game. Our **Beginning Java** and **Learn Java GUI Applications** tutorials are pre-requisites for this tutorial.

We also publish several advanced Honors Level Self-Study or Instructor-Led "College-Prep" and College Level Computer Programming Tutorials for Microsoft® Visual Basic® Professional Edition and Visual C#® Professional Edition:

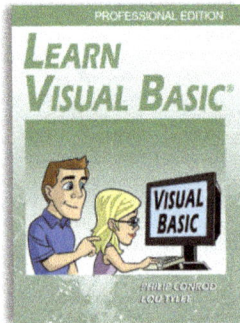

LEARN VISUAL BASIC PROFESSIONAL EDITION is a comprehensive college prep programming tutorial covering object-oriented programming, the Visual Basic integrated development environment, building and distributing Windows applications using the Windows Installer, exception handling, sequential file access, graphics, multimedia, advanced topics such as web access, printing, and HTML help system authoring. The tutorial also introduces database applications (using ADO .NET) and web applications (using ASP.NET).

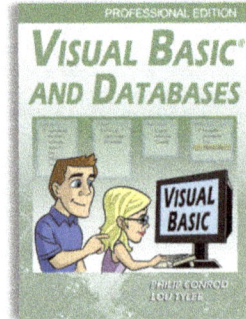

VISUAL BASIC AND DATABASES PROFESSIONAL EDITION is a tutorial that provides a detailed introduction to using Visual Basic for accessing and maintaining databases for desktop applications. Topics covered include: database structure, database design, Visual Basic project building, ADO .NET data objects (connection, data adapter, command, data table), data bound controls, proper interface design, structured query language (SQL), creating databases using Access, SQL Server and ADOX, and database reports. Actual projects developed include a book tracking system, a sales invoicing program, a home inventory system and a daily weather monitor.

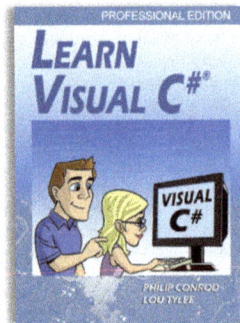

LEARN VISUAL C# PROFESSIONAL EDITION is a comprehensive college prep computer programming tutorial covering object-oriented programming, the Visual C# integrated development environment and toolbox, building and distributing Windows applications (using the Windows Installer), exception handling, sequential file input and output, graphics, multimedia effects (animation and sounds), advanced topics such as web access, printing, and HTML help system authoring. The tutorial also introduces database applications (using ADO .NET) and web applications (using ASP.NET).

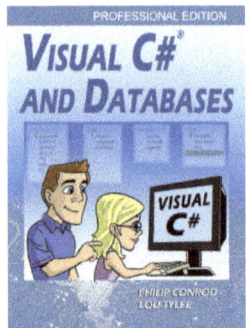

VISUAL C# AND DATABASES PROFESSIONAL EDITION is a tutorial that provides a detailed introduction to using Visual C# for accessing and maintaining databases for desktop applications. Topics covered include: database structure, database design, Visual C# project building, ADO .NET data objects (connection, data adapter, command, data table), data bound controls, proper interface design, structured query language (SQL), creating databases using Access, SQL Server and ADOX, and database reports. Actual projects developed include a books tracking system, a sales invoicing program, a home inventory system and a daily weather monitor.

www.ingramcontent.com/pod-product-compliance
Lightning Source LLC
Chambersburg PA
CBHW080906220326
41598CB00034B/5496